DON SHERWOOD

The Life and Times of
"The World's Greatest Disc Jockey"

LAURIE HARPER

Prima Publishing & Communications
P.O. Box 1260LH
Rocklin, CA 95677
(916) 624-5718

Copy Editing by John Faulkner
Typography by Howarth & Smith Ltd.
Production by Robin Lockwood, Bookman Productions
Interior design and illustration by Renee Deprey
Jacket design by The Dunlavey Studio

Prima Publishing & Communications
Rocklin, CA

89 90 91 92 RRD 10 9 8 7 6 5 4 3 2 1

Printed in the United States of America

To Hap

A man set apart, not only by his unique ability to make the impossible happen, but even more so by his generous and wholehearted efforts to help others do the same.

Acknowledgments

I especially wish to thank:

ROBIN COHELAN-SHERWOOD, who from the start was gracious, trusting, and open with all that is closest to her heart, assuring me that this endeavor was worthy of the struggle. It was indeed worthy.

THE SHERWOOD FAMILY, for their confidence and for giving me access to all the material.

The late CHARLIE SMITH, for giving me tapes of Don's shows so that I could truly become a fan. Charlie died shortly after I spoke with him. He was loved by all and will long be remembered.

EACH OF YOU in this book who took the time to tell me stories, answer questions, paint word pictures, and help give me a better sense of it all.

JANET GLUCKMAN, my personal editor and friend, who sacrificed her health and sanity to teach this often rather stubborn pupil the finer points of the writing craft. Doubtless, I stretched her limits of patience; nonetheless, she ever so eloquently persisted. I am forever grateful.

BEN DOMINITZ, a gentleman and publisher with the treasured combination of vision, sensitivity, and a sense of good fun.

MY APOLOGIES to those individuals I either could not locate or was not made aware of. Had I continued interviewing for this book, it would never have been completed. Such was the life of Don Sherwood.

Contents

Foreword

Don Sherwood is hard to capture on paper. He was all nuance and inflections, sudden flashes of extemporaneous humor and sly innuendo. And then there was that famous dirty laugh.

For what seems, in retrospect, only a brief, shining hour, he was King of the Hill in a San Francisco that isn't the same now that he is no longer a part of it. Back then, it was still, largely, an innocent city. Don, innocent in a uniquely wicked way, fit the scene perfectly and soon dominated it.

To those who came along too late for him to be a part of their daily lives, conversations, joys and sorrows, I can only say—too bad! As a disc jockey on radio station KSFO, he played an occasional record, but mainly he rambled— and my, could he ramble. Although he also did TV, radio was his forte. His voice was made for radio. He had the timing of masters like Jack Benny and Johnny Carson, and more natural wit than either.

Like all geniuses, he was complicated, by turns generous and mean-spirited, dedicated and careless. With his marriages and affairs, his wit and wild ideas, his mercurial style, he was great copy for me. We were friends in a bantering, edgy sort of way. He was great company. With his high-voltage intensity, he could raise the atmosphere to dangerous levels. And yes, he smoked and drank. A lot.

For those who remember him in his giddy prime, who turned on the radio every morning to find out if he'd be there, he will always be the best part of the best possible time in San Francisco—the crazy guy we never really knew, who became "part of the family."

Don Sherwood will forever remain hard to capture on paper, but it is impossible to think of anybody who could have come closer than Laurie Harper has in this chronicle of a legendary character—one who left us laughing through our tears.

Herb Caen
San Francisco
1989

Introduction

After Hap Harper and I were married in 1982, virtually every place we went people said to Hap, "I remember you from the Sherwood days! You guys were crazy!" Then stories of the "old days" tumbled out, starting with "Remember when Don said . . ."

Don Sherwood's radio and television career set San Francisco on its ear from the early 1950s until the late 1960s. He was not only the talk of the city, he *was* the city, gaining an unprecedented 25 percent share of the market in radio—*one in four people*.

Over a million people acquired a taste for Don's wit and charm, joining in his mad parade. They noticed their worlds becoming brighter, funnier, and infinitely more interesting. Don challenged everyone, convincing them that there was more to life than work, schedules, bills, news, chores, and barbecues. He became a part of their families, a part of their everyday lives.

His gifted imagination and renegade attitude encouraged people to break free and take a chance, bringing out that little bit of Sherwood in each person. This "little bit of Sherwood," cleverly disguised behind crooked grins, sideways glances, and often prematurely grey hair, distinguishes Sherwood fans. Their eyes gleam with secrets that come from being part of Don's special "club."

Who was this self-proclaimed "World's Greatest Disc Jockey"? How did the son of a piano teacher from the Sunset district of San Francisco, the juvenile outcast of every school, come to dazzle this city and claim it as his kingdom?

Part of the answer lies in Don's childhood and early years, which set the stage for his rebellious nature. The other part lies in the opportunity that radio and television provided, enabling Don to convert the seeds of failure into success and freedom.

What did not change was his ingrained low self-esteem, which spread like a cancer into all the critical areas of his life. He had the gift of a quick, brilliant mind, and the curse of that mind never being satisfied. He made other people's lives more meaningful, yet he could find no meaning in his own.

The laughter and shenanigans that characterized him, and were an integral part of his success, largely masked his own confusion, pain, and despair. Don was not being facetious when he said to Jerry Van Dyke, "I now realize that I was overqualified for this life."

Throughout his life it was apparent that Don was more than simply a product of his childhood; he was a captive of it. Despite his obsessive search for ultimate truths, he never accepted the answers he found.

In 1976, at the end of his rollercoaster success, Don retired from radio and the public eye. He retreated, without fanfare, to his houseboat in Sausalito, seeking refuge in his beloved world of the sea.

When Don Sherwood died on November 4, 1983, KSFO suspended regular programming for an all-day tribute that had to be extended as telephone calls backed up. People from far and wide, of all ages and walks of life, called the station to reminisce about Don. The station's tribute turned into an outpouring of affection for a man who had been many things to many people—a unique man whom San Francisco had the fortune to call its own.

In the Beginning

WHAT THE STARS PREDICT
Children born today will be
very brainy. They will be
successful in whatever they
undertake.

San Francisco Examiner
September 7, 1925

Monday, September 7th,
1925: Labor Day. "If you don't step on it, mister, this baby
will be born in your cab!" Inga moaned as another contraction gripped her.

"Hold on, lady, we're almost there!" Just my luck to
get a lady who waits till the last second, the man thought.
"No baby's ever been born in my cab, and I'm not starting
now!" he added aloud.

"Everything's going to be just fine, Inga," Marie murmured. "You'll be happy to know I'm a nurse," she said a
little more loudly to the cab driver.

He did not look relieved.

"You just relax, Inga. We'll manage. This baby's going
to do just fine." Marie Christiani's voice remained typically
calm as she reassured her older sister.

3

The cab driver's nervous foot pumped the pedal erratically, tossing the women back and forth as he dodged the city traffic.

Inga was not excited about the prospects for her future. This baby was her first and, she determined as her groans became more frequent, most likely her last.

By the time the cab careened to a halt at the hospital, Marie was excitedly announcing that her sister's baby was coming at any second. But the nurses were not convinced it was time. Furious, Inga locked herself in the bathroom. Only Marie's insistence finally got her into bed. "I thought she was going to disgrace me forever and have that baby on the commode!"

The baby was kind enough to wait until his mother got under the covers, though not a moment longer. At 1:57 p.m. on Monday, September 7, 1925, Inga's seven-pound, eleven-ounce son, Daniel Sherwood Cohelan, was born to the unsuspecting city of San Francisco.

★ ★ ★

Twenty-eight years later—with three marriages, three children, and a couple of career-related scandals behind him—Don Sherwood, born Daniel Cohelan, arrived at KSFO radio in San Francisco armed with a "carte blanche" agreement. It was March 6, 1953. The *San Francisco Examiner* announced: "KSFO introduces its new personality parade this morning, beginning with comic Don Sherwood. Formerly noted as the 'Noodnick' humorizer of KROW radio, this program could make this boy one of the best known local names before the year is out."

For the first time in his young life, Don was going to get paid to do exactly as he pleased and be exactly who he was from 6 to 9 each weekday morning on a leading radio station. And for the first time, he had a large audience to talk to and play with. Up to this point, his experience was of the sort often called "valuable."

Don had started in radio with a temporary job at KCBS. When that ended, he went to see Russ Coughlan, then the program director at KROW radio—today with KGO-TV. Russ remembers their first meeting well—

RUSS COUGHLAN:

Don had given away his belongings as part of some Eastern religious belief, and being broke, he decided it was time to eat again. There he stood in his T-shirt and jeans, which was all he had left.

He was a very good announcer and I needed one, so I hired him. Of course he couldn't come to work looking like that. He didn't have any money, so I bought him a suit and shoes—for which he never repaid me!

He did a good job. This was before he became successful, so he didn't pull any pranks. He was a good disc jockey with a unique sense of humor.

Al Torbet came in as Station Manager, and I started a disc jockey format like Los Angeles was doing. We started Don doing the "Nick & Noodnick" show as part of the first two-man disc jockey team in California. I was the afternoon guy, and Don eventually became the full morning guy. We did well and became the number two station, KSFO being number one.

Al Torbet liked Don's breezy manner, and it was a good time to be at KROW. Torbet was trying to build up the station and was giving his staff room to experiment.

The 6 to 9 morning show, "Nick and Noodnick," was called a "snappy rise 'n shine hilarious show combining comedy, music, time signals, guests, and singing weather reports" by a San Francisco newspaper. Torbet said it was the first time anyone realized that Sherwood had comic ability. It was also the first real press or publicity Don received.

Then Torbet created a noontime program for Don. The show was called "Sharps, Flats, and Sherwood." This was in addition to the "Nick and Noodnick" program, where by this time he was paired with deejay Ray Yeager.

Rod McKuen was an as-yet-unknown KROW staff

person, and Phyllis Diller was the continuity girl at the station. She was also writing jokes for "Nick and Noodnick." Phyllis and Don were friends from the start.

PHYLLIS DILLER:

I recognized a great talent in Don, a completely unused, fantastic, gigantic talent, but he was emotionally crippled from his mother, always being told "You're going to grow up and be like your father—a drunken bum!"

He had this rich, wonderful voice, and such an imagination, but he had no self-discipline. We both had the same sense of humor and were both terribly musical. We were soul mates.

He'd have me come into the studio and say on the air, "Good, good, goody-good morning" in this funny voice. That was my first real professional show-biz thing. He'd tease me and talk to me, clowning around.

It was a small, independent station, so there was no one breathing down your neck. These guys did all kinds of wonderful, fun things that no one can do anymore. Al Torbet believed in Don, and in me, and let us do anything. That's why we both later ended up at KSFO. Don thought I was such a Pollyanna . . .

All Don did at KROW was chat and play records. By the time he arrived at KSFO in 1953, however, he was formulating a rather different concept of the disc jockey *he* wanted to be.

He did not want to just spin records, read commercials, and give news, time checks, and station identification. He wanted to *wake people up*, get their adrenaline pumping and their minds in gear, and start their days with music that could lift their spirits. Don called it "adventures in music." Above all, he believed that people needed a good belly laugh to arm them for the day ahead.

Don loved language and the sound of names, so anything that tickled or fascinated him was likely to become a spontaneous, unscripted 'bit' on his show. Over the years, Don created a cast of characters that became part of his show: Skoshi, the little Japanese; Fenton, the know-it-all English puppet; Mort, the engineer; Bart Hercules, the musical monster with a Liberace voice, who taught weight control to women and peddled yogurt from goats "who cared enough to give their very best"; Sledge Hammer, the detective; Crash Footlocker, hosting "The Crash Footlocker Show—'The Man's Show' "; Fidel Trueheart, M.D., the doctor who lectured on the human body and its "care and prevention"; Rosita, the lead in "Just Plain Rosita," the soap opera that asked the question, "Can a woman over thirty-five . . .?"

When he wasn't being one of his characters, Don frequently read stories to his audience, such as the adventures of his beloved Tom Swift or the Rover Boys. What he did wasn't, of course, straight reading. In addition to his voice imitations, he gave new meaning to well-known stories through innuendo and his throaty, dirty laugh.

Herb Caen—who remains "Mr. San Francisco" to this day—was destined to have an enduring love-hate friendship with Don. In one of the first of his many commentaries about the deejay, the three-dot columnist noted in his *San Francisco Chronicle* column: "Don Sherwood is the only man in the world who could make The Rover Boys sound dirty—or haven't you been listening to his readings from 'The Classic' these mornings?"

Dick Nolan wrote in his *San Francisco Examiner* column, "My teenage son is going around these days practicing his 'Don Sherwood laugh.' Hevvins . . ."

Don's characters and his love for stories can be traced to his kindergarten year, when he was confined to bed with a rheumatic heart condition.

"He had to be kept quiet even though he didn't feel sick," his Aunt Marie, now in her eighties and living in Marin, recalls. "I would take the newspaper and read it to him. He'd try to follow along, asking 'Where are you now, Auntie?' He taught himself to read before he ever went to school."

Don spent a year in bed. He retreated into his own world of enchantment and beauty, a world he would never want to leave. Lying in his bed, he created characters and stories: "The space between the end of the bed and the wall became a deep river, the window ledge a great mountain," Don once said in an interview. "I was Tarzan, Tom Swift, Winnie-the-Pooh. All this shaped the talent and ruined everything else."

Will Sherwood Show?

Don Sherwood's listeners were quickly captivated by the characters who lived in his head, as was Don. A lesser talent might have been tempted to stick with what worked and let it go at that. Not Don.

Besides the character bits, music, and readings, Don delighted in impersonating certain singers, like Tony Bennett and Vaughn Monroe. When he went into his imitations, it was almost impossible to tell if it was Don singing or the record playing. In order to pull this off, he needed an engineer who could read his mind and be his right hand—someone equally talented. Only one person fit the bill: Charles Homer Smith.

Many people have said that the late Charlie Smith "made" Don Sherwood. Charlie had an extraordinary talent for entertainment and music, in addition to his consummate skill as an engineer; everybody recognized his genius.

Don and Charlie were a once-in-a-lifetime match-up, which was as much of a thrill to both men as it was to the audience. Charlie's nickname was Max, and Don referred to him as "The Oldest Man in the World."

In 1988, shortly before he died, Charlie reminisced about the early days with Don.

CHARLIE SMITH:

I had long since left Art Linkletter and come to KSFO when Don arrived at the station. He was kind of a dissipated bum there at first, coming in half-swacked, telling all about his wild episodes. I wondered who hired this guy, how anyone could work with someone like that! But I quickly found out that even if he was feeling bad, if he'd been up half the night before, he fit right in.

I worked for KSFO for thirty-five years. Don was one in the succession of early morning men that I worked with, and none of the others had his talent. The guy could step into the breach and do anything.

We'd start. No notes. Just a stack of commercials and a stack of records. Then Don would pick out what he wanted. If he didn't like a selection, he'd turn off the power and let it drag to a stop.

With the singing imitations, I gave Don the pitch, he started singing, then I segued into the record while he faded out. No one could tell where Don stopped and the real singer began. He would sometimes mess it up just so people would know *he* was singing.

Both of us loved sounds; I actually collected them. People knew this and sent me all kinds of strange sound recordings. I also recorded my own. I had cannon shots, rifle sounds—everything imaginable.

Don would say, "We have the wind, twenty-five miles per hour, range six hundred yards. Are you ready? Fire!" I'd turn off the music, fire the shot, and play the sound of falling junk or something. By working like mad and getting twenty things in your mind ahead of time, and having good equipment, you could do it. I'd fire one sound after the other on the turntable. He'd catch what I had in mind and jump in.

CHARLIE...

If we had tried to rehearse any of this, including the singing imitations, it would've sounded terrible. When you work that closely together, you get to know what the other guy is going to do.

One afternoon, I spent about thirty minutes stringing a bunch of unrelated music together and writing a script to go along with it. During the next show, without any warning, I put the needle on the record, handed the script to Don, and said, "Here, Don, try this."

Don did the whole thing. He played the parts of all the different characters, doing a miner's dialect, babies crying, and everything. As each episode ended in the script, the music would change, and he'd switch into another character. He did everything perfectly! Ironically, this script was called, "Lips That Touch Liquor Will Never Touch Mine."

By September 1953, Don's radio career was taking off. His name was showing up in the newspapers daily, he was the talk of the town, and the question most frequently being asked around the city was, "Did you hear what Sherwood said today?" Don was moving into the limelight.

His personal manager, Hugh Heller, of the San Francisco MCA (Music Corporation of America) office—now semi-retired and living in Missouri—says that from the moment he met Don in 1952, he saw the limitless possibilities of Don's talent. He began sending clips of everything Don was doing to MCA offices around the country, hoping to interest them in using Don for something national. For that to be a real possibility, his ratings had to be impressive.

Don himself informed the listeners about ratings: "You're listening to KSFO, and I have to keep reminding you of that because it's coming up to what they call 'ratings week.' One week out of every month little people go around with little pads and pencils and ask 'Who do you listen to in the morning?' and everyone says Doug Pledger!"

One of the first things Hugh did for Don was have a team of professionals handle his affairs. Given his drinking and his vulnerability to other people's ideas and schemes, Don was likely to squander everything. The team Hugh put together included Lemm Matthews, a personal attorney, as well as an accountant who monitored every financial transaction.

"Don owed about sixty thousand dollars to the IRS when I met him," Hugh says. "When I saw his checkbooks and saw that every check was written to 'CASH,' I said, 'How do you expect to talk to the IRS?' "

By November it was reported that Don, "hot as fire these days," had an offer from KNX in Hollywood to do a daily deejay show, and from Seattle, to air one hour of each Sherwood show.

But Don had already developed an illness that was to reoccur increasingly throughout his radio career: "radio sickness." He was playing hooky. The station tried sending cabs to pick him up and bring him to work; they charged him hard cash for shows he missed. It was all a futile exercise.

His malady didn't go unnoticed in the newspapers. Herb Caen noted:

> Don Sherwood's appearances on KSFO have become so unpredictable that the station has changed the name of his program from "The Sherwood Show" to "Will Sherwood Show?" Don Sherwood, madly in love and living it up, missed three of his five shows on KSFO last week, which cost him a pretty pfennig. But I guess she's worth it . . .

Don, apparently, was worth it, too. His many live-in characters, his famous singing imitations, and now his absenteeism, were getting a lot of laughs. In addition, he'd found a new source of amusement—his sponsors. While he never knocked their products, he gave them a real going over. After reading the script, he'd throw in a few ir-reverent comments such as, "I tried it and it didn't work."

The reaction after Don first clowned around with Les Vogel Chevrolet commercials was overwhelming; busi-nesses all over the Bay Area tried to jump on the band-wagon. Don's quoted response was, "I'm a disc jockey on the morning shift. My customers got money in their pock-ets. My job is to get it!"

Barnaby Conrad—portrait artist, author of *Matador*, and at the time, owner of a club by the same name—remembers one particular commercial: "This is brought to you by the man's deodorant—Splat! It comes in a bucket and you put it on with a trowel. Yes, this is a *man's* de-odorant. None of that sissy stuff!"

Every media person in San Francisco was watching Don. In December of 1953, Raymond Pierce of the *San Francisco Call Bulletin* wrote:

> Don Sherwood is one of the strange animals called a disc jockey. You'll pay little or no attention to the records he plays. People listen to him for the commercials—they are the most entertaining part of the show. Other disc jockeys, among themselves hardly ever chummy, listen to him to pick up pointers on how to get away with murder on a radio station. The show is "sold out" solid. What kind of creature is this adliberizer of zanology that has college professors writing him fan letters?

> For one thing, he's completely loony in as well as out of the studio—just doesn't give a whoop—has even burped loudly on the air—yaks at his own yaks. An en-tourage follows him around—two straightmen and a "coordinator" and a publicity agent. The trio is battier than the Marx Bros. Do they go home with him?

> He shifts accents like a chameleon changes color; does a French one, too—"cherchez la femme." He is getting more settled down now, though, after 3½ years of happy marriage.

While the station was allocating an enormous advertising budget for Don, word of mouth was building Don's popularity. Each morning, simultaneously, alarms went off and radios came on tuned to KSFO. The first question groggy listeners asked was, "Is he there? Is it Don?" They had begun to believe that if Don was there, it was going to be a great day; if he wasn't, it was going to be rough.

Last of the
Juvenile
Delinquents

Within the industry, record promoters were courting Don. Guy Haines, a promoter with Capitol Records now living in San Francisco, remembers his early attempts to persuade Don to play Capitol Records' selections.

GUY HAINES:

Before the Top 40 came in, we promoted individual records at the stations. Don, of course, only played what he wanted to, hit or otherwise. He jumped on the bossa nova from Brazil about a year before anyone else even started to listen to it.

One time I was hired by Marshall Naify of United Artists to promote a new release. I told Don how important it was to me. He yanked it off before it was finished, saying, "That's the worst thing I've heard!"

Don got first pick among the deejays, and KSFO got first pick among the stations—which irritated the hell out of the other stations.

Mecca Records, which ultimately became Pennant, was owned by Sidney Mobell and Tom Spinosa. Mobell, now a prominent San Francisco jeweler known worldwide for his unique creations, also wrote songs. When KSFO was promoting his music, he got to know Guy and Don. "Unfortunately," Mobell says, "Don never did buy any jewelry from me!"

In November of 1954, riding high on the success of their golden boy, KSFO took a major step. Not only did they move the studios to the elegant Fairmont Hotel, the station's management decided to create flashy studios to reflect their success.

Dick Swig, president of the Fairmont Hotel, says, "I'd listen to Don's show on my way to work to see what was going on at *my* hotel! There was a lot of crazy clowning around in the KSFO area. Don would call me almost every day."

Dwight Newton wrote many commentaries on Don in his *San Francisco Examiner* column. In the first of these, he wrote:

> It took me a long time to "get with" Sherwood, per-haps because it took him a long time to get with him-self. What he does now is neither precise, clear cut, nor routine. It's just original Sherwood; voicings by a man who at last is in command of himself. . . . Actually, the "Sherwood Show" is a two-man show, for one must include his engineer, Charlie "Max" Smith. Sherwood is gifted with a voice appeal I've heard femme fans de-scribe with a three letter word: s-e-x. That won't hurt his career. He's with us for no one knows how long—because in his short breaks between records, he's ex-posing the sort of drollery that could make him another—but entirely different—George Gobel.

Newton was doubtless referring to the fact that Don was gaining national attention. In a series of profiles done on the nation's best disc jockeys, George Coffey of United PressRadio in San Francisco wrote:

> Don Sherwood, the self-styled "hottest radio prop-

erty in San Francisco" says he got that way by hating people. "I also hate children, flowers, dogs, birds, and housewives," he says.

Sherwood is referred to by his co-workers as the last of the juvenile delinquents. "They told me I need a psychiatrist," he states.

Disregarding time signals, Sherwood is apt to tell his listeners, "If *you* don't know what time it is, you have no business holding down a responsible job!"

As for his goal in life, Sherwood says deadpan, "I'd like to float to Hawaii in a Martini shaker."

Locally, Herb Caen wrote in his column:

Found Don Sherwood hunched over black coffee, looking pale, wan. "Just had an electrocardiograph," he muttered, running a hand over moist brow. "Think I had a heart attack Sunday. I was sitting home, watching the 49ers, and all of a sudden it felt like somebody hit me in the side with a pickaxe. I fell to the floor, writhing, and all I could think was 'Gee, I haven't been having much fun and now it's all over.' " Asked solicitously, "Did your whole past flash in front of your eyes?" "Even worse," he groaned. "My whole future!" Made note—Must put these things in writhing, and crept away, shaken. Life without Sherwood—unthinkable.

The various newspapers in the city recorded Don's every move or quote:

human interest:

KSFO's elegant Don Sherwood got a call the other day from a Mrs. Galli. Seems that her little girl had fallen into the duck pond in front of the Palace of Fine Arts—whereupon a nice man jumped in and rescued her. Trouble was, the nice man left before anybody could get his name, and Mrs. Galli wondered if somebody could identify the hero, so she could thank him. Don told the story. "Sorry, Mrs. Galli. No news about the man who rescued your little girl from the duck pond. However, we've had three calls from men who claim they pushed her in!"

on San Francisco parking:

A man of the cloth had an appointment, but could find no place to park. He finally stopped in a yellow zone and left a note which read: "I have driven around this block twenty times, and if I didn't park here I'd be late. Forgive us our trespasses." When he came back he found a traffic citation and a note: "I have driven around this block twenty times and if I didn't give you a ticket, I'd lose my job. Lead us not into temptation."

on sausage:

The only thing that worries me about salami is—how did it get around when it was alive?

on government:

Government statisticians collect facts and draw their own confusions.

on income:

Every man's income runs into four figures—the figure he makes; the figure he tells Internal Revenue; the figure he tells his wife; and the figure she passes on to her bridge club.

tip for remembering to turn off car lights:

When you get in the car and turn your lights on, un-zip your pants. When you get to work and forget to turn them off, you'll walk in and someone will tell you your fly is down. Then you know you left the lights on.

Don typified a unique era—San Francisco in the fifties.

Throughout the years ahead, it would be fondly remembered as the best of times. Russ Coughlan describes it this way—

RUSS COUGHLAN:

The city was Enrico Banducci's *hungry i* and the *Purple Onion*. The *Purple Onion* was where they'd have amateur night and all of us, including Phyllis Diller, would go and do our acts. Don worked clubs too. We had done some things together, singing in a club. One time we both sang for this contest that was for a new suit, and he won. Well, he had no taste in clothes; he picked this ugly polyester suit! He was so hurt, he thought it was classy. Then there was George Andros' *Fack's I* on Market Street. The city had a lot of little clubs with good acts. Barnaby Conrad's place on Broadway was great. He was a wild bastard!

We didn't do dope, we did booze. We dressed in shirts and ties, and had decent haircuts—we weren't going for the absurdity then like now.

It was a really good time in San Francisco. It was before the sleaze. You could walk at night and not get killed. It was a town of class, not a dominance of social people, which you have now. It was the working guy's town, blue collar, good clean fun. We had more real humor then, not dirty humor.

San Franciscans saw themselves as special, much more so than now. We didn't have racism to speak of. There were districts, and everyone had theirs. Everyone stayed in their own, generally; there wasn't transportation.

It was a healthy town, you didn't have the stress you have now or the racial tensions. As musicians, we were just musicians, we weren't black or white musicians. There was a spirit in the town, and an innate loyalty to the city and to San Franciscans.

We worked very hard and were social among ourselves. We'd hang out till four in the morning telling

RUSS...

stories, having some laughs, because it was a good time, and we were all poor. It was the post-war era, all of us trying to get organized and get our lives together.

For Don, "getting his life together" was not all that easy. At twenty-eight, the web of people already in his life presented him with staggering responsibilities.

Young Rebel

From Don's first breath, his life was an emotional seesaw. He did not go home from the hospital to the tune of "Mommy and Daddy, and Danny makes three."

Inga and Marie took baby Daniel home to their mother's house on Twenty-sixth Avenue. Although she had not yet officially separated from Daniel Cohelan, Sr., Mother Inga had by then moved out of the apartment Don's father and she had lived in since their marriage, and moved into her mother's house. Inga, her mother, and Marie lived there together.

"For the first eleven weeks of Don's life, his mother couldn't get out of bed due to her phlebitis," Aunt Marie says. "I took care of both her and the baby. She never touched him. His father never came home even when he promised to, so he was no help. Don was really *my* boy."

"Daddy" was a nondescript, ordinary man who drifted from one job to another and never accepted responsibility for his son or his wife. He was an alcoholic and completely unreliable. Inga and Don were essentially on their own, and her apparent physical and emotional rejection of him prevented any normal bonding between them.

Inga was an intelligent, opinionated Irish-Scandinavian. Her whole family was reportedly creative, and she was a talented pianist. She may well have had great aspirations, but she had to support herself and her son. Her only option was to spend long days trudging from house to house throughout San Francisco, giving piano lessons.

There were periods when Inga did respond to her small child, but they were sporadic because of her overriding bitterness about having a child to raise. While other young women were being wooed by the upbeat tunes of the day, dancing the Charleston in their stylish flapper dresses, Inga was trying to cope with a failed marriage, an unplanned baby, and her financial situation. In an era where everything promised good times and romance, there were no such prospects for Inga. On her income from piano lessons, even staples like milk at fifty-six cents a gallon and bread at nine cents a pound must have looked expensive.

"It has now been four months since his father has seen him," Inga wrote in Don's baby book in July 1927. "He never telephones and doesn't send us any money unless we ask for it." Two months later, she added, "Your birthday came and has passed and no word or present from your father." Almost two years down the road, things had not changed. "Another birthday and two Christmas days and no presents, money, or message from your father." Finally, in September 1929, she wrote, "Divorce granted with full custody, no alimony or child support. No opposition or arguments."

With the divorce final, Inga nearly put a hole in the page erasing "Daniel Cohelan" from her son's baby book. She substituted "Donald Sherwood Cohelan," Sherwood being a name she pulled out of the air. His name was legally changed to "Donald Sherwood Cohelan." Inga later explained, "His father didn't have anything to do with rearing him, and I didn't see why he should have his son named after him."

While Inga worked all day, Marie took care of Don. "He was such a sweet boy. I adored him, and he was devoted to me, of course, since I was like his mother," she emphasizes.

A natural bond between Don and Marie grew out of her consistent love and attention, creating friction between the two sisters. Inga had to rely on Marie to care for Don and she certainly did not want to play mother, yet she became increasingly jealous of Don's genuine attachment to his aunt. This jealousy eventually caused a permanent estrangement between Inga and Marie, making Don a victim of their emotional tug-of-war.

Don was about ten-and-a-half when his father, of whom he had no memory, died. Most reports were that he died of a heart attack; Marie remembers it differently. According to her, he was coming home late one night after a regular visit to his mistress; he walked around a stationary streetcar, only to be hit by an oncoming car from the other direction. Either way, he died young.

Inga took Don to the funeral in Los Angeles. Daniel Sr. had not only neglected to tell his family that he had remarried, he'd also failed to mention his marriage to Inga to his new wife.

"How do you do. I'm Mrs. Cohelan."

"Oh, how nice to meet you. I'm Inga Cohelan and this is Daniel's son, Don."

"Dan . . . Da . . . son . . ." That was that. The newly widowed woman fainted.

The funeral was now Don's only memory of his father.

With no male role model during his early years and in constant conflict with his mother, Don almost inevitably became an inveterate rebel by the time he was a teenager. He disregarded any instruction he was given by Aunt Marie and the church—he was confirmed at the Church of the Incarnation on March 3, 1940—and chose to rely solely on his own observations and wit. Any pictures drawn for him of such things as love, family, trust, honesty, and security seemed to him to be contradictions of his own reality. He opted to live by more tangible beliefs.

At this early stage of his life, Don's belligerent attitude toward authority and conformity was fixed, and while it didn't win him any medals then, in later years it became a significant part of his appeal.

Don told a reporter: "My mother was a dynamo, bright as hell, with a great sense of humor. She was a real woman's libber. But she was afraid, raising me alone, that she'd be too gentle with me. So she beat me all the time with a broom handle, until I was about thirteen. Then I took the stick away and broke it over my knee and the beatings stopped. We were never close." In fact, he threatened to kill her if she ever laid a hand on him again.

Don bounced between high schools, always getting expelled. His grades were a disaster.

"I wasn't a rotten kid. I was confused," Don said. "I took puberty pretty hard. In fact, I went bananas. It took me five high schools to get through the eleventh grade, majoring in recess and tea dancing. Actually, I never stopped long enough to really major in anything. I just tried to stay one step ahead of the principal!"

Marie recalls that Don didn't have many friends because he was always in debt to all of them. "He'd borrow money and never pay it back. Then he'd come to me to borrow some, and I couldn't give him the money."

At sixteen, after seeing "A Yank in the RAF," Don hopped a bus north hoping to join "the boys." He lied about his age and was inducted into the Canadian Tank Corps. Shortly thereafter, however, when the announcement was made that they would be in England by Christmas, Don rushed to confess his true age and hightailed it home.

Back at school, he still did not graduate. Few people knew that he never finished high school, yet it remained a source of great insecurity and self-consciousness to him. He was an avid reader and had the mind to learn, but he lacked the self-discipline to follow any program.

After leaving school, Don drove a sandwich truck during the day and took continuing education courses at night. It was the principal who suggested Don go to radio school, emphasizing that with his smooth, deep voice he would do well. On this good advice, Don enrolled in the Samuel Gompers School in San Francisco, later bragging that he completed the whole course in a matter of weeks, fast-tracking so he could go to work as soon as possible. But, having completed radio school, he found there were no jobs in radio.

The best jobs going appeared to be serving in the Merchant Marine, so he promptly signed on. It was both the beginning of his love for the sea and an introduction to the world at large. Once away from home, he faced a serious dilemma: what to do about women? In this early letter from sea to Aunt Marie, Don purportedly seeks advice on this matter, although he clearly knows what he wants. This is classic Don:

Dear Auntie,

I've been writing mush to Pat [the girlfriend down the street], but deep down I'm beginning to wonder whether it is the real thing, or if it was brought about by my lonesomeness at being sent to a place like this. Will you please write me a letter, man to man, and give me advice, as you always have, on what I should do next. Whether I should begin to ease off slowly, or just come outright and tell her there has been an emotional strain put on me for the past two months, that prompted me to say such lovey-dovey things. . . . Now don't get me wrong, I meant everything I said to her, when I said it, but now I've been sorta callused you might call it, and I don't want to look forward to a home or anything. . . . After all, I'm going to see a lot of girls and life in these four years, more than I had expected. When I joined the Navy I didn't plan to be in longer than a year. . . . Now I just want to be a sailor and raise hell.

Love,

Returning from the sea in 1944, Don landed a job as a radio announcer at KFRC and moved back into Aunt Marie and Uncle Andrew's basement apartment. About the third Saturday at his new job, Don left the house, saying to Aunt Marie, "I'm going to do something you won't like."

When Marie caught up with him a few days later, Don announced: "I got married!"

Don was nineteen years old and his bride, Svetlana, was a few years older. No one knows where they met or how they got together. "My mother brought me up under the strict rules that you don't sleep with someone unless you're married," was Don's explanation.

The marriage lasted a year.

"I came home one day, and their place was stripped clean," Marie remembers. "Everything was gone, including Don's things. I called Don at work and said 'You better come home.' "

Svetlana had gone home to her parents. The couple reconciled and Svetlana came back, but one morning shortly thereafter, when she came home after staying out all night, everything blew.

Marie heard Svetlana screaming, "Don't kill me! Don't kill me!" as she ran out the door. Don came up the stairs right behind her, his face all scratched up, his hair disheveled. That was the end.

His wife was not the only thing to go. While Don had a great baritone voice, perfect for an announcer, his job at KFRC was short-lived. He had only been hired as a temporary replacement, and his time was up.

Don took off for Los Angeles, hoping to get radio work there, but with no contacts or references to speak of, his futile job search kept him near starvation. After a year, he gave up and headed back to San Francisco. He found the competition even tougher than it had been in Los Angeles which forced him to take a job with the Armed Forces Radio Service.

He headed back to sea. After only six months as a radio operator on an Army transport, he was drawn back to San Francisco.

There were many things that Don did not particularly like about his life, but San Francisco was not one of them. In sickness and in health, for richer or for poorer, till death would them part, this little city was his home.

Baby Diane

KGO radio, at 100 Sansome Street, was the first building in town to have automatic elevators, air conditioning, and no windows.

Don decided to take a stab at getting a job there. He waltzed into the station cold. Following his uncanny instincts, he tried to sweet-talk the pretty, young brunette receptionist, Sally, into helping him.

"He came to me saying, 'Put in a good word for me.' He told me that he was just out of the Merchant Marine. His face was all broken out and his hair was getting thin, 'from an exotic disease I got in Korea.' "

Don didn't get a job at KGO and went to work instead as an announcer at KCBS in the Palace Hotel. He did not, however, give up on either Sally or KGO.

SALLY :

He came back one day, and between the elevator doors opening and closing, he managed to run over to my desk to leave a bouquet of violets and a poem he'd written, and get back in the elevator! Then he came back another day and asked if I wanted an ice cream. He ran out, spent his last dime on it, and brought it back to me.

I was nineteen years old, a very immature nineteen, I might add. This was a very grown-up, sophisticated job

SALLY...

for me, to be the receptionist. I had started wearing silk stockings and heels.

KGO was having a cocktail party one night, and I thought it would be a good way for Don to meet people. Of course, I didn't drink; I'd never even had a cup of coffee. We went to the party, and he talked to everybody. That night was our first real date. He took a cigar band and placed it on my finger and asked me to marry him, and I said yes!

The next day I was telling all the radio announcers. They took me for coffee breaks, advising me to think about it. I said, "Oh I have! I've thought about it." That's how it happened—on our first date.

When he took me to meet his mother, Inga, I didn't know where we were going. He said, "We're going to see someone." We went to Fairfax and drove up a rural road. The house was up on a hillside, and we had to walk up all these steps. It was a bright, sunny day, but the house was very dark inside. My eyes adjusted, and there sat this woman with a band on her head, looking like a Gypsy. I thought he'd taken me to see a fortune teller! There were two huge pianos in the room, and cats. It finally dawned on me that the "Gypsy" was his mother.

I loved the name Danny, but he'd told me his mother never called him Dan. I was not to slip up and call him Danny. I remember being so disappointed that his name was really Don.

His mother was very eccentric, completely different from anyone I'd ever met before. But then, Don was different too. I'd only gone with high school boys to this point, and Don was a *man*. He was twenty-one, he'd been married before, he'd been to sea, and he was a radio announcer.

Don and Sally—today a legal secretary and living north of San Francisco—were married in August of 1947 at the Church of the Wayfarer in Carmel. Bill Martel, Don's best friend from his starving L.A. days, was there, along with his mother. Sally's parents were there, too, and one of her girlfriends. Don was late, of course. "My father was furious, thinking Don had stood me up," Sally says. "I didn't know better and never for a moment believed he wouldn't show."

Don and Bill arrived; their car had broken down, and they'd hitchhiked to the wedding.

This time, instead of moving in with Aunt Marie, the newlyweds rented the downstairs apartment from Mother Inga in Fairfax. Don was working at KCBS. Things went relatively smoothly in the house, considering the relationship between Don and his mother. Inga easily dominated Sally, who was a timid girl.

One day, the two women went to select linoleum for the kitchen floor in the young couple's apartment.

"I was afraid to speak up about what I liked," Sally vividly remembers. "His mother intimidated me, so when she picked out some stuff that looked like liver spots and vomit, I didn't object. When Don got home and asked how we did, I told him that his mother liked this. 'Well, what do *you* like?' he asked. I told him which one I liked. He marched upstairs, and he and his mother went at it! Of course, I was afraid that now she would know I had complained and caused this blowup. She called him a son-of-a-bitch and he yelled back 'Yes! That's exactly what I am, a son of a *bitch*!' He told his mother, 'She's going to have the linoleum she wants, and you're not going to put that shit on there!'

"I'd never heard a mother and child fight like that. I never talked back to my mother. It was a whole new world for me."

Sally, however, did see Inga's affection for Don. She says that, to his mother, Don was the "immaculate conception." Inga told Sally that Don was her Jesus Christ, since his father had so little to do with it. "She was proud of Don. She bragged about him to all her friends, even though to his face, she would put him down and criticize him. If she heard him playing piano, she'd say, 'Oh, Donny's so talented!' " Ironically, years earlier, Don pleaded with his mother for piano lessons. But Inga had flatly refused to teach him, forcing him to go to Aunt Marie's house to play *her* piano.

Don opened the KCBS station each morning, going on the air from 5:50 to 6:00—a whole ten minutes. He played a couple of records, talked, and gave the news. Then he had to hang around for *eight hours* to do the two o'clock news and station breaks. It wasn't much of a radio job, but it *was* a job.

According to Sally, "When Don was really happy after a show, he'd call his mother and ask, 'Did you hear the show? What d'ya think of it?' He wanted her approval so badly. But she wasn't the kind of woman to praise him to his face. She would pick out the one part of the show that went wrong."

Sally, a soft-spoken woman, recognizes that Inga didn't have it easy either. "She was a single mother in the days when hardly anyone was. She had to go around and teach piano lessons. Don used to say to me that he was the only little boy who didn't have anyone to call him in when it was dinner time. Everyone went home to their own house, to their family. *His* mother would be teaching. But she always left macaroni and cheese or something for him, or dropped off a hot lunch for him at school if she wasn't going to be home for dinner. And Aunt Marie took care of him."

Having lived around both Inga and Aunt Marie, Sally could understand Don's attitude about women, and these two women in particular.

"Auntie was your perfect lady, so feminine. Everything was just so. Little tea cups . . . everything done in small portions, dainty, with a special plate for this and special flowers on the table. The table was cleared before dessert. Even at dinner, it was like you were at someone's house for tea. She was all love and caring.

"Inga was totally the opposite! She'd slop the food on the table. You'd have your cake or pie right on top of the plate you had your meat and gravy on. Half the time, the dessert would have ants on it! You'd think it was little chocolate things on the frosting. She'd bake the cake and frost it and then put it in the cooler room on top of the fridge—and the ants would come. She also had a cat that was always on the counter, so you'd see cat hair in everything.

"She was a very strong woman, and one thing was for sure—you always knew where you stood."

By Thanksgiving, only three months into their marriage, Sally had morning sickness. They had not planned on a baby just yet.

"Everything was so new, and happening so fast," Sally says. "I was not the girl he'd met and courted a few months ago. I had been through so much in such a short time. Now I was someone who was sick all the time, getting fat and grumpy. He wanted us to be happy, and mostly, he wanted our child to know it was loved. I frowned all the time because I wasn't feeling well. He would say to me, 'Now we've got to *smile* around this baby, because we want it to be a *happy* baby!' "

Sally didn't know how to cook; she had never made a bed or done her own laundry. On top of that, mother-in-law Inga's place was "rustic" and Don was fastidious.

"Everything had its place," says Sally. "He was so organized. He'd run his finger along the window sill to see if I'd dusted. He was a cleanliness nut. We didn't even have a phone, so I'd have to run upstairs if I heard the phone ring, pregnant and all. The washing machine was an old wringer, and I'd never done that. It was all quite difficult."

When baby Diane was born, on July 29, 1948, Don announced her birth on the radio, telling everybody that his daughter was born at four that morning. The letters he received from listeners congratulating him confirmed that he already had fans—even from a mere ten minutes on the air.

During this period, one of Don's close friends and drinking buddies, Frank Haggerty, then the guitar player in the Ray Hackett band at the station, suggested to Don that he audition for the band singer's spot, which had just opened up. Don auditioned and got the job, which gave him the chance to build a modest reputation as a singer. "Young Man with a Song" was the name of his show.

"Hackett wasn't the most amiable man in the world," Frank Haggerty says with a chuckle. "He'd throw Don a lead sheet of a song nobody had ever heard of and tell him it was going to be on the show the next day." Don had never learned to read music. "I'd get out my guitar and we'd spend hours working on it so he'd have it ready for the show. Songs were not arranged within Don's range, of course, so lots of times he was squeaking and squawking."

Don and Frank would stop off for drinks after work to play shuffleboard and relax. Don began to come home later and later.

By then he had met Shirley.

Shirley was a script typist at the radio station. She was a "mature seventeen-year-old," described as a cute, bouncy, curly-headed girl. Don and Frank had talked about her to Sally and other people, but Sally hadn't thought anything about it. It came as a complete surprise to her when Don packed up and moved out, leaving her in the basement of the dragon lady's house.

Baby Diane was eighteen months old. Sally was now to be the divorced mother of a young baby, forced to go back to work to support them.

Don was doing to Sally what his father had done to his mother—and to him.

"Inga used to tell me, 'You'd better watch out. Donny's a very handsome man, and there are lots of women who would be interested in him.' I was so naive," Sally reflects. "I told her, 'Oh, but he's married to me!' I didn't know that sort of thing went on."

History had begun to repeat itself.

Love
and
Scandal

Don started in radio during its most glamorous period. In the late forties radio stations were nothing like the electronic studios of today. Each had its own live orchestra and band; studio pages darted about; there was a Hollywood excitement in the air. Stars were being made. Television was still relatively young, and most people had been raised on radio, which was still very much a part of their lives and a major source of entertainment.

Shirley, Don's new love, had been working for KCBS for several weeks by the time Don came into her life. She had taken the job temporarily; her ultimate goal was to go to Hollywood and study acting.

"I fell in love with Don the moment I heard his voice, and I never fell out of love with him," Shirley says. "It was a long love affair that never ended."

SHIRLEY :

The first day I saw him, I was coming down the stairs

SHIRLEY...

from the music library. This guy was laughing and talking to the program director. I saw big shoulders in a grey, striped, flannel suit, and heard a deep, resonant voice. I managed to think of several reasons to walk by so I could get a good look.

The flirtation grew and grew. Over a period of weeks we became friends. He was married, but he told me his marriage was rocky, and a divorce was inevitable. He moved out of his mother's house and separated from Sally, and we started seeing each other.

Don was really torn, not wanting to hurt his daughter, and I was trying to convince myself that he would have divorced Sally even if we hadn't met. No one knew we were seeing each other until one writer, who was interested in me and jealous of Don, went to the station manager and told him of our involvement and Don's separation from Sally. This was not the image the station wanted. It was all a big scandal, and CBS fired Don.

No one suggested that I leave the station; Don was seen as the bad guy, and I was the "innocent child." Of course, I quit anyway. That night I made an unsuccessful suicide attempt, which added to Don's growing feelings of guilt and misery.

Don was fired from KCBS on May 29, 1949. Completely stunned to be suddenly out of work again and flat broke, he moved back with his mother. Sally had already moved out of the house. Shirley was living with her own mother and had found another job in San Francisco. Don, on the other hand, couldn't find work. He later commented that his firing from CBS was the beginning of his "deep hatred for network executives."

Don took jobs working in a warehouse and as a truck driver, and then a job at a lumberyard. He was able to borrow the company truck to meet Shirley for sack lunches on the waterfront.

They really began to get to know each other during this time when there were no diversions.

"Life was so uncomplicated," Shirley adds, with a sad smile. "We had so little, and we appreciated everything—a walk in the park, time spent with good friends. Many years later we both talked about this period in our lives that for each of us was the best of times."

Don became interested in Eastern religions at this point and gave away all his clothes, keeping only one tweed suit.

"He was going to live the simple, pure life," Shirley says. "He withdrew from the rat race—mainly because he couldn't keep a job! It was a good time to not be into materialism."

For Don's ex-wife Sally, now living in San Francisco, life was more complicated. She was trying to find a way to work and take care of baby Diane, but there was nothing resembling today's day care. Places that took care of children kept them around the clock. "It's hard on the children whose mother doesn't come," a woman told Sally.

Aunt Marie and Uncle Andrew offered to take care of Diane. It was the only good solution. Sally says she saw her daughter on weekends and holidays. "Having Diane stay with family was certainly better than with strangers, but it was a very unhappy time for me. I've blocked a lot of it out."

Aunt Marie was only too happy to care for Diane, just as she had cared for Don as a child. Her comments are reminiscent of earlier days. "I was her only mother for a long time. Sally would come on the weekends. Don would come to visit her sporadically. She was such a sweet child, and she got very attached to me, of course."

"I'd visit Diane on a weekend. She'd fall and scrape her knees or something and run to Auntie," Sally remembers, with tears in her eyes. "Diane lived there for two years. It was Auntie who cared for her. It hurt me so much when she ran to Marie and not to me, but it was understandable. I hated to leave her, but what else could I do?"

Meanwhile, Don struggled to keep the jobs he could get, although his temper and independence sometimes got the better of him. In his early twenties, with an ex-wife and a child to support, he didn't have the luxury of options.

Don's contact with Marie, outside of occasional visits, was frequently by letter:

Dear Auntie,
Here is a measly ten for the week of the 13th, the weeks of the 20th and 27th will be forthcoming. I kind of juggled finances a bit to enable me to have my teeth pulled, something that just had to be done or I could never go to work!

I now look like someone's grandmother, and am told I shall remain toothless for 10 days or more.

I certainly hope to drop over and have some soup with you in the near future—maybe Tues. or Weds? I shall call before hand.

Thanks for being so patient, once again, and I shall get caught up with my bills.

Love to all,

★ ★ ★

Dear Auntie,
I'm awfully sorry there isn't a check included in this note.

Once again, I must reassure you that I'm not taking advantage of the fact that my daughter is with you, rather than at a home with demands being made constantly for remuneration.

I shall make good every commitment but as I said, because of the present circumstances, it may be slow.

I shall definitely be over to have lunch with you next week. I get my teeth tomorrow! I do feel we have a great deal to talk about.

Love to you,

When it became possible for Diane to go home with Sally, inevitably it couldn't be done without hurt feelings.

Sally says: "Auntie Marie told me that the doctor advised against taking Diane back, saying she would need psychiatric help to make this break. I just fell apart and called Don. 'That's a bunch of bullshit! You make an appointment with that doctor, and we'll go see him,' he said.

"Don was always very supportive—he was there whenever I needed him all through the years.

"We went to the doctor, who said, 'No, I feel the child should be with the mother, in most circumstances. You know, too much love can be harmful.' That was the nice way he put it. He knew Don and I were decent people and that I wanted my child back."

Sally took Diane to her grandfather's place in Wyoming.

"There were a lot of misunderstandings," Sally explains. "I think Marie thought I was a cold person, but I was just ignorant about many things. We were all so young."

In the interim, Don and Sally had gotten a proxy Mexican divorce through a friend of Don's who sent the papers off. They came back mostly in Spanish.

One day Don called Sally in a panic. "I don't think that Mexican divorce is legal!" He and Shirley had been married a few weeks before, two years after they'd met.

"You mean you married Shirley on August twenty-third—*our* wedding day?" Sally gasped. She reassured him that she would get a California divorce.

Everyone had tried to talk Shirley out of marrying Don, which was a familiar scene. "I kept saying, 'But this is different, we love each other!' " Shirley says.

Having lived with one wife at Aunt Marie's, and with another wife at mother Inga's, this time Don moved his bride into a studio of their own in the Richmond district.

Shirley got pregnant immediately.

"There we were, so poor and so happy," Shirley remembers. "We'd walk from Seventeenth Avenue to the beach, in order to have money for pie and coffee at Max's Green Apple Pie Shop. We'd walk all over, talking and holding hands. Gradually his interest to revive his career took hold again, as well as the thought of getting revenge on CBS."

Marriage on-the-Rocks

This was when Don first went to Russ Coughlan and began at KROW with the "Nick and Noodnick Show. It was just in time. On June 1, 1951, his son Greg was born.

"All was well," Shirley says. "Don started doing commercials. He did a Kilpatrick's commercial and had to ask them for quick payment so that I could get out of the hospital!

"I remember Sundays, when we'd go over to his mother's house for dinner. It never worked out. As soon as they were in the same room they'd start fighting. I'd change the subject, trying to herd if off so we could eat the beautiful pork roast I saw in the kitchen, but most of the time we never made it that far. Don would storm out saying, 'I'll be in the car.' I'd beg him to be nicer to his mother. 'She's the ax murderess of Marin!' he'd growl."

Inga and Don were both opinionated and strong-willed. They were both well read, and usually at opposite ends of an issue. Neither of them could stand to be disagreed with.

"And they both drank," Shirley adds. "Inga was very dramatic and would fake a heart attack as we were about to leave. She would get so mad at me for not taking her side in their arguments because she believed that women should stick together against anything a man said. I kept my opinions to myself!"

Don's ex-wife Sally and current wife Shirley were friends-of-sorts and occasionally even took care of the children for each other. While they were very different physically—Sally was tall, thin, and brunette; Shirley was shorter, "more voluptuous," and blonde—both women were soft-spoken, gentle, loving, and totally supportive of Don.

"I could see that Shirley was going through exactly what I'd been through," Sally says. "I'd go over and baby-sit when Greg was a baby, so Shirley and Don could get out together. She'd tell me she was alone so much, like I had been. They had me to dinner a couple of times. I always liked Shirley."

While Shirley was spending more and more time alone, Don was experiencing the thrill of being noticed around town and, at KROW, the staff was beginning to find out what he was all about. At KROW, the staff was beginning to find out what he was all about. He clowned around in the studio, making faces at people in the booth while they were trying to do their show. He was the joker.

As Don and Shirley's marriage got increasingly shaky, though, his attitude changed. He moped around the studio, becoming gloomy and morose. He'd go up to the office, with its big French windows and no balcony, and threaten to kill himself as he took a running leap toward the windows. Phyllis Diller would scream, falling for his stunt every time, as Don stopped just short of the window, a grin on his face.

Turmoil in Don's personal life seemed to be as much a part of him as breathing; right now he was chomping at the bit with family responsibilities.

Phyllis Diller took Shirley out to lunch one day to try to help Shirley understand Don better, and to help her see how she should handle Don if she hoped to keep their marriage together.

"Phyllis was kind and understanding," Shirley says. "Don and I both loved her. She explained to me how Don was different, that he was never going to conform and that the harder I tried to make a suburban husband out of him, the more he was going to fight it. The best way to keep him was to let him go, so he would always come back. I became determined to give Don the space he needed."

A major silence was developing between Don and his loyal friend, Aunt Marie, to which Don responded with the following letter:

Dear Auntie,

I sat down purposely in front of a blank piece of paper because I felt there was something I should say, but I'll be switched if I can think of what it is. Monetarily I feel that over the next few months I will have completely repaid you for the specified amount. I do fully realize, however, that payment in full will not, and can never be forthcoming.

What you have done in time of need for Sally and myself and Diane can never be measured in dollars and cents.

It seems that over the years we have gradually drifted apart, mainly because of the things you have DONE for me. The old philosophers were certainly right!

Another factor in the infrequency of our get-togethers was Uncle, whom I can't blame too much. Now that there is this great new gap brought about by your loss of Diane, and the part I may have played in same, I can't see what is going to happen.

All I can say is, I do appreciate you for what you've done for me, both recently and in the years gone by. But with the picture painted in such somber tones, how, I ask you, can I ever prove this?

If I have caused you concern in the past with my failure to pay for Diane on time it, believe me, was due to the many tricks of fate . . . and a gradually subdued idea that I had some right to live my own life.

Thank you for the Valentine's card to Greg.

Love,

Then Don's life took a new turn. Al Torbet—General Manager of KROW—left to go to KSFO. Don was right behind him. Al had secretly signed him to the new station.

KSFO offered the opportunity to make everything Don had worked for worthwhile. He didn't waste any time saying "See ya later" to his buddy, Russ Coughlan. It quickly proved to be the right move—at least for his career.

"Everything was wonderful until his career clicked and he got attention and notoriety," Shirley says.

With things now going his way, Don began casually courting people at KPIX-TV. The publicity he was getting made him a welcome face all over the city.

"His ego grew and women adored him," Shirley says. "He lapped it up, and everything was downhill for us. He loved it all. His success became more and more important to him, and his drinking problem burst forth. He was a bad drunk, getting out of line and picking fights. I'd get a cab home by myself, so embarrassed with his behavior. Our daughter Robin came along at the time when he wasn't handling his newfound success very well."

Sally vividly remembers September 14th, 1953—the day Robin was born—

SALLY :

I used to go to the *Drawing Room*, a bar on Van Ness. I was dating the owner at the time. Don went there a lot, too, because it was near KPIX-TV.

Don was sitting at a table with Suzie. I'd heard rumors that there was someone new. I saw *red*!

I'd talked to Shirley that day, at the hospital. She was waiting for Don. While she's waiting, he's sitting with this loud, foul-mouthed woman!

Don thought Suzie was wonderful. In those days women didn't use language like that, but Suzie and Don could be at the Fairmont Hotel, and she'd use foul language. He loved the fact that she "had the guts to do it."

I marched up to their table and said, "Don, you better get to the hospital. Shirley's waiting for you. You'd bet-

SALLY...

ter get there and see your baby!" Then I walked him to the door to make sure he left. I wasn't jealous for myself, but I was furious to think he was going to put Shirley through what he'd put me through. I knew what it felt like.

So, by now, did Shirley.

When Don finally arrived at the hospital, he offhandedly tossed a carton of cigarettes on her bed and made a remark to the effect of "What's all the fuss about?" This was hardly the "Congratulations, darling, I love you," she'd wanted. She didn't understand his callousness until she watched from the window and saw him leaving the hospital, laughing and joking with another woman—Suzie.

Don and Suzie had met at a cocktail party. Soon after, Suzie left her job to become his personal secretary and quasi-manager. She was considered a good stabilizing force in his life.

"You have to let Don have his head," she said to reporters. "You can't try to lead him, he'll do the leading." Asked about his frequent absences, she replied, "Every once in a while, Don's got to simplify his life. He goes crazy when he has all these commitments."

When Robin was three months old, Shirley — ever so reluctantly — moved to her mother's in San Jose, going back and forth as she and Don tried to work things out.

As usual, Don promised things he couldn't possibly do.

While America was embracing the "Ozzie and Harriet" dream, Shirley watched hers crumble. "He wanted to be together," Shirley says, "but I just couldn't stay with him. He made a sacrilege of marriage and women. The kids were subjected to his jaded point of view. It was insulting to me when Don would talk about his wives on the air. Everyone heard it, everyone knew everything, and when we were married, everything was in the news. You couldn't have a private squabble.

"I didn't handle it well, obviously. I've always wished I had. Looking back, we would both have been so much better off if we'd stayed together. He wanted his wife and his children, that security, but I was too young to handle his type of marriage. I couldn't keep hurting like that, wondering what was wrong with me. I was nineteen when I married him and in my mid-twenties when we divorced. He didn't want a divorce, he wanted *freedom*."

Don knew all too well what it felt like to be betrayed, to be rejected, to be left behind. But he was caught up in his own actions and reactions, the headiness and intensity of his increasing success. He wasn't considering how his actions affected his family's lives. He was creating his own world, and it was a day-to-day proposition.

"Don was a good guy," Russ Coughlan says, "there wasn't a mean bone in his body. Sure he was a womanizer. That was the way he was, and the women knew who he was before they ever married him. He never hid what he was. You knew he was a bad drunk, and this or that. There was nothing subversive about him, no pretense. The adoration people had for him came out of that believability."

In fact, no matter how much he hurt his friends and loved ones, Don was always forgiven—except by his mother and Aunt Marie.

KGO
and the
New Deal

With his personal life tucked away, San Francisco's newest young star had all of the city as his playground. Every door was open to him; everyone wanted to buy him a drink, tell him a joke, be his friend.

Nineteen fifty-three was the year the scrapbook of his life started. It was too soon for people to wonder where he'd come from or how he got there. All that mattered to them was knowing he would be there when they turned their radios on.

By 1954, the chats Don had been having with KPIX-TV paid off. Roman Wassenberg offered him a television spot. It was only ten minutes a week on Tuesday nights—the time frame that seemed to start everything for Don. He gladly accepted.

Wassenberg said it was the best television Don ever did, because "he just pulled up a chair and entertained." He was free to do whatever pleased him. This was to be the primary key to his success, both in radio and on television. His material came out of his own experiences. Being out with people all over the city every day gave him plenty to talk and joke about. Because he could make anything that fascinated him equally interesting to others, he was able to relate to his audience unusually well. People watching his show did not step into another world; Don stepped into theirs.

As a result of his initial venture into television, Don was being closely watched by KGO-TV, along with every other major station. Soon Al Torbet, over at KSFO, was having to fight off network overtures toward Don. The big question on Torbet's mind was, how could he hold on to his star?

Torbet figured his best bet was to find an additional local showcase for Don that would keep him in San Francisco, yet allow KSFO to share him. KGO-TV made the winning offer.

On Janury 15, 1955, Don debuted on KGO-TV with a Saturday evening show. "Pop Club" was a half-hour show that combined playing records with "experts" rating them and dancing girls encouraging audience participation.

Paul Speegle wrote in his *San Francisco News* column:

> Don Sherwood, KSFO's child of nature, slid into a new medium last Saturday and came up smelling like a rose. The relaxed, off-beat manner which is Mr. Sherwood's stock-in-trade contributed to a very easy, comfortable half-hour of viewing.

Terrence O'Flaherty wrote in his *San Francisco Chronicle* column:

> KSFO's sleepy-eyed disc jockey has added another dimension to his present 3-D personality (radio, recordings and cafeterias).

> "Pop Club" has two ingredients which put it far above similar shows: its amusing decor (old-fashioned soda fountain) and an amazing emcee (Sherwood, the soda jerk). Sherwood . . . has a line of ad lib chatter that bounces like a barrel going over Niagara Falls. The commercials for Belfast Root Beer fit in gracefully between bounces.

Herb Caen commented:

On the basis of his first show, I'd say that Don Sherwood is the best thing to come along in local TV since Lee Giroux was a pup. Keep an eye on this boy. He won't be around long . . .

Dwight Newton of the *San Francisco Examiner* added:

When you tell me local television is dying, I'm not listening. . . . Don Sherwood's new "Pop Club" premiered with a production polish unseen in this area since the arrival of the erudite "Science in Action" . . . and "Success Story" programs.

Any local show can be as successful as a network show if people will look at it. People will look at this one—especially "pop" music devotees.

Don was now doing two radio shows for KSFO and KGO's Saturday evening TV show. His early morning KSFO program was called "The Where's Sherwood Affair." The one in the afternoon, from Mannings restaurant (where Don had worked as a bus boy in 1943), was called "The Why Sherwood Affair." This show was devoted to interviews with prominent stage personalities playing at San Francisco night spots.

On January 1, 1955, Dwight Newton announced his annual Day and Night blue-ribbon winners for local television and radio performances. Capturing the award for Man of the Year/Radio: Don Sherwood. Don won a second award for Best Deejay.

Dwight wrote:

This slap-happy refugee from the "Nick and Noodnick" program is building a wildly talked about reputation. He is cussed and discussed, panned and praised, but seldom ignored. His subtle humor is a refreshing tonic in a crassly-commercial disc jockey era. His star is rising, possibly to network heights.

"Don would come in and tell me whatever he planned to do before he'd do something," Dwight Newton says.

"He was always the first to tell me. He was a genius in his field, but personally, I saw him as a two-edged knife."

Fan clubs were emerging, official and otherwise. An ad that ran in a local paper is a typical example of Sherwood's loyal audience:

RIDER WANTED

To and from Belmont or San Mateo, door-to-door. Rider must like sportscar, top down and Don Sherwood. $5.00/week.

By February 1955, even as he was increasingly absent from his morning radio show, Don was feuding with KSFO over "loot, loot, and more loot." In April, the joke around town was that KSFO would have to get more writers on staff to keep coming up with explanations for Don's absences. It got to the point where everyone was surprised if he *did* show up.

All the newspapers in the area were getting letters, asking questions or expressing opinions. The *Oakland Tribune* was getting enough Don mail to practically fill their daily "Question & Answer" section. Judging from the witty answers they consistently came up with, the staff at the *Tribune* enjoyed the constant dialogue.

These questions and answers, over a long period, actually chronicle public response to Don—a type of rating system in itself.

Question: I heard somewhere Don Sherwood hardly sleeps at all, that he goes out late every night and still does his KSFO show starting at 6 a.m. Is it true he's trained himself to go without sleep?

Answer: Not true—The ability to go out at night and still be bright in the morning is peculiar to light bulbs.

Question: How come Don Sherwood calls himself "the world's greatest disc jockey" all the time? It becomes a little nauseating.

Answer: His radio show comes on at 6 a.m., the hour when roosters crow the loudest.

Soon after making the arrangement for Don to be on both KSFO and KGO-TV, Al Torbet left KSFO. San Francisco being the small city that it was, and even smaller within the media community, Roman Wassenberg became general manager at KSFO. Once again, he was Don's boss.

Don had his Saturday night television show for only six months before KGO made him the offer to take over their ailing "San Francisco Tonight" variety show, which ran from 10:50 p.m. to midnight. Don was more than primed for it.

The Don Sherwood audience now woke up and went to sleep with him five days a week.

His schedule was: 6 to 9 a.m., on the air at KSFO; 2:30 to 4:00 p.m., tape last half of afternoon show for KSFO; 4:00 to 5:00, do first half of radio show on KSFO; 5:05, rehearse "Pop Club" at KGO for live airing at 6; 9 p.m., back to KGO for "San Francisco Tonight" rehearsals; 10:50 to midnight, on the air at KGO.

TV Guide—promoting shows such as "I love Lucy," "Dragnet," "Topper," and "Lassie"—made mention of Don's mad schedule, saying, "Don has one advantage, though. He has no trouble waking up—mainly because he seldoms gets to sleep." Don did not yet know his own limits.

Terrence O'Flaherty of the *San Francisco Chronicle* had some illuminating things to say about Don's new "San Francisco Tonight" show:

> Don Sherwood has made a successful switch to the after-dark world without loss of life, laughter or blood. . . . It's safe to predict this daring young man will float through the air with the greatest of ease for some time to come. Whether you'll float with him depends on how much fun you have on his trapeze. His between-act patter is low pressure in the style of Benny, Garroway and Gobel, and he works easily with outside celebrity guests. . . . Sherwood is lucky to be surrounded by some lively musical talent. Barbara McRitchie has a clear, warm voice and a personality to match. There are very few gals in the pop song field

who can top her when she's at her best. . . . The
George Cerruti Trio, Phil Bovero's boys and George El-
liott are noisy and fun and their good-natured feud is
an amusing touch. . . . "San Francisco Tonight" is tai-
lored for Northern Californians who prefer live performances to old movies. It is also recommended for
insomniacs, cleaning ladies, tavern keepers, older deb-
utantes and other flowers that bloom in the night.

Don's name was showing up so regularly that Herb
Caen felt left out: "It's been weeks since I printed Don
Sherwood's name. There. Now I feel better." Shortly
thereafter, he noted that when Phyllis Diller heard about
Don's television pilot, she demanded to be the first guest.
"One way of judging the good guys of this world is by
their capacity to attract good and loyal friends," Herb
wrote. "By this standard, Sherwood rates high."

Dwight Newton added:

In Don's first solo series, "Pop Club," he has received generous applause from press and public. But
he has no illusions about the future of his nightly marathon. He's doubtful if any late night show can be a
"smash" success here. "They are big in New York,
Chicago, Los Angeles," he says, "but it takes more
people to run those cities at night. Are enough people
awake here around the midnight hours?" . . . Perhaps
the greatest change in Sherwood came when he absorbed some sound advice from former KPIX Program
Manager Bob Wassenberg. "There are two types of
performers in this business," Bob told Sherwood.
"One type takes this attitude—I have an act; please like
me. The other takes another attitude—I like you; and
that's the type that succeeds, if he has the talent to
match his attitude." Sherwood said he hopes to never
forget that advice. He'll have a new theme on his show
based on his new philosophy: Let's Be Friends. And
he'll have the best wishes of the radio fans who have
made his KSFO show so successful. And mine, too.

Then, two days later:

The best thing about Sherwood's new show is Sherwood himself. . . . He is a dominant, warm, engaging personality. He can sell commercials with the greatest of ease and good humor. He has a fine talent for voice impersonations. He is RELAXED. . . . He can be sincerely philosophical as well as comically corny. . . . I wouldn't be surprised if ABC-TV, in its search for a Steve Allen of its own, finds the answer in its latest San Francisco acquisition—Sherwood!

"San Francisco Tonight"

"San Francisco Tonight" was a major production. As such, its success or failure rested upon the combined efforts and talents of many people— not all of whom were visible. Without the right on-stage support-musicians, the right guest selection and handling —without a well-coordinated production crew—Don would have been hard-pressed to make it work, even with the best possible promotion and publicity, the right time slot, and the backing of generous sponsors.

Don, of course, concerned himself with as few of these details as possible. His attitude was "Take me or leave me, what you see is what you get."

Fortunately, the same masterful timing that worked for him on radio, worked equally well on television. He operated on instinct, on his own natural sense of what worked and what didn't.

The orchestra for Don's show consisted of four saxophones, one trombone, two trumpets, guitar, bass, drums, and piano and accordion played by George Cerruti. There were also writers, arrangers, and extras. Phil Bovero, a long-time staff orchestra musician for various studios around San Francisco, brought Don this professional musical team. Jimmy Price doubled on trumpet and trombone and did some of the arranging. John Markham was the drummer.

"Before television these orchestras would have up to a hundred people on staff—everything was live," Markham explains. "You had harp players and string groups, copyists and arrangers. All the music was written for that particular show; you couldn't just go down and buy it."

George Cerruti also had his own small group on the show—accordion, bass, and guitar—a band within the band. Don horsed around with George in much the same way Johnny Carson does with Doc Severinsen on the "Tonight Show."

"Phil Bovero and Don didn't hit it off," Markham says. "Phil was of a different generation. He was older than Don and naturally had a possessiveness about *his* band. He showed his authority and expected it to be respected. Don's special attention to George created jealousy."

Marty Paseta was the talented staff director at KGO, "a hot, young guy" who would later go on to be a big-time Hollywood director. He got along fine with Don, even though Don clearly did not like to rehearse or pre-plan the show.

Jimmy Price remembers their first rehearsal: "Marty was running around, very nervous and efficient, telling us all precisely how everything had to be. Don walked in and watched Marty doing this for a moment. Seeing that everyone was uptight, he leaned over and said, "Marty—shut up!" Don was flexing his muscles and letting everyone know that, in the end, things were going to be done his way.

"San Francisco Tonight" offered Don a format he could enjoy: none. Not only did he get to act out his famous characters from the radio show in costume and do skits, he could also meet and talk to new, interesting people. Some were celebrities, many were not. The show was a constant challenge to Don's quick mind.

Quickly dispatching with the preliminaries, Don got

down to the nitty-gritty. "Sometimes he got his guests so angry, you thought they were going to jump up and punch him out," Markham comments. But Don also had the knack of knowing where to draw the line. By getting them laughing, he eased things off.

"I remember when Esther Williams was on," Markham says. "There were all kinds of sexual innuendoes. She said, 'Oh look at that musician over there—what a big instrument he has!' There was a lot of that."

People were not the only guests on the show. One night, Don chased a greased pig around the set! He was likely to do anything; nothing was sacred, especially not his sponsors. Using his popular radio gimmick, he continued to display utter irreverence for those who were paying his bills, like Biggie Furniture.

"During one show, Don went to open the refrigerator and the door came off in his hands!" Jimmy Price says. "Another time he sat down on a mattress and box-spring combination, and it collapsed! These were the perfect things to happen to Don because he would always make something great out of them. Biggie Furniture loved it!"

Falstaff Beer was another sponsor which, for years, subjected itself to Don's peculiar inspiration.

"One time he went to pour the beer for the commercial, and nothing came out—it was frozen in the can," Markham says. "He made so much to-do about it, shaking it and carrying on, giving the floor people a bad time, that one guy got him another can. But he shook it before he threw it to Don. Don opened it, and we watched it explode all over him!"

Herb Caen was quick to point out Don's success with the show. In his column he wrote, "KGO-TV discloses that the Don Sherwood Shows were the top mail-pullers during the month of June with 7,572 pieces of mail received."

During all of this, Don was drinking heavily. Louise Jorjorian of KGO's publicity department worked closely with him, handling his promotion. She remembers him being hypertensive before the show and getting, in Don's terminology, "juiced."

Don's buddy, Russ Coughlan, was one of the on-call stand-ins.

RUSS COUGHLAN:

Don and I got reacquainted when he started doing the KGO television show. We hadn't seen much of each other since the KROW days. At this point, I was a salesman for KGO.

I'd get a call at the last minute saying, "Don's got a heat on, so you've got to come back and do the show." I'd come out to do the show and the studio would be jammed with people—standing room only.

I'd say, "Good evening, ladies and gentlemen, I'm Russ Coughlan. I'm sorry to say Don won't be here tonight." Everyone would groan AWWWW. What a great way to do a ninety-minute ad-lib show!

I'd call Don afterwards saying, "You bastard!" There was no time to prepare, and you had an antagonistic audience! It was great training.

Dick Brill was Don's writer/producer. He was a big factor in the show's success.

Don gave the goofiest interview in the world. He said whatever came to mind. When he interviewed Esther Williams they ended up in a hugging and kissing match. He didn't know what to do when she took him on.

Total spontaneity. That was the charm. Today, most of these people haven't paid their dues and don't know how to ad-lib. If Don's guests were working well, he'd lay back and respect them. Of course, if they weren't, he'd antagonize them and be sarcastic.

He was very nervous about it, and wouldn't go on without three or four drinks. He needed it to get through. It was live, and that took a lot of guts.

George Cerruti, from the band, also covered for Don on many a missed show. "At the last minute I'd open the show for him while Suzie tried to get him in shape for it, and then he'd arrive. He was a wide-awake drunk! I'd announce, 'And here's Don Sherwood,' and he'd jump in."

Del Courtney, a deejay at KSFO, was involved in television during its early San Francisco days. Del had done a KPIX three-hour-a-day variety show that began in 1949, a forerunner of the Merv Griffin/Johnny Carson/Mike Douglas type of variety show. He could well understand what Don was up against doing his show—

DEL COURTNEY:

You worked under hot lights and did everything live. For commercials there was no "We'll be right back after this message." You had no prompter, no idiot cards, and you had to direct the camera. I'd be pointing to what I was going to do next.

While Don was doing his "San Francisco Tonight" show, I was broadcasting live from Al Williams's *Papagayo Restaurant* at the Fairmont Hotel, the late-night spot where everyone came after their shows. It was a four-hour, late-night show on KSFO.

I'd known Don from before KSFO. When he was back at KROW, I had an orchestra playing at the St. Francis and the Fairmont, and Don auditioned to be a singer for my band. I told him, "Don, you have a good voice but it's not what I'm looking for. Try some lessons."

John Markham echoed Del's sentiment. "We'd always go to another studio to rehearse, and Don would sometimes attempt to sing a song. He had no sense of meter. We'd go over and over it with him, counting it out for him, but he was always out of sync. One night, finally bored with it all, I got up and slammed my brushes down and said, 'Aw, for Christ's sake, what are we doing here?' Don quickly snapped back, 'Well if you don't like it, you're fired.'

"I did the show that night, and the next morning I got up early and caught Don after his KSFO show and explained how I felt. Of course I 'admitted' I was out of line. I was really scared that I'd lost my job!"

George Cerruti remembers Don wanting to sing on the show. "I taught him 'Volare' in Italian, but part of the way through, he started making it up in English as he went along, until finally he just said, 'Ah, to hell with it!' "

Frank Haggerty, Don's close friend from the early KCBS days, liked Don's singing. The two of them wrote their own songs. Many of their songs were not fit for public performance, of course, but they had a fun time writing them. One that Frank remembers and still plays was called "Gold Leaf on My Saddle":

> There's gold leaf on my saddle,
> where I met old dangerous Bill.
> He made my false teeth rattle
> and my bung hole's puckered still.
> His six guns are a smokin'
> where he shot my knockers off.
> I wouldn't say he scared me
> but he started me to cough!
> There's gold leaf on my saddle —
> if you're wondering why I'm pale,
> there's a damn good pair of knockers
> lying out there on the trail.

"I was on Don's television show once in a while," Frank says. "One night he had the Four Freshmen on the show, and I mentioned to Don how much I liked the guitar that one of the guys in the group had. The next day, Don showed up at my house and gave me one just like it, which I still play today. He had a heart of gold. When he got drunk, he got sloppy, but I never saw him mean or out of line."

Don wasn't just getting a lot of heat about his drinking, he was also being crucified for his attire on the show. He didn't believe in dressing any particular way and, lacking any taste in clothes, this usually resulted in T-shirts and baggy, old pants—not the general public's idea of proper attire for a television host.

The ever-interested Dwight Newton of the *San Francisco Examiner* wasn't missing anything:

> I smell trouble ahead. Don's "hangover" gags about "shaking hands and red eyes" sounded for real instead of make believe.

> Look friend, for a long time we've been your biggest booster around these acres. We liked you on the radio (named you Man of the Year this year) and we had high hopes for you on television. Stop looking like a slob! Change the pace. Tone it up. Smarten up. Put on a tie once in a while. Add style to the show, the thing you need most if you ever hope to hit the big time. And lay off those whiskey jokes. Spend more time with your writers and directors. A major sponsor is interested in you. Don't bolt the door before he knocks.

Public response was divided, as usual:

> If he wears the same size hat at the end of this year, then and only then will he pass the test to become a star. I have my doubts.

> Sherwood can't hold a candle to the good shows that Rusty Draper put on.

> Sherwood is hotter than a two buck pistol at a shotgun wedding.

> Tell Sherwood to straighten up and fly right!

A woman named June Marsden wrote in:

> This horoscope is free, gratis, for nothing. Tell this crazy man to watch his manner all during the 1950's because what he does during the '50s can backfire on him in the '60s.

> He'll probably be able to get away with almost anything so long as he angles for the favor of the womenfolk. Tell him the worst is over—for this part of his life.

"Sherwood's Place"

As far as Don was concerned, however, the worst was far from over. His frenzied work schedule left him pulled in too many different directions at the same time. He'd have had to clone himself to keep up with it all. Something had to give—and it did. Exhaustion set in, contributing to his battles with Wassenberg, his KSFO boss.

Management was telling Don to knock off the "goofy stuff" and play it straight on his show; in other words, they wanted him to stop doing the very things that had made him successful. Presumably, this included his sound effects, his wild stories, his family of invisible friends.

Don did as he was told, and complaints poured in. Wassenberg tried to convince him it had all been a mistake. Don didn't budge. Wassenberg withheld a paycheck. Don snapped back to his usual self.

Wassenberg "apologized"—he bought malted milks for all the picketing Sherwood fans outside the station. Life appeared to have resumed in all its color, but Don was running out of steam, and his fans could sense it.

Herb Caen wrote:

Most intriguing sightem at Sunday's 49er-Cleveland
game at Kezar: TV's Don Sherwood sending his gal
friend and willing slave, Suzie Pierce, downstairs
through the mob to fetch him a hot dog and cuppacaw-
fee! However, Sherwood wasn't ALL bad. He let her
see the game. Didn't make her wait in the car.

By August 1955, Dwight Newton was filing this status
report on Don:

My desk is littered with letters bitterly protesting
and frantically praising the antics of "our favorite
slob." That would be Sherwood.

Someone writes: "You have carried casualness,
which can be an art, to the point where it is sloppy and
downright insulting to those wanting genuine entertainment." Another says, "If Mr. Sherwood wore a
suit, a dressy shirt and tie once in a while he would
look twice as handsome."

Sherwood's most ardent admirers direct their heavy
artillery at me for criticisms printed here a while back.
Sherwood took them in stride (like a dignified dinosaur
racing through mud up to his neck) but his fans are furious. "George Gobel has told whiskey jokes so why
can't Don Sherwood?" and "If you can't say anything
good, say NOTHING AT ALL!" . . . "Why don't you
retire? It must be pension time."

These comments and dozens of others indicate a
healthy state of affairs for local television's leading
screwball. The worst fate that can befall a performer is
when fans give him the silent treatment. Few seem to
be silent about Sherwood.

If he learns to discipline himself, he may yet outlink
Linkletter, who was once the pro and con talk of Our
Town. As Sherwood is today.

Surprise!

In December of 1955, Don turned in his resignation to

KSFO—again. It was his fifth resignation. Whereas most of them were accepted as Don's expression of frustration and thus ignored, this one was for real.

The December issue of "America's Coolest Teenage Magazine," *Dig*, ran an article entitled "Where's Sherwood?":

> Don Sherwood has been panned, fanned, named and blamed, fired and re-hired more than any one yo-yo head in Bay Area radio and television. He's a strange animal. He's his own best audience. He goes through material faster than five writers can write it. He's contradictory and wonderful. He's as artistic as a barefoot Bohemian and as commercial as a parking lot.

After Don's resignation from KSFO, Wassenberg commented to the press: "Sherwood has no talent, something I've just realized in the last three or four months. I used to think he was loaded with talent. The point is that Sherwood has to keep trying to top himself. He starts out by making sly little cracks on radio or TV and then his jokes get rawer and rougher. Pretty soon he's got to undress in front of the camera or pull some equally shocking stunt. Eventually, he runs out of shockers and he has nothing to fall back on."

KSFO was protected in their market by Don's contract, which prevented him from working for any other Northern California radio station until August 1956. KSFO's lineup was now Bob Colvig, Del Courtney, Bob Hansen, Bill Heyward, Wally King, and Dick Cook.

With his days free, Don had the luxury of time on his hands. He was still doing his KGO television show at night, but he needed something new to fill the void.

What to do?

"Hey! There's a bar for sale on 18th and Geary," someone suggested.

"Christ, for all the money I dump in bars, I might as well own one," Don said.

The press soon announced: "Don Sherwood, the Peter

Pan of the local airways, has been operating the old Rumpus Room on Geary under the new name of 'Sherwood's Place.' " In "Talk Around Town," David Hulburd described the opening celebration:

> Notes by a free-loader at preview party at Don Sherwood's new saloon at 18th & Geary. . .
>
> Saw fellow pacing up and down outside wearing sign reading: *Congratulations Don! Best wishes for success of Sherwood. Listen to the Dick Cook Show, KSFO 6:30 to 9:30 a.m.*
>
> Inside packed with people promoting themselves. Small blonde bombshell roared up decked out in low cut, tight, brilliant red dress, dark glasses. Suzie (Don's secretary and manager) Pierce.
>
> Grabbed Sherwood by elbow and said, "Nice party." "Know what you mean," said Sherwood, hurrying off. "Used to be a free-loader myself."
>
> Distraught looking individual in Sherwood's wake identified himself as Hugh Heller, Sherwood's agent. Said place pretty far out and had never done well as Rumpus Room. Hoped would do better now, what with Sherwood expecting to promote it on his shows. . . .
>
> Suzie appeared again. Someone asked what she did there. She said, "I'm Sherwood's folly."

The old Rumpus Room had been the training grounds for a few greats like Rusty Draper. Don redecorated the place and put in the popular Frank Haggerty Trio. Many fans came to the bar hoping to meet Don and have a drink with him.

It all seemed like a good idea at the time.

Don did himself a favor and started 1956 with a retreat to Hawaii. It was a brief one-week vacation, but by the time he returned, his "radio sickness" was in remission.

Within a couple of weeks, he was working for KYA radio in the 1 to 3 p.m. slot, backed by a sixteen-page contract.

February was consumed with plans for a television anniversary special of his "San Francisco Tonight" show, including pre-publicity for the $50,000 spectacular at the Opera House.

On March 1, the ninety-minute program was broadcast from the San Francisco Opera House, with guest stars Jonathan Winters, Vivian Blaine, Dizzy Dean, McDonald & Ryan (dancers), Johnny Mathis (then a local singer performing at the Fallen Angel and recently signed to Columbia Records), singers Steve Rossi and Julie Mason, and other local talent. KGO and Don's long-term sponsor, Falstaff Beer, teamed up for "San Francisco's first home-grown television spectacular."

Don's first year on television had already won him the local TV award for "Best Male Performer" of 1955—"when he performs," Terrence O'Flaherty was quick to add in his column. "I'm afraid that being a bad boy sometimes pays off."

The reviews for the much-awaited special were not what was hoped for. The general consensus was that it lacked warmth and spontaneity.

Dwight Newton wrote:

> "Thursday night was just a stylized, faulty, poorly produced imitation of the Ed Sullivan show. What happened to Don Sherwood, the laughing boy of the Falstaff frolics? He had a faraway look in his eye. . . . I may be wrong, but I suspect that Sherwood could have strangled Nelson Case when he interrupted a few of Don's commercial gags. And vice versa. A whole column could be written about the joyful sight of show people rubbing up against each other with smiles on their faces and blood in their eyes. Johnny Mathis got the brush off from the production crew and cameramen. His selection, 'The Wrong Face,' was the wrong song."

The first mistake the producer made was to try to do

the standard showcase special, requiring a strict time schedule and rehearsals. The second was to expect Don to go along with that.

Bar Fly

Don was getting weary, and it showed in his comments to the press. He told Herb Caen's assistant, Jerry Bundsen, how lucky he was to be who he was and not a celebrity—to be able to eat lunch without somebody hitting him on the back to say hello, just as he took his first bite of food.

The pressures and frustrations of maintaining his success were gnawing at Don.

"You get somewhere in this business, and then you worry about slipping," he said in an interview. "Look at Sinatra. He's at the top, and he doesn't know which way to turn. He's done everything. The only way he can go is down.

"I'm always worrying about drying up on TV. When you stop worrying, you're through. When I was on radio alone, I did all kinds of things I thought everyone understood. But on TV, I do things I think are funny, and nobody digs them. I can't do the same things over and over again. All the excitement, the fun, goes out then, and there's nothing left. The audience *knows* it, and the audience is in on every blessed thing you do.

"I'm not a comedian or a comic or a gag man, exactly, and I'm not a singer. . . . I don't know what I am. And I don't care about recognition or fame. What do I want? I guess I want money. I'm afraid to not have it. But now the more I earn, the more I have to earn." Don was not only in a high tax bracket, he had two alimonies, child support, and personal staff on his own payroll. "If I have fifty-seven dollars and fifty cents a week left, I'm lucky."

The pattern of Don's seesaw personal life continued. When his career was on top, his family and personal life were on the bottom, and vice versa. Asked where he was living, he replied, "I'm living in Marin with a woman I believe is my mother, planting a few flowers, and drinking a little beer."

Nothing had changed in the Inga-Don arena. By now Don had sent his mother to Europe and to the World Series. He kept trying to do things for her, to impress her, but it was never enough. With the innocence of a child, he continued to believe that one day there would be a magic moment, and things would change between them.

Don and Suzie Pierce were still together, and everyone was curious about them. The *San Francisco Chronicle* reported that Suzie's mail was "piling up on her hall table, including a letter from monologist Mort Sahl from Los Angeles." The mention of this letter was enough to make gossip fly because Don and Mort had had a falling out. Don said, "I won't even go over to his side of town until he apologizes to me." Nobody ever found out what that was all about.

Enrico Banducci—another dearly loved and deeply admired San Francisco legend — owned the *hungry i*, a discovery club. He promoted such talents as Phyllis Diller, the Smothers Brothers, Barbra Streisand, Bill Cosby, Flip Wilson, Shelley Berman, Mort Sahl, and many more. He also owned *Enrico's Restaurant* on Broadway, where Don spent a great deal of his life. Enrico and Don were destined to be great and lasting friends, enriching each other's lives as no one else could.

ENRICO BANDUCCI:

Don used to come into the club to see Mort Sahl, and that's how they became friends. Then Don did his own

ENRICO...

comedy act at the *hungry i*, right off the top of his head like everything else he did. He'd insult the people, and when they got mad and he bombed, he got mad and gave them hell—making him bomb even worse!

I remember the day Irwin Corey was on stage, and Don came in. Corey started screaming, "In the toilet with you! In the toilet!" He went right over to Don and escorted him to the bathroom. Corey had a microphone on him, so it played everything back to the audience. It was all planned between Mort and the audience, and Don fell for it. He kept saying, "Why are you doing this to me? I don't have to go!" The audience loved it. Don insisted, "But I came to see *you!*"

When I first met Don, I didn't like him. I wouldn't speak to him. I'd heard he was real tough on people, and I didn't want any problems with him, so I'd walk away from him. Then one day he said to me, "Hey, Banducci, come here. Why do you always walk away from me?" I said, "I don't like you!" and he said, "You don't like *me*—well, I don't like *you* either!" Then I got to know him and really got to like him. It's the old thing—fear of the dark, fear of the unknown. Then one day he said, "You know, you're starting to take to me. You're understanding me. You're getting a sense of humor!" I told him, "I've always had a sense of humor—you just weren't funny to me!"

After that we always traded insults and loved every minute of it. He would say, "I only come to *Enrico's* because it's convenient, not because the food's any good!"

Don also went to Barnaby Conrad's club, *Matador*, and sometimes he and Barnaby would have lunch together with Herb Caen. Barnaby went to Don's opening act at the *hungry i* and thought Don was terrific: "He sang and did imitations, singing into a wastebasket like he always did, which gave his voice such resonance. His improvisations were truly wonderful."

Russ Coughlan and Don were playing together all over San Francisco, "getting drunk and disorderly!" They didn't really have to chase women, since most women threw themselves at Don and Russ first. According to Russ, Don was not really a womanizer, in the true sense of the word, because he didn't *pursue* them. "He'd admire them," says Russ, "but not really go after them. I always got the feeling that he didn't like women for anything other than going to bed with them."

Don would get an inflated image of himself after an evening of heavy drinking—

RUSS COUGHLAN:

One night, after being out most of the evening, we went back to his place, which, of course, had nothing but cheap, ugly furniture in it. Don got very mad at me for something and started being a real horse's ass. He had a lady he'd brought with him, so I told her to go home and proceeded to put her in a cab.

Don didn't handle his booze well and was getting crazy. He said to me, "Ah, I'll fix you. You always think you're a big tough guy," and all that kind of stuff, because I used to be a boxer. He'd fake around with me once in a while. That night he slammed the door and was taunting me with stuff like "You son of a bitch, you're not going to get out of here."

I sat down and said, "Okay, rant and rave, do your craziness—but if you say the wrong thing, I'm going to beat the shit out of you."

He started playing the big tough guy, saying, "Okay, get up and do it right now." I kept telling him to watch out, or I'd really give it to him. He kept it up, and finally, I got up and started for the door. He grabbed me, ranting, so I slammed the door and said, "To hell with this!" I turned to him and said, "Okay, c'mon, take your best shot." He took one look at me and ran away! That was the end of that.

With his life spread all over the newspapers, Don's actions were generating more than mild speculation about his marital life. Don told everyone, "I am unmarried—presently and forever. And you can put down that my love life is very temperate." Asked if he thought he was oversexed or undersexed, he replied: "Probably. That's my answer. If you really want to know, I'll give you an expert medical opinion. My doctor said, 'You ought to be in a cage.'"

The *San Francisco News*, reporting on one of Don's more bizarre radio bits on KYA, confirmed that at the very least, he was totally uninhibited and proud of his image as "the man every woman wants":

> Sherwood turned into a girl last Monday at 1 p.m. In a voice dripping with primeval urge, this young lady distinguished herself with some of the more tasteless references to the romantic prowess of Mr. Sherwood, and generally contributed to what must have been a rather interesting afternoon to housewives bent over an ironing board or a sudsy tub of detergents. How much can you get away with under the name of Sherwood? Or "What price KYA?"

Interestingly enough, two weeks later KYA was playing taped reruns while Don was taking another "rest." After only a couple of months at KYA, Don was reportedly angling for a Hollywood contract. Discussions were going on, but no one was beating his door down to grab the $150,000 a year package.

His renowned absenteeism surely had an effect on potential buyers. Terrence O'Flaherty of the *San Francisco Chronicle* addressed this in his column, quoting one of Sherwood's former employers:

> We have long ago given up the idea of psychoanalyzing any of our performers, but Sherwood is a guy who must have something to fight. When he finds out nobody is against him, he cracks.

Sherwood responded with "They don't love me—

let's face it. But they know I sell. Every 13 weeks I get to make noises."

About this time, Don was regretting buying into the Geary Street bar. "Night after night people come up to me at the bar and say one of three things," he told Bill Steif at the *San Francisco News*. "They say, 'I can't stand your show, but I love you,' or they take me to one side and say, 'Why can't you get a new singer on your show?' or they say, 'My wife hates your show, but I love it,' or the other way around."

Don had quickly reached the point where he could not stand to go into his own bar. By June, he was out of the business.

Falstaff
and
Other Troubles

By mid-1956, Don had missed thirty-two television shows.

"Old, faithful George Lemont," as the newspapers called him, filled in as emcee for Don, with as little as a half hour's notice. The situation had escalated, however, to the point where getting paid, no matter how much, wasn't worth it to George any more.

Don was absent for the thirty-third time. George Lemont refused to do the show.

"If Don's sick again, tell him I'm sick, too—with sympathy pains," he said. George Cerruti, from the band, took over and opened the show, saying, "Don's sick, George is sick, and I'm getting sick."

One newspaper added, "And I'm getting bored. There have been many explanations for the laughing boy's failure to show up for work. Maybe he pulls out when the script looks bad. Maybe KGO had better start grooming another understudy. Or is that what Sherwood bought the mountain lion for?"

Yes, Don had bought a mountain lion. Herb Caen

noted, "Don Sherwood must be going mad, mad, ma-ad. He has bought himself a mountain lion cub—a BIG one—and drives it around in his Thunderbird."

Shirley, Don's ex-wife, faithful friend, and mother of Greg and Robin, remembers when Don brought the mountain lion to her house in San Jose. They put the lion in the garage while they all went off to Santa Cruz, during which time the lion continuously charged the door. When they returned, Don got into the garage, at the same time as the lion got out, forcing Don to chase, tackle, and finally shove it back in the car to go home.

What's a few scratches between friends?

Don also took his lion on the "San Francisco Tonight" show. He put a heavy chain on it and brought it out on stage. The cameramen backed up for a long shot—chains are one thing, lions are another.

Jimmy Price, playing trumpet and trombone in the band, distinctly remembers what happened: "Jim Green, the head cameraman, had the camera on Don, as Don was looking right down the throat of this lion. Then Don said, 'I can see its vulva!' He meant *uvula*, and as soon as Don said vulva, Jim looked over at the band with this long, slow turn of his head, the priceless expression on his face saying, *What* did he say?"

Even with moments like this, audience sympathy was wearing thin. The ratings at the start of the show were 5.1 percent of the Bay Area audience. At 10:45 p.m., they dropped to 4.5 percent; at 11 p.m. to 3.5 percent; and during the last fifteen minutes, they dropped to 2.8 percent.

OAKLAND TRIBUNE

Question: Please leave Don Sherwood's clothes alone, I like them. On him an old sweatshirt looks natural, and in a suit and tie he looks inhibited. If some people don't like the way he dresses, they don't have to look.

Answer: Believe us, we'll leave his clothes alone. We wouldn't touch them.

Question: On Don Sherwood's radio and TV shows, he seems real zany, always laughing and happy-go-lucky and not caring about a thing. Is he like this when he's not on the air?

Answer: In private life, Don is sober, industrious, impeccably dressed, well-groomed, bespectacled, concerned about taxes, supporting his children, and being a good citizen. We suspect the REAL Sherwood is the one you know on radio and TV.

Question: I've detected some signs that Don Sherwood is finally becoming civilized. He seems to have given up that deplorable sweatshirt in favor of wearing a suit, shirt and tie.

Answer: Don't get over-optimistic. Rumors are he's wearing the sweatshirt underneath.

The battle between George Lemont and Don continued. George wrote in the *San Francisco News*, "I went into a restaurant, and I was sort of surprised. They were treating me exceedingly well. The best table, etcetera. Then the maitre d' came over and said, 'Awfully nice to have you with us, Mr. Sherwood.' I said, 'I don't eat for him, too!'"

George also had told the *San Francisco Examiner*, "Sherwood was thinking about going into the circus with a lion act, but had to give it up. He couldn't get that big fat head of his into the lion's little mouth!"

As if this and all the other bad publicity weren't enough, Don came to do the show one night and appeared to be drunk. Management said he was "sick"; others said he was "well lubricated."

Don later explained to Terrence O'Flaherty at the *Chronicle*: "About that night, when people said I had a heat on—it ain't true. The doctor gave me some green medicine, for my nerves, but he didn't explain that it didn't mix with alcohol. I had a glass of wine with dinner and whammy! When I got on the show, I stumbled all over the place. I felt like I was inside a robot that couldn't turn the wheels to make anything move."

Drunk or not, he was headed for trouble. On one

show, he had a twelve-year-old boy, the son of a friend, read the Falstaff beer commercial for the audience. In his high-pitched, little voice, the boy endorsed "America's premium quality beer." This was all Falstaff needed to hear.

"The day after, the studio was stripped clean," Jimmy Price remembers. "Until then the studio was full of Falstaff props, behind Don's desk and all over, and there were cases of free beer for all of us. Now, not only was the free beer gone, but all the props had disappeared. There was Don, sitting behind this bare desk, with a twisted smile on his face."

What did Don do?

He grinned at the camera and announced, "There's something I've wanted to say on this show for a whole year—and I haven't been able to. Now I can. *Budweiser!*"

OAKLAND TRIBUNE

Question: On Don Sherwood's recent show, he divided his time between chortling with the orchestra, admiring himself in the monitor and clipping his nails with a clipper borrowed from the audience. I thought this was definitely a new low in performance for Sherwood.

Answer: Sherwood is used to coping with hangovers, but a hangnail is new to him. However, don't be too hard on Donny-babe. His happy irreverence for custom, his flagrant disregard of the sponsor and his completely casual handling of commercials is something there's too little of in TV. Television "propriety," where everyone is to sit at attention while a commercial is delivered, is ridiculous. At least performers such as Sherwood help keep the image on the TV screen in some perspective. We kid Sherwood on occasion, and we'd really like to see him wear a necktie as a sign of maturity, but more Sherwoods are needed.

Question: I had respect for your opinions until you said we need more Sherwoods on TV. A comment like that is disappointing, as Sherwood gets by on gall alone.

Answer: We secretly feel the key to Sherwood's success is that elusive quality Arthur Godfrey speaks of—humility.

Question: It came as an enormous shock to see your statement that Sherwood's success is due to his "humility." If he has humility, it's well hidden.

Answer: We were being facetious. For Sherwood, there are no middle-of-the-roaders. When his name is mentioned here, it's like mentioning Liberace; it brings a flood of mail either violently for him or violently against him. Sherwood comments here are running 50-50.

Question: Well, Sherwood has done it again. He announced that he was bowing to popular demand and wearing a new suit, and out he stepped in a suit of long woolen winter underwear. He proceeded to do the entire program in this rather unconventional attire. Chic, don't you think?

Answer: Sherwood in his long woolies is appealing to slobs. The day he appears on camera in his birthday suit is the day he'll have overdone being a "character."

After all the Sherwood bashing and commentary, Don claimed he had laryngitis. His replacement for the show was Ray Goman, Jr., a very popular entertainer.

Everyone seemed ready for a break from Don, and Don was definitely ready to take a break from them. He returned expecting to have been sorely missed. To his dismay, Goman's reviews were very good. Don's show mysteriously improved.

The rumor mills churned about Don and Suzie. "Don is like New York," Suzie responded, "wonderful to visit, but I wouldn't want to live there!" Reporters teased fans, telling them to stay tuned—the announcement would be along. Instead, what was announced was that Don had started taking flying lessons from his former apartment neighbor Hap Harper, of Harper Aviation in San Carlos.

HAP HARPER:

Don took the flight lessons over a very short period of time. Within a couple of weeks, he'd completed the basic phase of training and was ready for solo. He picked up flying easily; he was a natural. He wasn't afraid of anything. If you told him to do something, he'd do exactly as you said. He could handle a plane very well.

Then we wanted to solo him, and while it was easy to get him to come to the airport for his lessons, it was much more difficult to get him to go to the doctor to get the physical exam for the medical certificate that he needed prior to the solo. Since he'd told everyone he was going to solo, and in fact was ready, we decided to fake it, so a film could be taken and shown, as promised, on his TV show. Don taxied the airplane out to the end of the runway and got out. Our chief pilot got in and made the craziest takeoff and landing you've ever seen! That airplane was all over the sky! After landing, our pilot got out. Don got in and taxied up to the hanger with a grin on his face!

No one ever knew the film was a fake—until now. That was the end of Don's flight training. From then on, he was content to take his trips with one of my charter pilots.

When Don finally went to the doctor for a physical, he was diagnosed as having an ulcer. The prescription: a vacation. Before he could get a plane reservation for Mexico —only Don would go *there* to cure an ulcer—KYA asked him for his "RSVP"—resign, s'il vous plait. Don's penchant for disappearing had worn thin. Their penchant for giving him rules had worn equally thin with Don. He was happy to oblige.

When he returned from Mexico, Don was still a bachelor; Suzie was still at his side. As planned and predicted, he was back on his television program.

KGO-TV management was the last to know that while Don was on vacation, he had decided to resign. Not only that, but he decided to "make an honest woman" of Suzie. In December Hap Harper's charter service flew the couple to Reno, where they were married. A telegram came back:

DEAR HAP—
JUST MAKING IT SAFELY IN ONE OF YOUR
ANTIQUES IS AN ACHIEVEMENT—I THANK YOU, MY
WIFE THANKS YOU, MY MOTHER THANKS YOU AND
IF I EVER HAD A FATHER HE WOULD PROBABLY
THANK YOU TOO—IN ALL SERIOUSNESS I CAN
NEVER THANK YOU ENOUGH, SO BEST OF WISHES
FOR THE HOLIDAYS AND COMING YEAR.
                              — THE GREAT DON
                              SHERWOOD AND WIFE

The fact that Don had married again, however, did not mean that he was joining the nationwide exodus to suburbia. He refused to be one of the millions moving to what the book *Chronicle of the 20th Century* calls "commuter paradise:" ". . . a land of swing sets, garden hoses and charcoal briquets, where mothers get behind wheels of wood-paneled station wagons to drive their kids from ballet classes to Scout meetings to piano lessons. Everyone seeds, weeds, mows and waters ungrateful lawns. Apparently even paradise requires upkeep."

A wife was fine; serene, domestic living was still absolutely O-U-T.

Every Man
for Himself

The year 1957 dawned bright with promise. Don's oldest daughter, Diane, now living in Eureka, California, says, "After Svetlana, he married my mother. I came along, and by then he'd met Shirley, so that ended that. Then Greg and Robin came along, and he'd met Suzie, so that ended that. I guess after my mother, the organized one, and Shirley, the cutesie one, he decided he wanted a 'real woman.' So he went with the sassy, foul-mouthed person, Suzie—real snappy, slick, masculine, and tough. 'Scary broad,' Dad used to say."

The two had barely set up housekeeping when things began to fly apart. After being together for years as business partners, friends, and lovers, marriage was the ultimate test of their relationship. True to Don's past, it was doomed. Commitment was still only a word to him. The forces within him conspired once again to prevent him from surrendering any deep part of himself.

"It was one week with him, the next week with Mother," Suzie told reporters after her attempts to hold the marriage together failed. "He's difficult to be married to. He has more energy than any three people. It was unfortunate to begin with. We should never have married."

Don's personal troubles were not caused by his success; they were compounded by it. Long after his childhood year in bed with the heart condition, the dreamer in Don was still struggling to survive and conquer. His energetic mind craved knowledge and equations for the world around him and for the state of mankind that he observed so closely; his emotions ricocheted between the need to belong and a cynical mistrust of anything or anyone that could fulfill that need. His personal pain, the great enemy, came from deep in his soul. His psychiatrist, Dr. Ernest Lion, said that if he'd ever told Don all that was wrong with him, he'd never have come back. "My life is like a bad play," Don often said to his friend Hugh Heller.

"In therapy he was told that it was too bad he was in radio, since he was an introvert and a paranoid," says Don's son, Greg, part owner of a successful San Francisco advertising agency. "There was a heavy cost to his being in that business, since he was so sensitive and self-critical. In show business, even if you're loved by ninety-nine percent of the people, you're only as good as the last funny thing you said. As a kid I thought, Gee, you get off work at 9 a.m., go home, have breakfast, and have nothing to do for the rest of the day. But the incredible pressure of it— what's next? What happens if it doesn't happen anymore? Dad was always haunted by this."

Hap Harper recalls: "He said to me many times, 'You've always got to look over your shoulder for that kid who's coming to town who's going to take it by storm.' "

Radio and television were a perfect outlet for Don's quick wit, curiosity, intelligent observation, emerging philosophies, and imaginative escapades. On the other hand, success brought with it consuming demands that threatened his very being.

Don was always hoping to find a way to balance his celebrity status with the demands of being husband, lover, father, and friend. "He was a major celebrity," Russ Coughlan says, "the most major one I've seen in this town. He collected stooges and had people hanging around doing his bidding, but he didn't get the truth from most people."

Don trusted few people to share his philosophical and spiritual struggle. What everyone saw was a significant off-shoot of that struggle—his drinking.

Don was an alcoholic, and not only because of the pressures of his career. Both his father and his mother were alcoholics, so he was environmentally, if not genetically, predisposed to be an alcoholic. Everything around him nourished his illness. The drink dulled the pain but cured nothing.

His moods continued to swing dramatically, and he was convinced that he was the greatest manic-depressive in the country. He told reporters that his dark moods were like "stepping on cats, ships sinking, thunderstorms, and holidays."

Diane was now eight, Greg five, Robin three. While Don continued to search for the meaning of life, his children were growing up with the same question that had haunted his own childhood: Where is my father?

"I didn't see much of him when I was little," Diane says. She didn't know until she was an adult that he had bragged about her on the radio when she was born, or that he worried about her being a "happy baby." He had even written a song for her. Later, her mother told the story of Don holding baby Diane in front of the open window, without a stitch of clothes on, giving her an "air bath"!

"My mother wasn't making it a point to be good friends with Dad, and he was too busy for us," Diane continues. "He'd drop in, but I didn't really spend time with him until I was about fifteen. When I was six, he took me for my first horse ride. He was always the one who introduced me to adventure and got me to take chances."

Sally did see Don occasionally after their divorce. "One time Don took Diane and me to the 365 Club for dinner," she recalls. "Diane was just a little thing. She wanted us to dance together, so we did because it was important to her. I looked over at her—sitting there with the sweetest smile. All I could think of was how tragic it was that she had so rarely seen her mother and father together and that she didn't have more family life than that."

Robin, Diane's half-sister, saw more of Don, as did Greg. Don and Shirley, *their* mother, had a closer relationship.

"I remember when I was three, Dad would come for Greg and me, and I'd apparently run out of the room saying, 'He didn't come to see *me*,' " Robin comments. "There was an amazing animosity between us early on. Dad was already calling me ugly names that you just shouldn't call a child.

"I tell Diane to this day that she didn't miss anything those first years. The way he treated us at that time, she was lucky she wasn't there. Of course, it changed as we all got older and wiser, but it was scary at first. Mom often claimed to be on the verge of a nervous breakdown. She knew Dad was a volatile man, and she wanted to protect me. But she also felt that any relationship was better than none at all. I pleaded for none at all. It was clear that he and I didn't get along. He scared me. Twenty years later I told him how he'd frightened me, and he confessed he'd been scared of me, too!"

"I knew that my father was different," Diane says. "Everybody kept telling me he was unusual. At one point, I remember he was carrying around the lion. One day I was visiting his mother, and he came to see her. When I saw him outside, I ran to my grandmother, saying, 'There's a tall, messed-up looking person at the door.' He'd just been playing with his lion. She [Inga] said, 'Diane, this is your father.' I thought, so you're the strange, tall person that brought me stuffed teddy bears and a television on my birthday."

Sally remembers that day at Inga's house. "My husband went to pick Diane up from her grandmother, and Don was there. Diane naturally called my present husband "Daddy," and that really hurt Don. I was always sorry for that, for Diane's sake. I probably should never have told her to call my second husband 'Daddy,' but I'd married him so we could have a home life in the suburbs, so she could be like other children. I was sorry my husband was there at the same time as Don, because Don stayed away for a while after that. 'Goddammit, I'm her father!' he'd say."

"I saw Dad often until I went to boarding school," Robin says. "We had fun in childish ways. Dad, Greg, and I would go to restaurants and have contests to see how long it would take Dad to make us laugh—two seconds. We'd start blowing the straw wrappers all over the place and make the waitress mad, or we'd roughhouse with him. He was fun at the child level. This was his joy.

"He was born on the seventh of September, and I was born on the fourteenth, so we were too much alike—two Virgos.

"One time we all went riding—Dad, Diane, Greg, and I—but there weren't enough horses. He had me stay behind all afternoon, waiting in the corral. Diane told me she's never forgotten how stoic I was. With Dad, there was no room for back talk. Outings would end abruptly if he thought you looked at him 'wrong' or sassed back.

"After weekends with him, where he was usually cruel, verbally and emotionally, I'd be home eating my breakfast of Cheerios, watching Mom listen to him on the radio. She was his fan, totally in love with him. It was hard to understand at that age."

"Don talked about Greg on the radio more than about Robin or Diane," Shirley recalls. "Don and Robin were both so intense. Dr. Lion insisted they should see each other, no matter what, but Robin kept saying she'd have been better off if he'd stayed away. She was outspoken. From the time she was a tiny girl, she would not play 'let's-get-along-with-Daddy.' Greg played the game, although I don't know how he felt about it."

"If he was talking to me and I looked away, he'd scream, 'Look at me, goddammit!'" Robin agrees. "He numbered my looks saying, 'There's number forty-nine, it says I hate you!' I don't recall having any evil intent, but I *did* want to be home, safe with my mother. He knew it and it hurt him. It made him paranoid."

Diane remembers his obsession with eye contact, too: "Early on it was constant strangeness. If you weren't devastated by him at least fifteen times a week, you weren't close enough, you weren't his friend. He could only deal with people one-on-one. More than one person was an audience, and he'd perform. One-on-one, he felt he was involved in a real conversation. You could only interrupt with really important questions. If you drifted off for a moment and lost eye contact, he'd say, 'Fine! You're not interested. Is there a fly on the drape that's more important than talking to me?' "

"I remember when I was about seven, we were having breakfast at *Sears Fine Food Restaurant*," Robin says. "He said to me, 'God is a fabrication, a device of human beings, a crutch. But if there is one, you're looking at him.' It was years before the impact of this statement hit me. To this day, I often slip and say 'Dad' when I mean 'God,' and vice versa."

"He was never really a father," Greg says, elaborating on his own perspective. "We were much better friends than we were relatives because of the nature of our lives together. He had a tendency to run away from relationships, including wives and children. But we kept coming back to him with needs. We had more motivation than others. We could never go away."

Don often said in his interviews that he hated children. He did not hide the fact that he wasn't good with them. All of his children agree that he could not relate to their younger minds; he could not communicate with them, and they had to be able to communicate at his level. Once they became teenagers and could speak to him as adults, they began to get to know each other and were able to talk about the painful, early years when Don resisted playing any traditional father role. He never could accept anything other than being a "person" to them, someone who challenged their minds and toughened their skin. Rather than making sure that his children would not suffer as he had, Don was teaching them not to *expect* love.

At a time when everyone wanted or needed a piece of Don, it was every man for himself. Fortunately for him, his close friends, family, and children were able to hold their own, hoping and waiting for peace in Don's world.

Chicago

Don had been doing the KGO "San Francisco Tonight" show for less than two years when it folded in 1957. He was negotiating with the new KGO boss, John Mitchell, when Mitchell came down with the flu. Negotiations were temporarily halted. Before Don could make his deal with KGO, a much-anticipated offer came from NBC-TV for Don to host a Chicago show, "Club 60."

Hugh Heller, who had been managing Don and several up-and-coming entertainers, saw his four years of hard work promoting Don pay off. Heller was being transferred to Chicago with MCA for their industrial show production company.

"There had been limited interest in Don to date because MCA was getting commissions on ten-million-dollar-a-year stars like Marilyn Monroe and Jimmy Stewart," Heller says. "San Francisco was not considered a mecca of show business talent, so I had my work cut out for me getting Don that offer!"

Here, at last, was the big national television offer all of San Francisco had been anticipating—

HUGH HELLER:

I recognized Don's superstar qualities, and in watch-

HUGH...

ing the "Tonight Show" format, I knew it was perfect for Don. It was the ideal marriage.

It took me about two years of work to get the attention of NBC in New York and to get them excited about Don's potential. I sent them tapes and kept talking to them. Then, when Steve Allen left the "Tonight Show," and NBC didn't want Jack Paar for the spot, they agreed to try Don. It was *the* huge opportunity, and everything was set.

But before we could get that going, NBC heard all about his drinking and his irresponsibility, and quickly decided that they better be safe and try Don in Chicago first. If he succeeded there, he would go on to New York. The Chicago show was an afternoon, half-hour daily network show.

The *San Francisco Call Bulletin* reported:

> Wither now, Don Sherwood? The latest word is Chicago. Sherwood, San Francisco's perennial bad boy of the video scene, has called an about-face to plans to stay loyal to local fans. Two weeks ago the news broke on arrangements to start a new series of shows here on KGO-TV and KGO-radio. Now it's announced that Don has signed a "juicy" new contract with NBC Chicago for five shows a week in color. It's to start in April, with circuits to Philadelphia, New York, Washington and Los Angeles. But not to the town that made him famous! Why not is not known locally.

"Before he left for Chicago," Sally says, "he was all subdued and sad. He came around to see his friends and family to say goodbye. He made it very dramatic."

Because it happened so fast, there was virtually no preparation. Hugh Heller had all he could do to get Don on the plane.

HUGH HELLER:

Don had never been east of Reno! Suddenly we have this deal for Chicago, so he and Suzie stayed up through the night packing and getting ready. The next day we arrived at Midway Airport in Chicago. Don had not slept, and when we got him to the Palmer House, they'd screwed up, and his suite wasn't ready. He called me saying, "There's hair in the bathtub!"

This was a classic statement, because Don, being a true Virgo, had a thing about cleanliness, and if he did nothing else, he kept his sinks and bathtub immaculate. When the room was messy and there was hair in the tub, it was all over!

I got him squared away, and he got to bed. Early the next morning, the NBC guys were on the phone calling Don to get him to an early rehearsal at the studio. They wanted to go over the schedule, figure camera angles, with the key people watching. The man told Don how the first *sixty seconds* of the show were going to go, and Don said, "Let me call you back." He called me and said, "No way," so I called the station people and explained to them, again, that Don didn't work like that!

I was working for MCA at the time, on location working with Magnavox, and could not be there as a right hand to Don and the NBC people.

I tried to convey to NBC that they had to turn Don loose, that they could not *rehearse* Don Sherwood. Like Steve Allen, Don was best the first time, he was not an actor. It was all a *moment*, not a replay. Now George Gobel, whom I also managed for a time, is a comedy actor who works by planned acts, right down to the hand movements. He could do his act in his sleep because it was practiced and memorized. Don Sherwood was the opposite. His best moments were accidents.

Dick Brill was the perfect writer for Don on "San Francisco Tonight" because he gave Don the premise, the set-up, and then let Don run with it. It was not scripted. He left it flexible, and it would play. Dick understood

HUGH...

Don well enough to be able to do that. Not many writers could have.

I convinced NBC to let Don get some sleep, but the next morning they were right back at it, trying to rehearse him again.

Don tried to call me, but couldn't reach me, so he sent me a telegram saying, "I know how much this means to you. I'm sorry it's not working out. Someday we'll see that it worked out for the best." He got on a plane and went back to San Francisco. He later told me, "I'd never be able to find anything to talk about in Chicago! Here, I can say I brushed my teeth and people are interested."

Don was back home before anyone in Chicago knew he'd checked out of the hotel. The San Francisco presses were rolling with the headline, "OUR HERO RETURNS!"

Dwight Newton's column read:

> The unpredictable winner of our local TV Favorite Program poll took a three day, dreary look at Chicagoings on and decided, "This ain't fer me, bub." In Chicago, yesterday, NBC officials who had given him a royal, police escort, were thunderstruck. "He just disappeared," they wailed on the telephone. "Why? What happened? Where's Sherwood?"

> He's home, flew in Wednesday night. Says Don: "I'd rather wash dishes in San Francisco than be a TV star in Chicago. It wasn't right. My talent has to be kept at room temperature. I'd have killed myself in a month back there. We arrived in Chicago 7:30 Monday morning. They rushed me to the studio. They made me watch auditions from New York that didn't mean a thing. They had no hotel room for us. They insisted on taking pictures. I hadn't shaved. I'd been thirty-five hours without sleep."

> That afternoon, Don told them flatly: "Look, I'm tired. I'm walking out. I quit." They induced him to

stay another day but it was more of the same. "They had the opening of the show timed to TENTHS OF SECONDS. I don't work that way. They think you'll do anything for money. That's all they talk about. Money. You can't do creative work when they want to kill your creativity."

Then Don and Suzie drove around Chicago and out to Evanston to see what the country was like, what the living was like. Said Don: "The snow was brown, the day was cold, the clouds were gray. They don't know what living in San Francisco means."

Don said Dr. Lion had told him not to go, that he wasn't ready for the pressure of network television. There was no question that Don had the talent to go beyond San Francisco, but as Dwight Newton had stated earlier, "Trained in the local school that produced Jack Webb, Art Linkletter, Ralph Edwards and Hal March, he [can] join them in the big time whenever network executives are convinced he will remain reliable."

"He never bombed anywhere, he bombed with himself," Enrico Banducci says. "I told him that I knew talent, and he had it all. But he never believed it. He knew he was an alcoholic and didn't want to risk falling from the big arena. He had this city in his hands, but he didn't believe he'd ever have the country. I told him, 'Stay here, *we* love you!'"

No matter how proud the city would have been to see Don go on to network television, everyone was thrilled to have him back.

The Police Captain's Sister

Clearly, the thing holding Don back from national success was the very thing that created and sustained his regional success—spontaneity, inconsistency, rebellion, and irreverence.

Equally apparent was the fact that Don was not about to change.

With barely enough time to get his feet on the ground, another crisis occurred. He arrived back in San Francisco from Chicago on February 18, climbed into his 1938 Buick, and drove straight to Jimmy's Liquors on Irving Street to play poker in the back of the store.

The next morning, after he left the game, he stopped for a few fizzes. Driving home from there, he turned a corner and accidentally hit a woman who was crossing the street. Before he could take in what had happened, he was at the Hall of Justice in police custody, charged with felony drunk driving.

The woman he had hit and seriously injured was the sister of San Francisco police captain, John Butler!

The newspapers had a field day. This scoop was

meaty—no trivial banter here. As Captain Butler put it when Heller called him from Chicago: "Kiss this guy good-bye."

Don told the police he'd been to a late-night party, then to a bar for a couple of Royal Fizzes. He was driving home at about 11 a.m. when he hit her.

Don's old friend George Andros lived nearby. He called district attorney, Pat Brown, and explained that it was circumstance, that Don was not at fault.

"The accident could have happened to anybody," Don told reporters. "With someone else it would have landed on page ten. Because it was me, it got on the front page. And I'm afraid that because of the publicity, the judge will be on the spot. He can't be lenient. I'm innocent. I wasn't drunk. I was up most of the night, playing cards with friends. I'd had only a few beers. They can prove it." Don claimed that his drunken, "bad-boy" image was a deliberate part of his publicity.

"I couldn't eat for two days afterwards," Don said. "And I couldn't sleep. I kept seeing Miss Butler and the wheel in my hand. I kept trying to stop. Even though I wasn't going fast—my car didn't even get a dent when I hit her—I just couldn't stop in time. It could happen to anybody at any time. But it won't ever happen to me again. I'll never drive another car."

He did, of course, but his long-standing fear of cars had been permanently reinforced.

The accident tested the public's true feelings for Don in a way that ratings never could. To his public, Don was one of them, not a celebrity on a pedestal. He was part of the family, the favorite son. Unlike typical celebrity fans, Don's were not fickle. They forgave him for things he hadn't done yet.

Mrs. Sven Tillander of San Francisco wrote to the paper:

> I, too, would like to add a few words in Don's be-
> half, as I am sure that no physical hurt Don could
> have, could compare with the deep sorrow and hurt he

feels now. Someone once said, "While going up the hill of prosperity, may we never meet a friend coming down." To which I add, "Take him by the hand and help him back up again." And this is what I hope San Francisco will do for Don Sherwood.

Before the case went to court, one of Don's fans, Tom Rooney of the annual San Francisco Sports & Boat Show at the Cow Palace, called up his friend Hap Harper and told him he was having a terrible time getting Don to come to the show. He explained to Hap that all kinds of gifts were to be presented to Don but that Don said he didn't want to come because "the people don't want to see me."

Hap worked to convince Don that no one's love for him was diminished. "He really thought no one liked him anymore," Hap says. "Finally, I told him that if he wouldn't go for any other reason, go and get the boat they wanted to give him and give it to me!"

Don agreed to go.

The *San Francisco Call Bulletin* reported:

> It looked like a new day dawning for Don Sherwood. There he was, with the crowd of people watching him while he was loaded with an array of gifts, and with everyone saying nice things about him. It was almost too much for the disc jockey/TV star.
>
> "This is certainly unexpected; I can't get over it," said Sherwood. He looked a bit pale, and even a little embarrassed—over the role in which he was cast.
>
> There wasn't any real reason why the event was held for Sherwood, except, as Tom Rooney explained, "to show him we think he's a great guy."

First they gave Don a fourteen-foot, two-seat boat, complete with an Evinrude outboard motor. Then water skis. ("Do these work under water?" Don asked. "That's where I do most of my water skiing.") Then a week's vacation at Lake Shasta, together with a tent, a sleeping bag for two, a boat trailer, camping boots, a yachting parka, and a year's free berthing at the Oakland Marina. Lastly, they put a yachtsman's cap on his head.

"Don, we're here to testify to you," Tom Rooney said over the cheers of the crowd. "You are our city's foremost radio and television entertainer, and we want you to know how we feel about you. You belong to us, and we want you here. We want to thank you for coming back to San Francisco. We want to thank you for being and wanting to be a San Franciscan!"

Don was truly overwhelmed. "I can't thank you too much. It's been a long road with no turning, but you brought about that turn. . . If I get real sloppy now, it just wouldn't be me, so . . . thanks, anyway." This was probably the closest Don ever came to believing that people loved him.

The boat that Don had been so hesitant to accept turned out to be the start of his passion for boats; he later graduated to bigger ones and lived for many years on a houseboat in Sausalito.

As he was instantaneously changed from everybody's "favorite slob" and star of the city to citizen under arrest—like Superman to Clark Kent—the public seemed shocked by the serious side of him. Many articles ran under headlines like "Deadly Serious Don."

The following piece ran in the *Call Bulletin*:

> Don Sherwood is two people: Don Sherwood the star and Danny Cohelan, the sensitive young man, who is deeply concerned about serious matters.

> "I'm not really a Dr. Jekyll and Mr. Hyde," Don says. "Being on television, I had a dual personality—what the public wanted and what I really am. The public likes a carefree character. They like to feel there's someone who doesn't worry. I don't think there's anyone on the face of the earth who worries more than I do. I've got an ulcer and can't sleep, to prove it."

> Referring to the accident, he says, "It's a terrible thing to think that you've hurt someone. As far as I'm

concerned, a career doesn't mean that much. I want to live just like anybody else. I've given up the idea of being a tycoon in the television business. It's true I had wanted to be the W.C. Fields of TV. Now I don't want to go on TV. I don't even want to talk about it. I just want to live like anybody else."

In March, Don's case went to trial. There was continued public support for him during the whole ordeal, and the press was generous in giving him his say. Hugh Heller notes that Miss Butler herself was a fan of Don's and told the court that she felt fine and did not wish to press charges.

On July 13th, people from all over the city packed the courtroom, awaiting the verdict. The silence hung heavy. People held their breath as the foreman of the jury handed the piece of paper to the clerk, who handed it to Judge Neubarth and then back to the clerk. After reading seemingly endless preliminaries, the words finally rang out: "Not guilty!"

No one heard another word. The courtroom erupted with screams and cheers. People clapped their hands and stomped their feet for more than a minute. Don, overcome with relief, could hardly stand up. He hugged his defense attorney, Harry Wainwright. He had survived intact. He'd been set free once again, and could now be at peace with his city.

The out-of-court settlement for Miss Butler's injuries was $59,000.

Right after the trial, Don got a call from Hugh Heller in Chicago. George Gobel had called again to ask Hugh to come to Los Angeles as executive producer of his television show. Was Don interested in being the announcer for the show, warming up the audience and introducing George Gobel? Don just laughed. "After what happened in Chicago, do you really think you can sell that?" he asked. Heller told him it wasn't up to the people in Chicago. "Well, I'll pass," Don said. "Why don't you hire Dick Cook? He needs the money!"

Cook, a disc jockey on KSFO, was not one of Don's favorite people. Although Don approved of him originally, trouble started when people noticed how much Dick Cook sounded like Don . . . and how good Dick's singing imitations were. Hugh Heller, despite the intended joke, thought about it. Dick Cook *did* have a good voice, so he hired him.

Ironically, when Don called later on and said to Hugh, "It's okay, Dick's got enough money now, you can let him go!" Cook had already made arrangements to go to a radio station in Hawaii.

With all that had happened to him during the year, Don had taken the time to do some serious thinking. After the Chicago offer, he had put his contract deal back together with KGO-TV for his variety show. Now he was starting to think it was time to do his radio show again.

By a strange coincidence, KSFO was thinking it was time to have Don back again. Fortunately, there was now a very special man at KSFO who could really make things work: Bill Shaw.

Bill Shaw
to the Rescue

The task facing Bill Shaw when he became general manager at KSFO was to take an ailing station and build it, once again, into the number one station in San Francisco. He had been managing a station in Los Angeles. All through 1957, he had been asking about Don Sherwood—

BILL SHAW:

The "smart" people like lawyers and accountants cried, "Don't hire him! Don't touch him!" Salesmen, secretaries, cab drivers, bartenders, and housewives said if we could possibly get him back, grab him.

We had initial talks with Don about coming back to KSFO before he left for Chicago. When that didn't work out, we talked again.

We had just about agreed on everything when ABC, here in San Francisco, made him an offer for both radio and television at about fifteen hundred a week. That was still more than we could pay. The station didn't have that kind of money. We agreed that he should take their offer.

BILL...

He was just about to go with KGO when he got involved in an all-night poker game and the car accident with Miss Butler. ABC bailed out of their offer immediately, leaving us standing firm with ours.

Don's recent trial had purged the timid, leaving only one courageous man in the ring—

BILL SHAW:

Morning man is the star position on a personality radio station. A good morning man is hard to find. There are only half-a-dozen in these last twenty years that have been outstanding. You can't pick one off a bush, you have to scour the country.

I figured Sherwood was going to be one of the all-time best. He was the one we wanted. We made our deal, and he came back.

We decided to sneak him back on the station—let him be "discovered" again. We put him on the air without a big prepromotion job. I've seen many examples of great talents that failed after a big promotion. It's a psychological thing. People like to discover things for themselves. If you over-promote someone on your station, the listeners think, "Okay, show me. Be funny." If he's not, they don't give him a chance. But if *they* discover him, it's a new guy!

Dwight Newton wrote:

I've found a new synonym for Showmanship. You spell it KSFOmanship. KSFO earns the distinction by returning Sherwood to his 6 to 9 schedule. Back at his old stand, shepherded again by Charlie "Svengali" Smith, Don is delivering the most interesting and versatile DJ program I've heard since he left radio. He is honest unto himself. He indulges in nonsense but is never a hypocrite.

The "KSFOmanship" was Bill Shaw. "When you hire a talent, you hire him warts and all," he says. "He knows more about how to run a radio program than anybody else does. We had an unwritten agreement that he wouldn't lose our station's license, and we wouldn't try to tell him what to do."

This was exactly what Don needed—freedom. He needed to be able to go back into his imagination and let his live-in characters, who had been closeted over the past many months, out. He needed free rein.

BILL SHAW:

Don was marvelous, very funny, and I liked him very much. He was a black Irishman, up in the clouds one day and down in the dumps the next. We knew all his faults—not showing up, skating the fine line between what's permissible on the air and what might get us in trouble. He walked it a lot, but never walked over it. He had an innate sense of what he could get away with, how far to go. None of his listeners knew that, and they kept waiting for him to step over the line, which was part of his charm.

He also knew when to leave a subject, topic, gag, or character, before his listeners got tired of it. He had an incredible sense of timing, like Jack Benny and others. I put him in that class because, in this city at that time, he was as important here as these others were nationally. I consider that he was, during this time, the best in the country. He had a twenty-five percent share of the market. There were twelve major stations at that time, before FM.

Bill Shaw, now retired and living in Marin, leans back in his chair and laughs, remembering how Don did not confine his show to the studio. He often went out on the balcony of KSFO, with the microphone, and told his listeners to wave at him as they went by. Sometimes Don waved back, sometimes he responded with shocking gestures. There was no telling what he would do next.

"One time he decided to visit the other 'morning men' around the city," Bill continues. "KJBS was the leading independent station. Don went over there and interviewed their morning man—on the air at KSFO, during that guy's show. It totally destroyed the other guy."

Dave McElhatton—then on KCBS radio, opposite Don's show, today the news anchor on KPIX-TV—had fun when Don showed up at his studio. It didn't rattle him at all. He jumped right in, and audiences got the benefit of both deejays. "You can't plan things like that," Bill says. "They have to come out of a fertile imagination like Don's."

Not only did Don do his morning program live on other deejay's shows, he made fun of his competition. Early in his KSFO career, he wrapped up a bunch of organ records and sent them around to the other morning men with a sarcastic note: "You might as well play this while I'm on the air."

DAVE McELHATTON:

I knew of Don from the KROW days. When they put me in opposite him on KCBS, I was a young, eager kid, too dumb to know how much trouble I was in!

Down the road, I beat Don in the ratings. I assured him it was a short-term victory, which it was! This started calls between us, on the air.

A salesman from my station would say to me, "Hey, heard you on KSFO this morning"—which was like booking passage on the Titanic!

Shaw is a very bright man who had a concept for that station few people could have. It was awesome to see

DAVE...

Bill Shaw in action. How many radio managers would
have the guts to believe a guy like Don is worth it?

Don was a cross between Peter Pan and the Bad Seed.
He was leading us all to Never-Never Land. There was a
texture about him. He had a magic voice—the Pied Piper
of Pandemonium.

Referring to Don's notorious absenteeism, Bill Shaw
says, "Part of his bag was being antiestablishment, and
station management was The Establishment."

BILL SHAW:

That was fine with me. He and I had a good relationship, and he never took off on me personally.

When he didn't show up for work, he was flaunting
his power. It didn't surprise me the first time he didn't
show up—I knew it was going to happen. In the first
contract we wrote with him, we had a penalty clause
written in because he *told* me there would be times he
wouldn't show up. When he wasn't there we'd put in
Aaron [Edwards], or later, Carter B. [Smith]. We always
had a guy there to fill in. They were good, so we didn't
lose a lot when Don didn't show, because everyone
knew he'd be back.

You see, with a guy like Don, you buy the good and
the bad. You're not going to change him. Of course, I
wouldn't permit that kind of behavior generally. You
can't run a station where everyone shows up when they
want to. Don got away with it because he was good
enough. If he hadn't succeeded, we'd have fired him.

DAVE McELHATTON:

What drove those of us working opposite Don crazy
was that he made higher ratings *not* showing up in the

DAVE...

morning than we got showing up! So when my boss told me he wanted me to do more unpredictable things, I left the show and went on remote to see Don. He was interviewing Ronnie Schell that day, so I sat in and broadcast from KSFO against my own station.

All the strong deejays were at KSFO. So were the Giants and Forty-Niners. The station was loaded.

One of the bits that livened up the morning show when Don *was* there was "Just Plain Rosita." Of all the "soap operas," "Just Plain Rosita" was a favorite—asking the question: "Can a woman over thirty-five . . .?" It starred Luze Morales, "a lady of easy morals."

"Just Plain Rosita" had started when a language course arrived at the station for Charlie Smith. "It was Portuguese phrases, but it didn't work very well," Charlie said. "So I found some Spanish ones and played with the idea, adding some Spanish theme songs. The sentences were short, like 'I'm going to the store' kind of thing. I played a few phrases to Don in Spanish. He'd translate them off the top of his head. Don, of course, didn't know a word of Spanish. It was nonsensical."

With this routine, Don got a whole audience of people wanting to know what was going to happen next to Rosita.

"Everyone listened to hear 'Just Plain Rosita,' " Herb Caen says. "Charlie Smith was a master—quick, the perfect foil—just amazing. Everyone woke up in the morning in a state of anxiety, not knowing if Don would be there. It's a terrible way to wake up! Turn the radio on and hope he's there."

Russ Coughlan admits: "I was a little jealous that he was as clever as he was. He had a faculty that sustained him beyond all his problems. His was a world that you and I will never have. I wish I could see things that way. He could be around reality, but he didn't see it."

Regardless of the chaos that reigned in Don's personal

life—he was drinking by ten o'clock in the morning—at the radio station, he was able to create a world based on his own particular vision.

For those three hours in the studio booth, he could be anyone or anything he chose. The listeners vicariously escaped with him and did not return to everyday reality until Don closed his show, saying: "Out of the mud grows the lotus." The Zen proverb was not only his professional trademark, it was the image he had of himself.

Aaron

About this time, Aaron Edwards joined the Don-Charlie morning team. He quickly became one of Don's favorite playmates on the show.

Aaron had been at KSFO since 1956, originally part-time, then full-time in the news department. Today, Aaron does special-assignment reporting for KGO-TV.

"There was never a planned thing between us," Aaron says of his days with Don. "I was there to do the news, but Don started to kibitz with me."

The two of them worked together off and on for more than seven years. Their repartee evolved into a one-way put-down routine, with Aaron at the receiving end. Good mood or bad, it was always "Hey, Aaron, come in here for a second."

AARON EDWARDS:

He would walk all over me. My mother was alive at the time, and she used to say, "Why does that man talk to you like that?" She didn't like it. I went along with Don's gags, and he always hung himself. If you gave him enough rope, he came out the bastard. He was mean and vicious at times, but we'd laugh about it off the air afterwards.

A lot of what he did was dirty, but it was done all by

AARON...

inference and through that famous laugh of his. A lot of people listened to see how far he'd go. He said with his laugh what he couldn't say with words!

Of the laugh that had become Don's trademark, Herb Caen wrote, "If you could put Sherwood's laugh into words, it would be unprintable."

His laugh usually began with a low, suggestive, throaty rumbling chuckle, coming from way down deep, erupting into a full-blown, hearty laugh.

On the same topic, one reporter wrote that if you were to peel away Don's facade, you would find an emotionally unstable clown. "My laugh is genuine," Don replied, "a mixture of cynicism and snickering." Referring to his child-like qualities of fantasy and his temperament, he said, "As an entertainer, it permeates you. All entertainers are basically children. I've been described as a Peter Pan with a libido."

AARON EDWARDS:

He liked to break me up during the news, on the air. We were always afraid it was going to make certain clients mad, because we'd be doing a serious report or story or commercial, and he'd break me up. It was an ongoing gag.

One of the sponsors we had was Foster's Restaurants. They were introducing English muffins. They hired a gal from Las Vegas—whom they referred to as Miss Muffin—and sent her around to visit morning deejays. She arrived at our studio one morning to talk to Don, wearing a full-length mink coat. Now you have to know the booth was small, maybe six feet by four. Don was at the console, and Miss Muffin came into the booth to sit on the chair behind him. When she sat down and crossed her legs, the coat fell open. She was bare right up to her

AARON...

ass! She was wearing a G-string and halter that you could put in a match box.

When Don saw that, his wheels started working. I went on the air to do the eight o'clock news. For years, the eight o'clock news sponsor was the Sir Francis Drake Hotel. Bill Shaw made it clear we were not to fool around with that one.

Out of the corner of my eye, I saw Miss Muffin take off the fur coat. I was surrounded by glass, including a glass door you couldn't lock. I saw her leave and thought she was going to the ladies' room or something. The next thing I knew, she was coming into *my* booth. I could see Charlie Smith and Don watching through the glass.

I was in the middle of my newscast when Miss Muffin started rubbing my back. I couldn't let on to the listeners that anything was disturbing me. I guess that made her want to try harder, so she started rubbing her boobs against the back of my neck! I kept reading my news, wondering what I could do. I thought, maybe if I clutched at her, she'd back away and that would be that. Never happened! I was reading and clutching at her, and her halter fell off!

Chairs crashed as Sherwood and Charlie fell over laughing, and it was all over! I quit, just left the room, and that was the end of the news. The listeners never knew what happened!

Aaron wasn't there during the Falstaff Beer fiasco, but he had heard about it. He had also heard about another of Don's antics with his Falstaff Beer sponsor—

AARON EDWARDS:

The owner/manager of the Falstaff brewers was coming to San Francisco. He wanted to meet Don. Don said fine, so the man agreed to pick Don up. The man

AARON...

drove up in his chauffeur-driven limousine and rang Don's doorbell. The door opened, and there stood this sweet young thing, stark naked. This was Don's idea of humor.

She said, "Oh, hello," like this was no problem at all. The guy didn't know where to look. He was ready to die when she said, "Oh, come in. Don's waiting for you." So they sat in the living room, he and the naked girl, conversing. All the guy could think was, "Is this what we're paying for?"

Sherwood finally came out half-dressed and said, "I'll be ready in a minute." After keeping his sponsor waiting sufficiently long for the desired effect, Don came out, and they left like nothing had happened. He loved to do this to people.

There were always two shows going on at KSFO—the one on the air and the one in the studio—

AARON EDWARDS:

Don would slip pictures of nude women into my copy book, while I was busy in the newsroom. I'd rush to the booth at the last second to get on the air, and flip to the copy book. There, in the middle of my news report, would be the picture, and that was it! I couldn't say anything—I'd just laugh, and he'd be in there rolling on the floor. The people at home must have wondered what the hell was the matter with me!

It got so whenever I saw Don coming around me in the booth while I was on the air, I knew there was going to be trouble. One day he walked right over and stood close to me. I was sitting, he was standing, so his belt came right about to my ear. I didn't say a word, I was minding my own business. The tension started to get to me because I knew something was going to happen. Don started unzipping his fly . . . zip . . . zip . . . zip,

AARON...

down, up, down, up—not enough to be heard on the air. But I'm hearing it, and it's up by my ear! Finally, he zips it down and sticks his thumb in my ear—and that was it!! The end of the world.

My wife would ask me, "So what did he do to break you up this time?" I'd say, "Oh, nothing."

Once Don and the guys put a recorder with a taped message in the wastebasket in Aaron's booth. It was timed to start talking when he went on the air. Aaron started his broadcast, and suddenly he could hear this faint whisper, "Aaron . . . Aaron, over here." He turned around, but no one was there. The tape paused. Aaron continued his news. "Aaron . . . can you hear me? Aaron, over here." Aaron couldn't figure out for the life of him where the voice was coming from, until finally he narrowed it down to the wastebasket. But he wasn't through reading the news yet, so he kept reading and shoved away the wastebasket with his foot, trying to push it out of the door without breaking up or falling apart in his newscast.

Suburbia was one of Don's favorite topics. Aaron was from the suburbs. One Monday morning, Don asked Aaron what he'd done over the weekend—

AARON EDWARDS:

I wasn't prepared for that, and I didn't want the intrusion into my privacy, so instead of telling him what friends we'd visited, etcetera, I told him I went to the dump. "To bring or to take?" Don asked, and that started it all. I asked if he'd ever been to the dump, and he said never. Well, after he got through, everyone kept asking me if I really went to the dump.

It became a thing. Every Monday morning he'd ask. "What did you do over the weekend? Did you go to the dumps? Meet any people there?"

When our kids were small, we used to go camping

AARON...

once in a while. Sherwood asked me, "Where do you go? What do you do? Are there bears?" One day he asked if he could borrow my camping equipment. I lent him the cots, stove, ice chest, folding table and showed him how everything worked. He and a friend went camping. They ended up somewhere near Redding in Lassen National Park.

The long and short of this weekend camping trip was that he was back by Saturday. They got up there in the heat of the day, moved to the campsite, and he started unloading all this stuff. The bees were all around him. The first thing he wanted to unload was the folding table. He was *not* mechanically inclined, mind you, and right off he pinches his finger, raising a blood blister. So that was it! He called me and said, "Son of a bitch— come and get this shit!" He brought the stuff back all bent and dented. He didn't understand how to put things back together, like folding a map back up! He gave me hell, like it was my fault. I laughed until I cried.

When Don didn't show up for work, for any number of reasons, Aaron filled in.

AARON EDWARDS:

I'd have to go on the air and make up these crazy reasons like "Don is going to be a bit late this morning, he can't find his brown sock." I'd carry the record show, just straight records, and try to keep it interesting, but I didn't try to do his show. I never let people forget I was just there in his place. I never got a nickel extra, which bothered me. I talked to Bill Shaw about it, but he wouldn't approve extra pay. He figured I was there anyway, so what did it matter!

When Don and I did things on his show together, I was his straight man, and I knew it. I accepted it and never tried to upstage him. Like with any star, if you

AARON...

ever try to outshine them or take the lead, you're looking for trouble. You either go along or you don't and I chose to go along and make a contribution. If I had crossed swords with him or dueled with him, he'd have gotten rid of me fast.

Traffic Watch—
Another First

Another addition to the show was Don's aviation friend, Hap Harper. Why not have Hap take his plane up every morning over the Bay Area and report the weather during his show, Don thought. He'd have another straight boy-next-door type to pick on.

It sounded like fun to Hap—something to do for a couple of days.

KSFO contacted the F.C.C. (Federal Communications Commission), which assigned the station the first radio frequency for airborne reports—a world first. They got all the radios, licenses, and permissions. Finally set, Hap flew off in his airplane and reported, "Sunshine in the Mission district . . . fog in the downtown area . . ."

"Something to do for a couple of days" became a couple of weeks . . . then months. By then, Hap was telling everyone how to dress for the day, whether to bring umbrellas or not, when to paint their houses, and whether or not to pour concrete.

While flying one morning, Hap spotted a head-on collision on the Bay Bridge and excitedly reported it during his weather report. Don saw the value of this type of information immediately: Hap could spot accidents from his plane and see whole traffic patterns. He could report traffic obstacles, like construction work, and even give commuters alternate routes and prevent them from getting caught in a traffic jam.

It also gave Don a private air force.

Traffic watch was born.

No one could have foreseen that it would become part of every station's service and information, nationwide. Actually, the timing was perfect. The suburbs were rapidly expanding, and commutes were getting longer, creating distinct traffic patterns at various times of the day. Thus, airborne reports proved more important than anyone could have anticipated.

The job that Hap figured would last about a month became a whole career—he is today the traffic reporter for KSFO-AM/KYA-FM. "I have now logged over two million miles over the Bay Area and never been out of sight of the San Carlos Airport!" Hap says. "Hugh Heller told me, 'Just keep doing what you're doing, Hap. I'll tell you when to stop.' He never called me, so I'm still at it!"

Hap developed a style of reporting that combined fun and humor with serious traffic reporting, and despite his brief air time, he and the Don-Hap banter soon developed a following. Don's barber told him, "Your show's okay, but you better not get rid of that kid in the 'egg crate'!"

"When he first recruited me to do the weather flight," Hap says, "he came down to the airport to talk to me. I was sitting in my office and saw Sherwood getting out of the car and crossing the parking lot. He wasn't concerned about all the people watching him. He marches right up to the front window of my offices, unzips his pants—I thought, 'Oh well, he's done that before'—and takes a leak on the window! Pees on it, right there in front of everyone!

"That was his way of saying, 'Harper, I don't give a damn about anything!' Our relationship was one of playful antagonism. Don picked on me the way he picked on Aaron."

Passengers occasionally flew the traffic watch with

Hap. Don did not always know ahead of time who was in Hap's plane.

"One morning, without telling Don, I had Vaughn Monroe flying with me," Hap says. "I told Don that I, too, had been practicing my imitations. 'How does this sound?' I asked him, handing the microphone to Vaughn, who started singing his song 'Racing with the Moon.'

"Don interrupted, saying, 'Well, Hap, you've almost got it, but not quite. Vaughn sounds more like this . . ..'" He did *his* imitation, which through the studio microphone *did* sound more like Vaughn than Vaughn himself.

"I said, 'I see. Okay, let me try again.' Then Vaughn started singing his famous 'Dance Ballerina Dance.' A few bars into it, Don said, 'Hap, that's *too* good! Vaughn, what are you doing up there?' "

Hap frequently joined Don's exclusive "breakfast gang" after the morning show in the coffee shop at the Fairmont Hotel. By now, Don had his boat up at Clear Lake. When he wanted to get out on the water, he'd broadcast the show from the airplane with Hap, who'd give his last traffic report up over Mount St. Helena.

Minutes later they were at Lower Lake, ready for a day of water skiing.

Hap's sincerity and sense of humor appealed to Don. While they were not "drinking buddies," they could still have fun in the same sandbox.

Each day sparked new ideas in Don. He looked, listened, watched, and read, constantly reacting to everything around him. He made everyone laugh at themselves and each other, but he also made them more aware of the world and of the human condition—"warts and all." He wanted listeners to learn, just as he loved learning.

When he discovered haiku poetry, for example, he started a KSFO haiku contest. Listeners happily joined in, and Don got the opportunity to teach them about this form of Japanese poetry. In the blink of an eye, *five thousand* haiku poems were submitted! Douglas Stout, an English professor at San Francisco State College, won the round-trip ticket to Tokyo.

Herb Caen lent his own perspective—

HERB CAEN:

> I don't know whether Don Sherwood's KSFO Haiku poetry contest is still on, but if it is, George Lemont has three entries: "I froze with fear as I felt the frog in my pocket slowly opening the jackknife." . . . "I massaged her scalp slowly, wondering where she might be at this moment." . . . "Just as the paper boat swirled into the culvert, I saw the little man waving frantically." Haiku?

"Everybody knows Don called himself 'the World's Greatest Disc Jockey,'" Aaron Edwards says, with a grin. "He would laugh and say, 'If I knew how to pick artichokes, I could be the best artichoke picker!' He was really saying, you are who you think you are. He laughed at himself, and he laughed at people who thought he was so great. He didn't think he was so great."

Don never did understand why he was special. He wasn't impressed with the gigantic size of his audience, or the fact that he had broad demographics within that audience.

Bill Shaw comments, "The breadth of his appeal is interesting. He appealed to truck drivers, cab drivers, bartenders, as well as college professors, high school and college students, and business people. He had an extremely good mind, a high IQ. He thought about a wide range of things and was intellectually curious, which added to his charm. He had a great knack for taking an obtuse subject and putting it in terms that made complete sense to the ordinary listener."

"When Don talked into that microphone, he was talking to each individual out there," Aaron adds.

"He never talked down to his audience, Don's son, Greg,

agrees." He was liked by the working-class people. He was an anti-hero."

His oldest daughter, Diane, says, "He was consistent with the notion that it didn't matter what you were doing as long as you were doing something."

Herb Caen explained to reporters:

> They all say the same thing about Don—"If he'd settle down, he'd be wonderful"—but he wouldn't be. He's the typical mixed-up man of the century. He hasn't got a peaceful mind, and that's why he's one of the freshest and most unpredictable talents on the air today. I hope he never learns to do things "the right way." Because that'll be the wrong way for Sherwood.

As always, Don's fans were keeping tabs on his personal life. How, they wondered, was his fourth marriage doing.

In November the papers reported that Don and Suzie were "working things out."

"I think you'll find that the situation has changed," Suzie said.

"Does this mean conjugal bliss has been restored?" the reporter asked.

"Yes, I think so."

Would they be living together again?

"Yes, I think so."

She wasn't leaving town?

"No, but you better talk to Don."

Don said, "I haven't talked to her lately."

Regarding marriage at this stage of his life, Don said, "You gotta work at marriage. The way I see it, there's no sense in getting married if you're not going to work at it. Four marriages are a little asinine."

Hap Harper told Herb Caen, "I can't send Don a Christmas card because, by the time I get through writing Mr. and Mrs., Mrs., Mrs.—there's no room left for the address!"

"I'm ashamed of myself," Don said.

As 1957 wound down, Don confided to Herb that had it not been for his regular visits with Dr. Lion, he would have been the next Golden Gate jumper.

By January 23, 1958, Suzie was in Reno filing for divorce on the grounds of mental cruelty.

Raid
on Stockton

Spring, being that time of year when all mortals are forgiven slight inconsistencies and often downright foolishness, was known to trigger haphazard thoughts and moods in Don.

As spring fever began its insidious assault on San Francisco, Don was inspired to share with his listeners his notion that the city of Stockton ought to be returned to the "recreation area" it once was—referring to its red-light district and open gambling.

It was apparently an idea ripe for the times.

Without warning, the subtle strains of a campaign began to develop. As the weeks went by, listeners commented on his idea, watering the little seed in Don's imagination. It was such a colorful picture.

Then a letter arrived from Stockton, telling Don to lay off: "Stockton's a fine city just like it is!"

A red light went off in his brain. The idea changed from "what if" to "when." "When I take over Stockton, I'll return it to the fun place it once was!"

He decided to take matters in hand and hit Stockton with a "blast of artillery" to show them he meant business. Charlie Smith got out his "cannon."

Don gave the word: "Fire!"

Hap Harper, in his plane doing the morning traffic reports, chimed in, "You need more elevation. Move it ten degrees to the left and put in a couple degrees of elevation. That oughta do it!"

The imaginery attack was on.

Don and Charlie continued firing shots, using Hap as the artillery spotter. By the third "salvo," Hap announced that they had scored a direct hit.

A few days later, Don received a call from the Chamber of Commerce in Stockton.

Herb Caen reported —

> Don Sherwood and his KSFO weatherman, Hap Harper, have been having a ball lately with their threats to "bomb" Stockton, but so many private plane owners have offered to help out that the Stockton Chamber of Commerce phoned Sherwood over the weekend, proposing to "negotiate a truce." General Sherwood is toying with the idea.

The infamous "Raid on Stockton" had begun—one of the greatest radio stunts of all time—building for several months as it took hold in Don's imagination.

He was going to "own" Stockton. He would be King of Stockton.

The plans took shape. "Threats" were dispersed throughout the heat of the summer of 1958.

Hundreds of fans began enlisting in the Sherwood Harper Liberation Expeditionary Forces of the Greater Bay Area, Inc.—the KSFO army and air force. Two fans, Gene Babow and Bob Cole, became a self-appointed task force to organize the ground mobile forces. Gene delivered a letter of agreement to Don at KSFO studios, carrying the briefcase handcuffed to his wrist.

Don named himself Field Marshal, Hap General, and fans honorary admirals and generals. Identification cards were issued. Light plane enthusiasts and small boat skippers from all over the Bay Area enlisted. Every listener wanted to get in on the fun.

The KSFO team issued one of the cleverest press releases ever written in the form of a wartime dispatch:

September 4, 1958: COMMUNIQUE issued from Jorge Jornocki, S.H.L.E.F.O.T.G.B.A.I. War Correspondent (Somewhere in the Bay Area)

Flocks of wildfowl, startled from their roosts in nearby marshlands, darkened the dawn sky as elements of the Sherwood Harper Liberation Expeditionary Forces of the Greater Bay Area, Inc. launched their first aerial raid against the City of Stockton on the San Joaquin River.

Dubbed a "complete success" by officers in charge, the raid was made without casualties.

The sortie was under the personal supervision of Field Marshal Don Sherwood, commanding officer of the S.H.L.E.F.O.T.G.B.A.I., while General Harper piloted the lead plane.

Early reports from the Stockton area indicated the citizens of that municipality were "stunted" by the suddenness of the attack. However, it has since been learned that the correct word was "stunned."

No definite information was released on the types and quantities of ammunition used. A usually reliable source in the ordnance section, however, indicated that somewhere between twenty and fifty thousand missiles were released over Stockton.

An aerial observer reported that the missiles appeared to be multicolored and rectangular in shape. He said that the city's streets were rainbow-hued as the flight wheeled onto its return route after the completion of the raid.

Field Marshal Sherwood cut a dashing figure as he hurried with long strides to his waiting aircraft as the raid was launched. He was wearing his now-famous gold uniform with scarlet breeches, liberally trimmed with gold braid.

The Marshal scornfully brushed aside an aide's offered pistol and carried, instead, as his sidearm, a four foot cavalry saber that had been used in the Indian Wars by a forebear.

"I come from a long line of simple fighting men," the Marshal explained, as he climbed into his plane, "who prefer the old reliable weapons of history."

A tense group of ground personnel, anxiously awaiting the Marshal's return from the raid, broke into a ragged cheer as the plane taxied back to its hardstand.

Asked for his personal evaluation of the Stockton situation after the successful attack this morning, Marshal Sherwood replied, between puffs on a large black cigar, that he thought the city was a "sitting duck."

He further elaborated by stating that the city would be his "before the frost is on the 'punkin.' "

This remark, which close associates have come to regard as typical of the Marshal's military genius, caused a spontaneous shout of "SCHARGE—on to Stockton!" to burst from the throats of his troops.

"SCHARGE," ("Charge!" with a drunken slur), became the slogan. The paper leaflets dropped on Stockton, carried the message: "CONSIDER YOURSELF BOMBED—STOCKTON SURRENDER—OR ELSE."

Following the first raid, Stockton pressed their truce offer by sending Don and Hap two harem girls in an armored car. They were delivered to KSFO headquarters at the Fairmont Hotel.

The two delirious rebels carried their trophies through the hotel lobby to the studios.

"I thought they meant peace offering," Hap says, "but Don thought it was a '*piece*' offering! He, being the wiser of the two of us, kept his for three days!"

Playing soldier has its own reward.

"Everyone assumed that because I was Don's friend and because we played together, we partied together. I soon had a much undeserved reputation for being a 'wom anizer.' My wife of that time was not exactly amused! Nor was she thrilled that I got letters from young women asking to fly with me. Of course, I assured her it was all in the line of duty."

KSFO issued "SCHARGE" buttons along with Sherwood Invasion Money with a printed worth of one thousand-and-a-half dollars, "depending on the success of the invasion of Stockton."

The date was set: September 21, 1958.

Official fliers were sent out.

Everything was readied.

EVERYONE in San Francisco and throughout the surrounding areas wore their "SCHARGE" buttons, business executives, construction workers, and cab drivers alike.

Only one question remained: "Will Sherwood Show?"

Indeed he did!

On September 21, Marshal Don and General Hap accompanied the flyboys—163 airplanes—to Stockton's airport. As Hap's air force neared Stockton, the Air National Guard out of Hayward joined up with them, flying in formation.

After landing in Stockton, Sherwood and Harper boarded their Sherman tank.

Other members of the aerial invasion were transported in the nearly two hundred cars that Bob Cole and Gene Babow had arranged for. The "fleet" of two boats was a little late—it arrived the following day. It was a matter of tiny motors and too many miles.

Lon Simmons, a well-known sportscaster who had recently joined the KSFO team, reported the siege for all the listeners who couldn't play hooky:

> As the troops make their way into town, there are still skirmishes on the outskirts of the city. . . . Marshal Sherwood and General Harper's tank is now rolling down Main Street. The crowds have parted like the Red Sea and line the streets, wildly cheering, waving flags and handkerchiefs. It is a proud moment for the Liberation Army as they come to a halt in the Stockton Civic Square. . . It is a tense moment, ladies and gentlemen. The dignified city officials stand at attention and bravely face their conquerors. . . Gallantly dressed in their flamboyant uniforms and brightly colored ostrich-feathered hats—despite oppressive heat—Marshal Sherwood and General Harper stride, with sabers glistening in the sunlight, towards the table prepared for the signing. . . All parties are seated. Marshal Sherwood passes the document to General Harper for review. . . Marshal Sherwood has now taken pen in hand. The crowd whispers amongst themselves. Ladies and gentlemen, the peace treaty has been signed! An unconditional surrender! They are all shaking hands. This is a momentous occasion. . .

The last of Lon Simmons' report was lost over the airwaves as a Stockton menace pulled the plug.

Before the ink could dry on the historic peace document, a pigeon flew over, dropping its mark . . . Splat!

So much for the peace treaty.

"Do you think he's trying to tell us something?" Don asked Hap.

The Sherwood invasion of Stockton was enough to interest Time magazine.

In their profile of Don that September, they noted, "He is the highest-paid record spinner on the West Coast and the electronic darling of the Bay Area . . . Last week signing a contract that will boost his yearly take past the $100,000 mark."

OAKLAND TRIBUNE

Question: What was Sherwood's invasion of Stockton all about?

Answer: Sherwood borrowed from Shakespeare—it was much ado about nothing.

Navajo

Just before the September Raid on Stockton, Don agreed to yet another KSFO show, "Sherwood and Friend," a two-hour nightly program that would air from 9:30 to 11:30. The new show was to feature guest interviews and some music in an informal, typically Sherwood setting. His long-time writer Dick Brill would produce the show, and Don would tape it after "Will Sherwood Show."

Déjà vu of earlier times! Don had pushed himself beyond his limits before, with disastrous results. Now he was getting ready to do the same thing all over again.

By October, the station had cut the show to one hour.

The first program—when the show was still two hours —showcased Don's buddy and San Francisco legend Herb Caen. In later shows, Don interviewed his local friends in the media and explored what interested him, without too much concern about whether or not the subjects were popular. He interviewed the known and the unknown, the wealthy and the poor; he covered sports, film, music, and restaurants. His guests included his old friend Phyllis Diller, Robert Merrill, Ann Blyth, Joe E. Brown, Harvey Ward, Victor Borge, Buddy Baer, Alfred Hitchcock, Jackie Cooper, Milton Berle, Horace Heidt, Art Linkletter, Dennis Day, Mel Blanc, Shelley Berman, Vincent Price, Errol

Flynn, Kim Novak, Earl "Fatha" Hines, Dean Martin, Lou-
ella Parsons, Drew Pearson, Jimmy Stewart, Buster Collier,
Wendel Corey, Shirley Temple, Ben Swig, and Trader Vic.

Besides actors, singers, comedians, and media people,
Don took full advantage of his opportunity to interview
and talk with authors, poets, and philosophers. Among
them were his friend Barnaby Conrad, Erskine Caldwell,
Lawrence Ferlinghetti, Jack Kerouac, Ken Patchen, and Allan Watts. He talked with Stanley Sohler, leader of the Nu-
dist Association; his buddy, cab driver Parkey Sharkey;
Albert Ward, cable-car bellringer champion; Juanita, Marin
café owner; and Jack Shoulders, Grand National Top Cow-
boy. Don wanted to establish a balance between his particular brand of bizarre, impulsive comedy and the
discussion of serious issues.

One fan, Virginia Bullivant, who worked for the *San
Francisco Call Bulletin*, was a volunteer with the charity organization Navajo Assistance. She set up citywide clothing
drives and did public speaking to inform people of the deplorable Navajo situation on the New Mexico Reservation.

Although encouraged by others to contact Don and be
a guest on his show, at first she shied away. "He could
make such a fool of people, I just couldn't!" Virginia says.
Then Paul Seegle, on the staff at the *Call Bulletin* told her,
"Don is very intelligent. He won't make fun of you." She
got in touch with Dick Brill and Charlie Smith, and was
granted an interview.

"Don was leaving for Los Angeles right after the interview," she says. "While he was interviewing me, the Fairmont Hotel barber was cutting his hair! Isn't that typical?
Still, I felt his electricity, his magnetism."

Don, immediately interested in the Navajo plight,
joined the appeal for food, clothing, and financial aid.

"I know I got through to Don because of his big heart
and because he was more than just a deejay," Virginia
adds. "He was interested in humanity. He wanted to help
people and enjoyed getting into something meaty and
meaningful."

Deciding he wanted to see firsthand what was going on and to meet Bert Pousma, the head of the organization, he flew to Gallup, New Mexico. He also met with California Congressman Clair Engle, who was on a committee that was investigating the disbursement of government funds assigned to the Navajo.

As his involvement grew, Don started reading newspaper articles on the air and talking about the Navajo on his morning radio show. He played the taped interviews with Bert Pousma on "Sherwood and Friend" and aired a home movie he had shot for his KGO-TV show.

All of this kept the press busy.

CALL BULLETIN:

Paleface Don Sherwood hit the tom-toms again today in his one-man war for the scalps of Indian Affairs agents neglecting the lot of the Navajo people. Wearing an old sweatshirt and a new social consciousness . . . Sherwood urges education of the generally illiterate Navajos with a view toward replacement of white Indian Affairs personnel by educated Indians.

HERB CAEN:

The Bureau of Indian Affairs in Washington is rapidly getting unamused by Don Sherwood's loud one-man campaign on behalf of the Navajo Indians, and especially by his implications that something mysterious is happening to the 100 million bux allocated annually to help the Navajos. From the sound of tomahawks being sharpened along the Potomac, I have a feeling Our Boy is in for a scalping. . .

Things were heating up.

Don challenged officials of the federal government's Indian Bureau to a roundtable radio conference. The officials informed KSFO management that Don had his facts wrong. Don flew in Bert Pousma and left repeated messages at the hotels of the officials, who were in San Francisco for a water conference.

The messages went unanswered.

Don told reporters, "I offered them the opportunity to speak."

That night, before his KGO-TV variety show, Don was warned by management not to mention even the word Navajo. They should have known better than to give him that kind of ultimatum.

During the show, while Don was interviewing actor Richard Egan, Egan noticed that his host was not acting his usual self and asked Don, "What's the matter with you?"

"Somebody got to somebody, and I'm not supposed to mention *Navajo* on this show," Don answered, "but I'm going to because I'm sore!"

Television screens all over the Bay Area went black. The station had pulled the plug.

The phones went wild, and before long a group of Sherwood supporters were outside KGO protesting. Sherwood pronounced, "I don't know what my status is now, but I know if I ever get a chance to go back on television again, I'll start right smack where I left off." He gave reporters one of his best lines ever: "I own my own program, but I don't own the facilities, and that's where they've got me, right in the facilities!"

The newspaper columns were full of heated discussion and public debate. Dwight Newton reported—

> If Mitchell [the KGO station manager] honestly believed Don's argument in defense of the Navajos was groundless, he should have turned the evidence over to Don to use on the show. . . How could Mitchell be so naive as to believe Don would accept a ban? If there is one thing that makes Sherwood see red, it is censorship—in any form.

> Mitchell committed an absolutely unpardonable sin. . . . He just left thousands of viewers hanging in midair, wondering what happened. For all they knew, Don had collapsed from acute indigestion. They had to

wait until the morning paper came out to read the truth. And believe me, it took a great deal of legwork and telephoning to uncover the truth.

. . . Mitchell made a fall guy out of himself and a hero out of Sherwood. Once again Don is a nationally talked about personality, and Mitchell is in the local, public dog house.

Yesterday morning, on KSFO, Don, unrestricted by management there, was not only talking about the Navajos, he was playing Indian music! And his new pet name for KSFO was Radio Free San Francisco.

This wasn't the end of the Navajo affair.

Don was subsequently given the freedom to tell his side of the Navajo story on his KGO television show, as long as the government's Indian representatives were given equal time to state their position. The *San Francisco Chronicle* called it "a struggle for peace with honor."

The popular vote was in Don's favor.

DWIGHT NEWTON:

I think it is time we stopped calling Don a clown. On Wednesday's Navajo show, he conducted himself with dignity and authority. His approach was deeply sincere. It was Don's finest hour. He has acquired intellectual stature through his many interviews with the low and the mighty. If he took the time and effort to really understand current events, he could become a very popular commentator.

When Don first raised the Navajo issue, people couldn't help but question his sincerity. Was he simply exploiting the issue because it was controversial, or did he really feel his involvement could make a contribution?

Did he, in fact, make a difference to the cause?

On a tangible level, he was personally responsible for generating significant donations of money, supplies, clothes, and blankets. He could not make a difference to the basic issue, but Congressman Engle continued to investigate and apply political pressure in Washington. In the end Don was vindicated for his early insistence that a problem existed: the Congressman's subsequent report showed that only fifty cents out of every dollar allocated for the Navajos was going to the Navajos; the rest was going to administrative costs.

Cause
and Effect

Should there be a fountain at
the foot of Market Street? What should be done to enhance
the Palace of Fine Arts? What about building controls?

Don was a typical native San Franciscan, proud of his
city. He was atypical in that he had the power to influence
the public's responses to such local issues.

When he waged verbal battles on behalf of building
controls for San Francisco, raging about the desecrating of
San Francisco's charm by "erecting 'big boxes' at the sky-
line," thousands of people applauded. When the focus
came to the San Francisco Bay, he crusaded to save it. He
organized yet another flotilla of boats—this time, not to
raid a city—but to clean up the bay by hauling in debris.

When State Senator McAteer's bay preservation bill
went to committee in Sacramento, Don got on the radio
and urged everyone to send telegrams supporting it. The
public responded, tying up Western Union's lines for
days. San Francisco seized the opportunity to control
landfill and bay development. Don was there when Governor Pat Brown signed the bill instituting the Bay Conserva-
tion and Development Commission (BCDC).

Don also wanted to tear down the Embarcadero Freeway in front of the Ferry Building, and was instrumental in preventing construction throughout the rest of Fisherman's Wharf and the Marina Area. One fan, John Miller, says, "I think he wanted us to tear down, each night, what had been built during the day!"

"Don was a whole lifestyle," Russ Coughlan comments fondly. "He was ahead of his time in many ways, always on the cutting edge."

Being on the cutting edge was an essential part of Don's volatile personality.

HERB CAEN:

Don Sherwood, covered around town last week by a writer-photographer team from LOOK magazine, begged to be excused one afternoon to keep an appointment with "the dirty doctor"—his psychiatrist. The writer asked if he'd made it up. "Nope," confessed Don. "Give the plug to my fourth wife. She's the reason I'm going!"

Don fascinated the media as much as he did his audiences. By 1958 people throughout the country were hearing about "this guy, Sherwood," his antics, and his crusades.

Dan Sorkin, a deejay in Chicago, knew of Don long before he came to San Francisco and eventually competed with him—

DAN SORKIN:

I first met him on the telephone. I had started a satirical, iconoclastic fifties campaign on my show about people who join marches without having any idea of what they're about. I was having a lot of fun with it.

Another woman and I got together and created a campaign based on a fictitious woman, Rose Bimler, with the purpose of saving her—never saying what we'd save her from. Someone donated buttons saying, "Save Rose Bimler." People didn't know there was no Rose Bimler.

DAN...

It all caught on, and the next thing you know the educational channel in Chicago asked if I'd produce a documentary about this woman, which I did. I called Don in San Francisco and someone else in New York, asking if they'd go along with the gag and distribute buttons. Don thought it was great, and he became the distributor for the West Coast. All told, we distributed more than two and a half million buttons!

It's wonderful what you can do when you're working with live radio! We called the Russian Embassy in New York and San Francisco, asking what had happened about the Bimler woman. They said they'd get back to me. A file was created on both coasts. At first I was told that they couldn't release any information on her. Then Don called the embassy on the air. Now the inquiries were coming from both coasts and Chicago, and a whole file was created for this nonexistent woman.

I talked to Don frequently but had not yet met him. We knew of each other and got news back and forth through the entertainers that were on all the shows. Jonathan Winters had been on Don's television show, so he told me about Don's accident with the police captain's sister.

The first time I actually met Don was during a McDonald's promotion. They were a sponsor of mine in Chicago. I was taking their plane, the Meat Wagon, around the country.

When I came to San Francisco, I went to KSFO to meet Don. This was right after *Saturday Review* did a piece on me because the Nielsen Rating Company claimed that I not only had the lowest ratings in Chicago, but that there were no numbers for me, period; it was an asterisk, no number! I went on the air reading this report, saying, "I don't exist, therefore you—the listener—don't exist. If you *do* exist, please write a letter to the A.C. Nielsen Company." They got bags and bags of mail, and everyone overloaded the Nielsen switchboard.

DAN...

Don got news of this. He called me on the air and made a plea to the nonexistent audience, saying he'd never spoken to an audience that didn't exist, since he had a "real" audience. He offered to "share some of his rating points" and mailed them to me.

"People always try to analyze Dad's success," Greg Sherwood says. "One important aspect was that he had the ability to communicate the truth. Also, his taste was proletarian—simple. He thought we might as well have fun, have a good laugh—relieve tension and stress."

Ronnie Schell was given a lesson from Don on another means of stress control besides laughing. Don took Ronnie to the ocean and handed him his gun. "Just shoot it right into the waves—like this," Don said, showing him. "No matter how you shoot them, they'll just keep rolling in." Ronnie tried it—what the hell. It worked! However, he did ask himself, "Can I get arrested for this?"

People kept trying to understand what made Don tick, what gave him the brilliance and the magic. Deejays and management people from radio stations around the country were sent to San Francisco with instructions to hole up in their hotel rooms, listen to Don Sherwood, and figure out how he was getting his high ratings. Who was this guy? was the big question. What's so great about him?

Initially they went away scratching their heads, mumbling, "I don't think he's that funny." As KSFO's publicity sheet said, "He's a young man with a touch of genius—beloved or berated, commended or condemned. But never ignored."

Bill Shaw had long ago deduced that it wasn't what Don did that succeeded, so much as who he was.

"In that era, Dad was the man in the gray-flannel suit, the anti-hero," Greg says. "We don't have those men today, because everyone's been co-opted so thoroughly, everyone bought off on the system. He presaged the beat generation. Today, with Robin Williams and David Letterman, Dad's stuff doesn't necessarily hold up; it seems archaic, but at that time it was amazing."

The full dichotomy of Don Sherwood could not be duplicated, much less explained in terms that most radio executives could understand or accept. Now, with the passage of time, there is perspective on Don's success.

Inevitably, along with success comes competition. Don was also unique in the way he handled that.

On the surface, it appeared that Don wasn't afraid of anyone who tried to beat him. Of course, that wasn't true. Even the most successful stars are well aware of how quickly a new talent can capture the attention of a fickle public. Don was different in that he hit the competition head on, challenging newcomers directly. He just picked up the phone and called them, live and on the air.

Hugh Heller, Don's former manager, remembers that while Don was very generous in scouting talent for the radio station and helping with recommendations and selection, he completely switched his tune once the person was hired.

Arrogant and conceited? Yes, perhaps he was. He had a sizeable ego—an inevitable outgrowth of being on the receiving end of an entire city's adulation. But the truth is that what came across as arrogance and conceit was a cover for massive insecurities.

From Hawaii
to Los Angeles

The Chicago episode in 1957 should have given everyone, including Don, a hint that he was, as his ex-wife Shirley says, "happiest in his own backyard." The theory was about to be tested again.

Hawaii's most renowned deejay was Hal Lewis, also known as "J. Akuhead Pupule" or "J. Fishhead Crazy." What Don was to San Francisco, J. Akuhead was to Honolulu.

What would happen if the two "greatest" switched places for a while?

J. Akuhead, who was from San Francisco, wrote to Don:

Sherwood, my boy:

I am simply delighted that your Mr. Shaw has seen his way clear to risk his radio station's reputation by having me appear in your place, because sometimes I get really sick. I have heard that you were a bum until about a year ago, and with my presence in your place, I would like to assure you . . . you'll be a bum again.

Our station manager, Richard Block (a Frisco boy), has also agreed that your show on this station should set Statehood back another 25 years. He is a former fan of yours

and tells me that some of the nutty things you do will un-
doubtedly cause the whole Island to slide back into the
ocean.

The mechanics of the switch I think are simple. . . I have
some promotional ideas we can go into in a later missive.

Regards,
Hal

Bill Shaw responded to J. Akuhead, "Sam"—

Dear "Sam"—

We approach this venture with the nervousness of a
porcupine making love.

By reputation, you seem to have the same strange hold
on the Islands that Sherwood has on the Bay Area. . . But
how you will do in each other's backyard is anyone's guess.
Nevertheless, it sounds like a very intriguing idea, and we
are prepared to go ahead with it, if the details can be
worked out.

Cordially,
Bill Shaw

By early July, Don was in the KHVH studio in Honolulu, and J. Akuhead was at KSFO. With a flurry of press
releases and publicity photo sessions on both sides of the
ocean, publicists did their best to make the exchange fly.
Both Don and J. Akuhead approached the switch with the
agreement that they would not try to fill the other guy's
shoes; each disk jockey would do his own show.

The two deejays ventured into each other's loyal fan
camp. Based on their significant egos, it was not done tim-
idly. Unlike substituting a regular deejay in someone's
spot for vacation relief, these guys were celebrities. This
essentially challenged the fans to defend *their* man.

A few of Don's San Francisco fans welcomed the
change, like the one who wrote, "I like your pigeon En-

glish story of Red Riding Hood and want to hear more."
Most of them wanted Don back and said so loud and clear.
"Ridicule should only be attempted by a clever person," a
representative fan wrote. "You are running this Hawaii
thing into the ground. I shall switch to Doug Pledger till
Sherwood returns."

Don did not fare any better over in the Islands. When
he tried to say Hawaiian words, they got all tangled up.
When he referred to deck sports being for the "people with
little funny hats and knickers," along with various other
quips, the listeners were not amused. In fact, Don's sense
of humor fell flat.

So much for that idea.

Lonesome Don went fishing. Sam Sanford, who had
written for Don's "San Francisco Tonight" television show,
was living in Hawaii and operating a fishing boat. He remembers the day he took Don out—

SAM SANFORD:

When Don had no luck fishing, he decided to scuba
dive, which he had never done before. He had no fear.
We strapped a tank on him, and over he went. He
caught his first turtle, which was about three feet across.
With turtles, if you grab them up from behind, you can
plane them—they act like a motor. Don didn't know
this, and he pointed the turtle down. We watched as he
disappeared into the murky depths! He wouldn't let go
of the turtle, and we couldn't get his attention. He kept
going down until he almost ran out of air. *Then* he let go
of the turtle.

He started to come up, and we went down to meet
him, to bring him up slowly. He had the biggest eyes
you've ever seen in a diving mask! "Did I do something
wrong?" he later asked.

This began Don's love for scuba diving. Upon his return to the mainland, he took proper diving lessons from

Ed Brawley in San Francisco—where there were no turtles. A few pink elephants, maybe, but no turtles.

Don chalked up the whole radio exchange to a dumb idea and gloried in a hero's welcome at KGO and KSFO.

Within the year, Don was bored with his television show. His intention to concentrate on radio alone was thwarted by Russ Coughlan, now sales manager at KGO-TV. Why not put Don back on television with an afternoon video deejay show Russ asked management?

"It was radio with pictures," Russ explains. "You were watching him take the calls. Don was clever and glib, and he had something to say about everything. He was just terrific, but he bitched and moaned, saying it was just like the old television thing, and he didn't want to do it anymore. The show lasted thirteen weeks, and that was Don's and my last professional association." Only Don had the luxury of starting and quitting shows, with a let's-see-how-it-goes attitude.

Hugh Heller had recently put together a partnership with Don, Lemm Matthews, himself, and a gentleman named John Rohnert. Rohnert had a farm just north of San Francisco. Heller put together a deal with a developer: in exchange for advertising and promotion, each of the partners received property. Don successfully promoted what is today called Rohnert Park, just outside of Santa Rosa.

This investment turned Don's finances around and provided long-term stability. He no longer had to worry about money; he was one of the highest paid deejays around, and his financial advisors had made profitable investments.

Don didn't have to have plans, since plenty of other people had them for him. Some of those people were his friends, others were not. He was focusing on his enormously successful KSFO show, when an offer came from a Los Angeles television station. Much to Don's disapproval, Bill Fiset of the *Oakland Tribune* leaked the news of the $75,000-per-year job offer. The first thing Don did was call Bill early the next morning and wake him up. He let Bill know he was not pleased about the column. Then he went on the air and read an "open letter to Bill Fiset," which was reportedly a script from one of Hitler's speeches.

The same question Don had faced several times before was raising its ugly head: Would he ever make it in a market outside of San Francisco?

KHJ-TV in Los Angeles had a program in mind, which they wanted Hugh Heller—the ever busy man of entertainment—to produce. The only catch to the deal was KSFO's newest efforts to curtail Don's temptations—a clause in his contract stipulating that he couldn't be out of the Bay Area after 9 p.m. any weekday night.

If Don wanted to do the show, he would have to fly into Los Angeles every Friday after his morning program, do the taping, and hustle back to San Francisco. The show would air the following Thursday night in Los Angeles and the following Saturday night on KPIX in San Francisco.

Hap Harper remembers flying Don to Los Angeles one day in his F-51 World War II fighter plane. He says squeezing Don into the back jump seat was "like Contadina trying to get eight big tomatoes in that one little can."

"On the flight home," Hap continues, "the weather started to deteriorate. I flew lower and lower, trying to stay beneath the cloud cover and sneak our way back, but we couldn't even make it to San Jose. Without any navigation radios on board, I was forced to turn around and eventually landed at Sacramento. We had to rent a car and drive back to San Francisco, leaving the plane there. Don was hopping mad! He kept saying, 'I could have taken a *real* plane with a *real* pilot!' "

Referring to California's long San Francisco–Los Angeles feud, Hollywood's *Variety* said of Don's show: "Viewers will resent his coming into their living rooms wearing a sweat shirt and striped sweater. Sherwood has nothing new or different to offer. Guts he's got, and a kind of confidence that may rub the wrong way. Despite his statement, 'I've got an awful lot of talent,' if truth be told, he hasn't. If Frisco can cut it with what he offered, then local TV audiences are to be pitied."

Terrence O'Flaherty of the *San Francisco Chronicle* snapped back: "The (Variety) reviewer's crack about southern California resenting the sweat shirt and sweater is, of course, pure bunk—or did he mean that viewers down there in the land of the flowered sport shirt and sagging toreador pants would consider Sherwood overdressed?"

Don started to refine his appearance for the show. He was restraining himself in every way to go along with the more conservative programming, but nothing he did made a difference to the Los Angeles audience. One northern California fan wrote in to the newspaper, "When Don was his rowdy, goofy, amusing self, he was torn to shreds. Now he is brushed and combed, properly buttoned and zippered, and he is still torn to shreds! Poor Don."

Some of Don's shows caught special headlines. On one occasion, Marie McDonald was his guest. Things were dragging a bit, to say the least. For lack of anything better to say, Don asked her what she had read lately. Silence. More silence. Then someone in the audience yelled, "She can't read!" Don did not reply. He just sat there, waiting for her to say something.

Finally, he said, "I suppose I could let you sit here a while longer."

"Yes, I suppose you could, since I didn't get a cotton-pickin' penny for coming down here!"

She proceeded to call him phony and pushy, and let him know in no uncertain terms that his show didn't have a hope in hell of succeeding.

Things did not go well with Zsa Zsa Gabor, either. Don and she got in a yelling match, and Hugh Heller remembers having to take the tape to management for approval to air it.

The media cautioned Don about such antics in public. Real pros, they said, do not indulge in "temperamental spats while entertaining."

KSFO:
"Sounds
of the City"

After interviewing a doctor who talked about the effects of stress, it was apparent to Don that he had to make a choice: "Sherwood and Friend" in San Francisco, or the Los Angeles television show.

He chose Los Angeles.

The San Francisco fans protested. They were losing the local show that allowed Don all the freedom he wanted, in exchange for the Los Angeles show that did nothing but stifle him. This wasn't their idea of fair play.

They did not have to feel cheated for long. The Los Angeles show lasted all of six months. Disappointed, but not unhappy to be rid of Los Angeles, Don commented, "I don't understand those people down in L.A. Next to being nice, doing nothing seems to be how you make it there."

He told Bob Foster of the *San Mateo Times*, "I'll never depend on television for a living. I'll never worry about ratings. I've done that. I've gone through all the stages of the 'artist,' including the Christmas when I was starving in my earlier Los Angeles days, with nothing to eat but popcorn off the Christmas tree."

There was one good thing that came out of Don's Los Angeles venture: he met Marilyn Walker.

MARILYN WALKER:

I was taking dramatic lessons and living at the Studio Club, along with Kim Novak and other now-famous actresses, when Don came to Los Angeles. I knew of him from having watched his "San Francisco Tonight" show when I lived and worked in Sacramento. I was in TV there, so I was very interested in him.

I found a way to get backstage to meet him. Then I worked very hard to get him to ask me out, though I knew he was dating Felicia Farr, who was also seeing Jack Lemmon (which Don couldn't understand when she could have *him*).

I wasn't even twenty at the time, and Don was drinking then, but I'd go with him to clubs after his show.

One time we ended up at Julie London's house. She sang some soppy song to Don, and he just melted into a pool of butter. He acted like it was the biggest thing to happen to him since coming of age!

There was no real relationship between us at that time. We were getting to know each other, and we both dated other people. I remember one night at the *Interlude*, Don was drinking, and he said to me, "See that woman over there? Well, she's a hooker, and I'm going home with her." I was put in a cab, in tears, and wondering what was wrong with me.

I was the kind of girl everyone wanted to protect. That was lucky in the sense that I got to go to many Hollywood parties, but was always sent home before all the trouble started—which it inevitably did.

After I moved out of the Studio Club into a house with some other girls, I got a call from Don. He was staying at the Hollywood Roosevelt Hotel and asked me to have breakfast with him. I remember when I got there, he was shaking like a leaf. I'd never seen d.t.'s or been exposed to any of that.

"Donny" at about five years old, soon to be completely enthralled with sailors' lore. *(Courtesy of the Sherwood family collection)*

Don's Pied Piper: little does he know this is exactly what he will become. *(Courtesy of Marie Christiani)*

1938 Lawton School class photo—San Francisco. The tall, gangly boy standing at the far left, third row, is Don at thirteen. He is already, in many ways, standing out in the crowd. *(Courtesy of the Sherwood family collection/Photographer: Frances Thompson Studio)*

Don and Aunt Marie on an outing in San Francisco. Much has happened since the early days when Marie was Don's sole confidante. *(Courtesy of the Sherwood family collection)*

Don's mother—"Big Inga." Once her son is a professional success, her life becomes much easier. *(Courtesy of the Sherwood family collection)*

Don and his second wife, Sally. Old enough to marry but not quite ready to "leave home," Don moves them into his mother's house. *(Courtesy of Sally Gilbert)*

Just as he is getting his first recognition on radio, at KCBS, Don becomes a proud daddy. His daughter Diane brings a new dimension to his life. *(Courtesy of the Sherwood family collection)*

Shirley is seventeen when she meets Don. Their lives are forever changed. Within two years they marry. *(Courtesy of Shirley Sherwood)*

Robin, about five years old. Dad is no longer at home. *(Courtesy of Shirley Sherwood)*

An increasingly rare moment when Don relaxes with son Greg and daughter Robin. The rollercoaster ride is beginning as Don's KSFO show catches on. *(Courtesy of Shirley Sherwood)*

A classic photo of Greg, about seven, having one of the 'those breakfasts' with Dad after his KSFO morning show in the Squire Room of the Fairmont Hotel. Having to maintain eye contact is not easy when you're trying to eat! *(Courtesy of Shirley Sherwood)*

Don and "scary broad" Suzie Pierce arrange for a chartered plane with Hap Harper. They're off to Reno to get married. *(Courtesy of Hap Harper/Photographer: Keith Cole)*

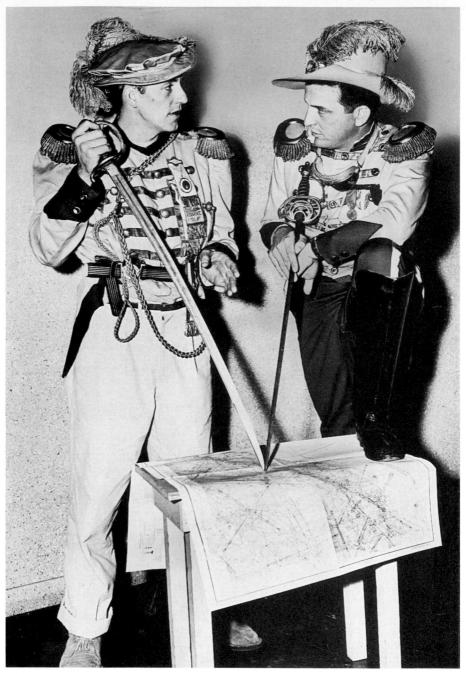

RAID ON STOCKTON: Marshal Sherwood and General Harper plan their strategic attack. There can be no doubt: Stockton shall be theirs! *(Courtesy of Hap Harper)*

Tension mounts as the moment draws near. Time to bite the bullet — or in this case, the cigar. *(Courtesy of Hap Harper)*

Stockton sends in a peace offering — two harem girls, but it's no deal: the raid is on. Sherwood and Harper carry off their war prize. *(Courtesy of Hap Harper)*

MARILYN...

When I was twenty-one, I flew up to San Francisco to see Don, which the *Hollywood Reporter* called "flying to the arms of her love." He was dating Caryl Paul and really liked her. I had been offered a contract with 20th Century Fox but was still making up my mind when Don said to come visit San Francisco before deciding.

That was the beginning of the end. If you ever wanted anyone to show you San Francisco, strictly first class, it was Don. He was sober—it was incredible. After a week, he suggested I go home, pick up my things, and come back.

Don didn't get a chance to tell Caryl about Marilyn before the press went into action.

HERB CAEN:

Don "All Clear" Sherwood and Caryl Paul, who announced their engagement a few months ago, have decided not to spoil their relationship by getting married . . .

About this time, Hugh Heller came back to San Francisco from Los Angeles to be program director at KSFO, under Bill Shaw. Al Newman was his assistant program director. Many new talents were added as Heller continued the efforts to build an invincible lineup.

One new person was Chet Casselman, who came up from Los Angeles to the news department. People would long remember Don teasing him about his particular way of saying, "This is *Chet*—pause—Casselman reporting."

"Don could take an enormously complicated issue and funnel it down to its most simple form," Chet says. "He did that with the news. If something didn't sound just right to him, his bear-trap mind wouldn't let go of it.

"In the newsroom, selection of material is dictated by one thing—interest. KSFO news was known for prompt and thorough coverage. We had our listeners calling in with tips, like the guy who called us when a Pan Am engine fell off, and the plane was making an emergency landing at Travis Air Force Base. If you do a good job with the news, your listeners will call in the stories and tips."

Once a month or so, Chet joined Don's breakfast gang at Squires in the Fairmont Hotel. "It was a remarkable scene. The waitresses took care of Don like he was a king. Everyone was there as Don's audience. No one could make a serious point, and I never wanted to for fear of being stripped naked and thrown out for everyone to see!"

Another key person hired was Elma Greer, the music librarian. Don frequently told his listeners about her legs—"the greatest wheels I've ever seen!" His pet names for her included "Bomba."

The music librarian is responsible for directing the music selection according to the station's format, which the program director establishes.

"She is a musical genius!" Hugh Heller says of Elma. "She could work with Don and all the deejays, and she knew the music better than anyone. She was a major element at KSFO."

ELMA GREER:

It was my job to listen to all the records that came into the station and place them in the library. I'd go over the list of selections with the deejays, who also had albums they wanted to play from their private collections. I was the one who had to battle with them when their choices didn't fit in with our middle-of-the-road format.

I pulled the records for Don's show, but he was free to ignore the list and go to his locker and get what *he* wanted to play. Nine times out of ten, he'd play what I'd selected, but I remember going on vacation once when I'd pulled a week of his shows. He threw them all away!

Working with those egos was worse than raising my own sons! I was a mother to all of them. You couldn't help but love Sherwood. He wasn't the sweetest guy in the world—he could be great one moment and then turn

ELMA...

around and be such a bastard. But I loved working with him, and worked closely with him for seventeen years, off and on. We'd fight, but he knew he couldn't push me around.

Not everyone loved the music Don selected. "He was really corny, and he loved corny music," Herb Caen says.

Many people agreed with Herb, but more believed Don had good taste in music. Don once explained his penchant for Latin music: "Somebody told me that it is close to the human heartbeat, and that's why it's so appealing, so relaxing. That's why I play Latin music in the morning . . . to get your heart started."

There was a method to his music programming. Realizing that his listeners were not fully awake at 6 a.m., he began the day with quiet, unintrusive music. As the show progressed, he livened things up according to the natural rhythm of the morning.

Bill Shaw and Hugh Heller were well on their way to having one of the strongest radio stations in the area. Their lineup of talent was continuing to strengthen, and now it was time for a sparkling new "jingle": a station break that sounded KSFO-ish.

Don and Hugh both hated the trite little tunes most of the stations created, so Hugh decided to do it right. He teamed up with choral director Johnny Mann and Allyn Ferguson, orchestrator and conductor for Johnny Mathis.

"Be sure you keep things short and upbeat," Bill Shaw told them.

Hugh proceeded to write the world's longest station break, a "tone poem," off-tempo and done in stereo for the first time, anywhere. With minor editorial changes from Don—"Don't call this city a town!"—SOUNDS OF THE CITY was born.

When Bill Shaw heard it, he said, "No way." After much debate, it was decided to sneak it on the night shift anyway. No sooner had it finished playing than the KSFO switchboard lit up. They tried it during the day, and again the phones went wild. Hugh Heller says the city "fell down loving it."

To this day, SOUNDS OF THE CITY is perhaps the most beautiful station sound package ever produced:

> The sound of the City,
> the sounds that are heard
> in San Francisco
> are mixed with daylight's glimmering rays
> and moonbeam's shimmering glow.
> When darkness settles on the City,
> homeward people on their way,
> chimes ringing softly in the stillness,
> fog creeping slowly 'cross the bay,
> hear the sound of the City,
> the sounds that are heard
> in San Francisco —
> on K-S-F-O.

Three Guys and a Gal: Ronnie, Vernon, Guy, and Marilyn

With Don only recently off television, KTVU Channel 2, in Oakland, grabbed him for another variety show—referred to by the press as Don's "Romper Room." A frequent guest on the show was his buddy Ronnie Schell, whom he called "America's slowest-rising young comedian."

"He was a great audience for me," says Ronnie, better known as "Duke" of the Gomer Pyle show. "I was working at the *Purple Onion* in San Francisco. Don heard about me and came in one night, a girl on his arm as usual."

RONNIE SCHELL:

After the show, I met him, and the following morning I went over to the KSFO studio. Don did a couple of "unmentionables," terribly filthy things (off the air) and just broke me up! We traded comments back and forth,

RONNIE...

and from that day I could always make Don laugh more than anyone else in the world, I was told.

I was to him what George Burns was to Jack Benny. I knew what tickled him, and that's what got the relationship started. I could get sicker than he could—I'd take what he said to the nth degree and then one step further.

Don came to see me at *Bimbo's 365 Club* on Columbus here in San Francisco, and would come to the shows in Tahoe or Reno. The greatest thing was when I got my first nightclub act at the *Blue Angel* in New York. He flew there for my opening night.

When I was doing a show in Indianapolis, I sent Don a letter telling him how lonely I was, and he told his audience to cheer me up. I got over eight hundred letters!

I was a total fan of his. I've traveled all over the world and never, to this day, seen an interviewer who could come close to Don. He was just as good on TV as on radio.

Women really fell for him. When Judy Garland did his TV show, they went to his apartment afterwards and got drunk together. But then he absolutely infuriated her, and she picked up his toaster and threw it out of the window—thirty stories!

And we all remember Esther Williams really liked him. Also Jane Fonda. When she was on his show promoting a new film of hers, Don showed me a note she passed him afterwards, saying she could take a later plane back to L.A. if he wanted.

The one thing Don and I never agreed on was my nightclub act, because he expected me to be the way I was with him—filthy and degrading! He'd say to me, "Shit, why not do the stuff we do?" I couldn't, of course, because I would have been arrested!

One of our "things" was to rib each other about who was the bigger star. We were having lunch one day at an Italian restaurant after I'd been on Gomer Pyle for a cou-

RONNIE...

ple of years. Some tourists came up to me and asked for my autograph. I looked at Don and said, "You see, I'm much bigger than you are now, Don."

While being "the bigger star" was a joke between Don and Ronnie, a part of Don took it very seriously. The night Don and Judy Garland had their fight, something else happened after she threw the toaster out of the window. She whirled around and snarled, "You're nothing. I know the real *Dave Garroway*!"

Over the years, Don repeated the story many times to his friends Ronnie Schell, Guy Haines, Vernon Alley, and, of course, Marilyn Walker, who recall some of the crazier moments.

MARILYN WALKER:

Don always kidded Ronnie about being fastidious, saying he was the only man in the world who combed his arm hairs! Once a gas-company man came to check the pilot on our furnace. When Don saw him using a long mirror on a tube, like a dentist uses, he conned the guy out of it, so he could give it to Ronnie with a note saying, "Here—now you can make sure your asshole's clean before going out on a date!"

The first time the three of us went on the boat together, Ronnie had to go to the bathroom. Of course, there was no head on this boat. I promised to look the other way. As soon as Ronnie started to go, Don turned the boat into the wind! "There's your first lesson in boating—never pee into the wind!" he told him.

RONNIE SCHELL:

One day a bunch of us guys were up on the Delta water skiing. I had just been skiing and needed help getting back into the boat. They kept faking help—you know,

RONNIE...

letting go of my arm so I'd fall back in. I saw Don disappear off the boat. Next thing I hear is "Hey, baby, I just took a big dump, and it's headed your way!" Sure enough, I'm in the water watching this big log drift towards me! That really made Don howl.

Vernon Alley was Ella Fitzgerald's long-time bass player. He met Don in the music clubs around the city. They clicked immediately, and Don arranged for Vernon to be on his ten-minute KPIX television show. Now Vernon was part of the KTVU band.

VERNON ALLEY:

Don caught me listening to the baseball game with an ear plug during the show. There was a home run, and I started jumping up and down. Don put the camera on me and said, "Now look, there's a bass player listening to the game, and I'm doing my funniest bit here, and he doesn't know anything about it!"

Don hired me to tutor him in voice lessons—he always wanted to be a singer! He rented a studio, I hired a piano teacher for him, and we had it all set. He had a good voice, but he couldn't keep time. I tried to get him to convey the meaning of the song, but he couldn't concentrate. He paid my retainer and the expenses for six months, but only showed up twice!

I had known Guy Haines, the record promoter with Capitol Records, before this. Nat Cole was a friend of mine. Guy would take Nat around when he was in San Francisco, which is how Guy and I got to be friends.

RONNIE SCHELL:

Vernon called us one night saying, "Get over here right now. Sherwood's dead drunk, it's a rainy night, and he's insisting on taking the boat to Sausalito." So we

RONNIE...

went over, promising each other that we wouldn't let Sherwood talk us into it.

GUY HAINES:

Some promise! Within minutes we were all in the boat with Don! I was on the bow with a flashlight, watching for logs and driftwood, and Don was going about forty miles an hour. Out by Alcatraz, he cut the engine and pretended to throw the keys overboard, saying we're going to drift out the Golden Gate! He was convincing as hell . . .

VERNON ALLEY:

We were out under the Golden Gate bridge another night in that little boat, and it was bobbing so much Don said, "Vernon, *you* get out on the bow and hold on to that cleat!" I was about two-hundred-twenty pounds. If I'd fallen in, no one would have seen me again. One of *us* always had to go out on that bow! Every time I went out on the boat, I thought I was lucky to come out alive.

I lived on Hyde and Bay, near Don, so anytime he had a party, he'd call me to bring up Scotch. At one party, Don got mad and started to wrestle me. I put him on the ground and held him there. He was so competitive! Mentally he could handle anything, but not physically. I was a pretty good athlete in my day, but of course, Don thought he was the strongest man in the world, so he always tried to arm wrestle me. I could put him down easier than I could a girl! He'd get so mad. I'd give him a chance, saying I'd use my left hand or that he could use two hands. He still couldn't win.

He never talked racial things with me. I don't think he was aware I was black—he just saw people.

GUY HAINES:

One night Don and I were in *Jimbo's Bop City* out on Post Street—the only two white guys in the place—and Don said to me, "Don't worry, I'm packin'." He had his gun with him. A big, tall guy recognized him and came over to our table and joined us. Don was half in the bag already. It turns out he and Don had gone to the same school, so Don said, "I don't understand—we're both raised in this town, we both went to the same schools, so why don't we talk the same? You have snaggy-mouth talk. . . ." Don meant it as an analytical thing, but this guy got pissed and started getting up. I saw Don reach for his back pocket, and just then, Jimbo came around and cleared the air. I thought Don was going to get us killed that night. He didn't mean it in a personal way. He was just curious about it!

Like Don, Russ Coughlan loved boats. "One of the times Don was down in Baja scuba diving, he called me, really excited, saying he'd fallen in love with a particular hotel. He wanted to buy it and have me run it. 'We'll have a great life!' he said. I seriously considered it, but didn't really want to give up everything I had to go down there.

"Don was doing well financially at this point, and yet he was the cheapest son of a bitch that ever lived! I would constantly insult him about it. He'd say, 'Why should I pay?' After this hotel deal, every time I'd mention he was cheap, he'd glare at me and say, 'I gave you a million dollars worth of talent . . . and I wanted to buy you a goddamn hotel in Mexico!' "

Since he didn't buy the hotel, Don decided to buy a Rolls Royce instead. Conspicuous material things were very much out of character for him, but for a brief time he played "Hollywood".

"This is a kick!" he told everyone. "I used to peddle newspapers on the street." Hugh Heller told reporters, "If you hear that Don Sherwood is making a lot of money, forget it. One of his chauffeurs is an awful liar!"

"You Can't Get a Decent Hamburger in Paris!"

As plans for Don's 1960 vacation shaped up, Marilyn was "sent away." "I knew he was about to have an affair, though I didn't know with whom," Marilyn says. "One morning he just announced, 'You're leaving. Pack up. I'm taking you to Guy and Bev Haines's house.' " Marilyn had no job and no money.

"Many of our arguments were the result of my immaturity and his inability to deal with that and with life in general. He'd taunt me by deliberately having an affair with a 'more mature woman.' "

The "more mature woman" in this case was someone whose name generated more than casual public interest—Jenny "Pia" Lindstrom, daughter of Ingrid Bergman. Since Pia lived in Paris at the time, it was no coincidence that Don's trip was to Europe.

Herb Caen had previously reported:

SCOOPS DU JOUR: Jenny Lindstrom Callaway, off Friday to spend the holidays with her mother, Ingrid Bergman, will scamper right back in three weeks to her beloved Don Sherwood. Despite the denials, this is one of the great loves of our time, exceeded only by Don's for Don . . .

One listener quickly wrote to Don: "Remember when you go abroad you represent all America . . . STAY HOME!"

With this sobering thought, and great trepidation, everyone wished him bon voyage.

HERB CAEN:

Don Sherwood, who's off to Europe on some sort of ill-will tour, was taken to the airport by his buddy, Ronnie Schell, the famous unknown comedian. They had breakfast in the wonderful Pancake Palace, where Don was surrounded by his admirers. Mr. Schell, ignored and crushed, perked up a little when a waitress kept staring at him. "Don't I know YOU from somewhere?" she asked. "Well," he preened, "perhaps you've seen me at the Purple Onion." She looked thoughtful for a moment. "Perhaps," she conceded. "Where do you usually sit?"

Ronnie's parting gift to Don was a butterfly-collecting kit. If only keeping Don out of trouble were that easy! Don grabbed Greg, all of nine years old and practically his father's constant companion, and off they went.

GREG SHERWOOD:

Dad and I got on the Lufthansa flight for Europe, and because it was a German airline, my father got me a couple beers, and we sat in the lounge drinking. He got me drunk for the first time and thought that was very funny. We got to Montreal and had a layover, so I walked into the bar there, said hello to everybody, and ordered a beer!

I had a hangover before we got to Frankfurt.

Dad and I would go out together during the day, and

GREG...

then he'd leave me in the hotel, so that he could go out at night. One night, at about midnight, he came back to the hotel with a couple of American guys from the army base, and he woke me up, saying, "Here's your Uncle Harvey and Uncle Bill!" They brought in their bottles to drink and carried on till all hours.

That same night, earlier in the evening, Dad had decided that all my problems in school were due to my being left-handed. He set about correcting my handwriting to make me right-handed. I kept saying, "You know I really can't do this!" We got all these sheets of paper and practiced making the letters bigger, because he was convinced that was the problem.

A few days later, we flew to Paris, and Pia met us at the airport. She didn't know I was coming along and wasn't pleased, giving me the ice. We were there for a couple of days, but they didn't spend much time together. It didn't seem to be working very well.

In Venice, Dad caught a cold, because he'd gone out walking with some woman in the middle of the night. I followed them; it was a safe place and not a lot of cars. They were in a water taxi, and I was walking along beside it. I got lost, but I had a good time finding my way back to the hotel.

Dad's cold got really bad, and he spent most of the next days in the tub. That's when he showed me what a "bidet" is all about . . . He was in the tub, and I sat on the bidet turning the nozzle, trying to figure out how it worked. The little nozzle was sputtering, not really working. I shoved it over too far, and suddenly the water jetted out. I flew off the bidet and jumped halfway across the bathroom. The water was spouting clear up to the ceiling like a fountain. Dad was sitting in the big Italian tub, watching me in complete hysterics, sinking into the water and almost drowning, because it was the funniest thing he'd ever seen.

GREG...

I had given myself the world's greatest enema!

When Don and Greg arrived home, Don was still sick. "You can't get a good hamburger in Paris," he bitched. There were other things he apparently didn't get in Paris.

Marilyn, back in favor, listened patiently to his tales of four cities. "In London, he went into the Soho district to a bar," she says. "The way Don told it, a beautiful girl walked up to him. He bought her a drink. When he made a move on her, she gave him her price, and he gave her the money. Then she said, 'This bar does not allow us to solicit, so I will have to join you outside. I'll meet you in five minutes at the third lamp post, around the corner.' He waited at that streetlamp for half-an-hour or so. Of course, the woman was long gone. So much for the big man about town! He was so disillusioned, and all I could do was laugh."

After seeing how well the Europeans got by on bicycles, Don bought a ten-speed and campaigned for Bicycle Power. One woman's husband took his message to heart and pedaled his child's rusty, blue bike to work one morning in Berkeley. "That was Friday," she wrote to a newspaper. "He hasn't been seen or heard from since!"

The listeners were overjoyed to have their Mr. San Francisco Radio back. While Don was off, supposedly unwinding in Europe, his fans were entertained by someone they knew and liked—Hap Harper.

Hap was by no means a deejay, but being the agreeable person he was, he gave it a shot. Of course, he had no idea of what it was, exactly, that Don did.

"The impression everyone has of a deejay's job is that you sit down, talk into a mike, and spin records," Hap says. "Sounds easy enough, and Lord knows, they make it seem easy."

HAP HARPER:

I quickly found out that you have to keep a log for everything—the music that's played, the commercials, the times! It's all very precise. Between keeping track of that and finding the next commercial to be read, I really had to concentrate. Since I wasn't a professional announcer, I was trying to glance through the commercial copy while the songs were on, so I would have some idea of what was coming. There was a notebook with sponsors' copy, which also noted if it was to be read live or if it was prerecorded. Many of the commercials had "tags"—special information for me to add.

Don knew the music and the stars, so when a song played, all Charlie Smith had to do was hold up the album jacket. Don could announce the song and performer, as well as talk about interesting aspects the average person doesn't know. I knew the songs, and I knew the performers, but I didn't know their backgrounds, so I didn't have anything to talk about. All I could do, when Charlie held up the album, was announce the song and the performer.

The second day, I couldn't even give the time checks anymore. There I was, a grown man—I had been telling time for a few years! I knew when the big hand was on twelve and the little hand was on seven, it was seven o'clock. In all the chaos, though, trying to have a few funny things to say, I'd look at the clock, and it told me nothing. I saw where the hands were, but I couldn't tell you what time it was. Maybe that's why they have digital clocks in the studios now!

By the end of the morning, I didn't know if I was coming or going. There were people walking in and out, handing me things to put on the air. I remember thinking, these three hours are worse than working a full day. I was drained! Anytime someone walked in, I'd try to get them to stay and talk to me.

HAP...

Fortunately, Aaron Edwards came in to help me with everything. The third day the show was all his!

Aaron took over until Don returned, at which point Aaron went back to news, Hap returned to the air, and the listeners settled back into their morning routines.

Sharing the Spotlight

The decade of the sixties was Don's heyday. He was at the top professionally, in a position to influence causes and to direct the course of people's lives. He had power; it was heady medicine. Sometimes this was to people's advantage, other times it was not. Don was considered to be a man of "iron whim," so everything depended on whether or not it was his idea and on how he felt that day—that *moment*.

While he couldn't or wouldn't take control of his own compulsions, addictions, and destiny, Don kept himself busy with other people's lives. He helped many people's careers, but he loathed star-hungry people, hangers-on. Ask Don Sherwood to advance your career, and you would be dead, but be one of those lucky enough to be *selected*, your career could take off.

Mostly, the help Don gave young performers came out of spontaneous enthusiasms. Early in Wayne Newton's career, when Newton was playing Lake Tahoe, Don went to see his show. He came back raving about it, telling everyone to "get up there and see him." If you go and don't like him, I'll personally refund your money!" Night after night, Harrah's South Shore Room was filled to capacity.

In Wayne Newton's case, and in those of others whose careers Don advanced, his plugs were a natural response to what he saw as talent. When he "discovered" someone, he was sincere and generous with his praise, and spoke out of his own enjoyment. If he couldn't do that, if he didn't like or respect the individual, he did nothing at all. You couldn't buy Don's blessing. He liked you and you were in; he didn't and you were ignored. Don did not compromise himself for anyone—ever.

Who were some of the people he did help? One was a young, upstart comedian appearing at the *hungry i*—Bob Newhart. Don was immediately impressed. He jumped in on radio and television to help in every way he could. When Warner Records brought out Newhart's first album, "Behind the Button-Down Mind of Bob Newhart," Don gave it a big drum roll. The newspapers chimed in:

> Locally, Bob Newhart got a generous and enthusiastic send off by Don Sherwood. Sherwood first played the disk last Tuesday and already the public is talking about the guy.

> This Newhart is great. He has a number of routines on the album record—a thing on a sub returning home after a two-year cruise, a driving instructor routine, etc.—and one which concerns baseball. Buy it, borrow it, or turn on the radio and hope for it. You'll laugh, and that won't hurt you a bit, will it?

Bob Newhart's career was off and running, and Warner Records presented Don with a handsome replica of the Gold Record in appreciation for his help in launching it. Of the first 100,000 albums sold, San Francisco bought 25,000 copies.

Shirley Sherwood remembers when Newhart first appeared in San Francisco. He was a virtual unknown. By then, she and Don had been divorced for a few years.

"Don enrolled Greg and Robin in a summer school in Marin for six weeks, and we were all going over there," she says. "Don casually informed me one day that he'd promised Bob Newhart he could stay in 'our' house while we were gone. Don didn't live there, and he didn't even ask me! I told him, 'You're going to move strangers into *my* home? No way.' He very nervously added that he'd already promised Newhart.

"I had never stood up to Don and flat out said no, but this time I did. Don could have killed me. Although we were divorced, the house he'd bought for us was in his name, so he threatened to sell it and put us out on the street! I stuck to my guns. Newhart didn't stay there, and we did not get thrown out on the street."

Another entertainer who caught Don's imagination was Steve Rossi. He was heavily promoted on Don's television show. Later, Rossi met and teamed up with Marty Allen and became part of "the nuthouse duo"—Allen and Rossi.

Johnny Mathis also got a big push on the television show. "He's a real pleasant and eager young man, a wonderful kid to work with," Don said. Mathis went up to Don one day and asked him, "Do you know anyone who'd be willing to manage me?" "Naaah, forget it," Don replied. "That life isn't for you. Stay in school, graduate, and get a decent job."

Buddy Hatton once quoted Fred Allen's book, *Treadmill to Oblivion*: "The life expectancy of a personality . . . is equivalent to the life span of a moth flying into a flame." This was similar to the advice Don gave Buddy when Buddy was just another upstart San Francisco deejay: "Rent, don't buy."

Not all entertainers felt beholden to Don. Danny Kaye was on Don's television show. Don asked him where he would most like to be, and Kaye replied, "In my hotel room, right now." Don liked Kaye, but the feeling certainly wasn't mutual.

Mutual admiration *was* the bond between Don and Tennessee Ernie Ford. They both had television shows, were equally successful, and needed nothing from each other.

"I called him almost every day on the air from my car phone," the singer recalls. "He'd say to me, 'Hi, Ernie. Say something country.' I was one of the fortunate people that Don liked. I don't know why, but he did."

At one point, both Don and Ronnie Schell were appearing at George Andros's *Fack's II*. Herb Caen was keeping track of everybody:

> Comedian Ronnie Schell is still mapping out his campaign to get married September 30. The way ol' Ronnie has it lined up —" On Sunday I'll select my best man and ushers . . . Monday buy a house . . . Tuesday arrange for the church and the preacher. Wednesday I'll buy a ring. Thursday night Don Sherwood will toss a bachelor party for me. And on Friday night, well, I guess I'll propose to Elma Greer." Or somebody.

Bill Dana was a talent Don admired and enjoyed. Hugh Heller brought Bill Dana to San Carlos Airport one morning to fly the traffic watch with Hap Harper. Don called Hap in for the weather and traffic report.

"Jose Jimenez" answered, "Hap stepped out for a moment."

"Jose, what are you doing up there? Can you fly a plane?"

"No, but Hap gave me this manual."

"Where are you now, Jose? Look out the window. . . What do you see?" Don asked him.

"I see my reflection."

Don and Bill Dana did Hap's entire report. It was all comedy. Hap says it was one of his best reports ever; he never said one word!

George Andros was a close friend of Don's. He remembers Don's help promoting his club when heavy rains were keeping people home and he was losing money. "Don volunteered to do a comedy act on the same bill as

Carmen MacRae," George says. "He told jokes and had everyone laughing and falling all over. He was a big hit.

"Don packed the place, but there was just one problem: everyone left as soon as his act was over! Don really loved Carmen. When he saw what was happening, he asked me to put her in first. It worked.

"He did this for me for a couple of weeks. It was very generous of him, and I appreciated it."

Obligation was still not an acceptable word in Don's vocabulary. Just as he chose to help particular entertainers, he *chose* how and when to help his friends.

Drinking, Hunting, and Figs in Winter

The only people who could sustain a relationship with Don were those who understood and accepted his parameters. Marilyn Walker's relationship with him was on-again, off-again. If there was anyone he might have made an exception for, it was Marilyn. She did everything she could to accept his terms, but that didn't mean she liked them. Typically, she kept hoping he would change. She repeatedly quoted to him from a poem by Edwin Markham:

> He drew a circle that shut me out—
> Heretic, rebel, a thing to flout.
> But love and I had the wit to win;
> We drew a circle and took him in.

MARILYN WALKER:

The times when I wasn't with Don was when he was drinking. You never knew when it was going to happen, but you could sense it—you could see the storm clouds coming.

173

MARILYN...

When we first got together, he was on the tail end of his Zen study, so we'd talk about Nirvana, the wheel, reincarnation. It was the end of the beatnik era in San Francisco, and North Beach still had that aura.

Our favorite restaurant was *Romano's*, where they wouldn't let anyone else know we were there or intrude. Otherwise, we were at the *Normandy* and always *Enrico's*.

A lot of Sundays, we'd go for a walk after breakfast down to Montgomery Street because Don liked walking around the financial district, with no one around, just newspapers blowing, a few stragglers here and there. Then maybe we'd take a cable car back up the hill to our place on Lombard, read the paper, or watch a football game on TV.

Don was *the* Forty-Niner fan, and for him, there was only one way to see the game, and that was from the booth. Lon Simmons was right down from us, and all the football wives and owners were there, which was fun.

Don's children were very young. Greg and Robin were coming to our place on weekends. I knew Shirley and the kids were more comfortable when I was there.

At one point, something had gone wrong. I didn't know what, and Don started drinking and was gone for a couple of days. I was in contact with Dr. Lion and Don's attorney, Harry Wainwright. I looked for him all over the place.

I found him at home, standing between the beds with my gun in his mouth—the one he'd given me for protection. "What in the hell do you think you're doing?" I yelled. I remembered him quoting parts of a poem about a man, Richard Cory, who everyone thought had everything. Everyone wished they were in Cory's place:

MARILYN...

> So on we worked, and waited for the light,
> And went without the meat, and cursed the bread;
> And Richard Cory, one calm summer night,
> Went home and put a bullet through his head.

I could hear the words in my head as I looked at him. The only thing I could think to say that would devastate him enough was "What am I going to tell the kids?"

He took the gun out of his mouth and pointed it at me! I took off down the hall, and he shot two bullets into the walls. I found a phone, and called Bill Buchalter. He was the only one I could think of who could talk to Don in that state and maybe get the gun away from him.

What I didn't know was that Don had gotten Dexedrine from his doctor. He'd combined the pills with alcohol and hadn't slept in days.

Bill went over to the house, and I went to my girl friend's. The next day, I didn't get an answer when I called home. I called Harry Wainwright, and we went to the house, both of us afraid of what we'd find. The front door was chained, so we went through the garage.

The whole house was silent. We found Don passed out on the living room floor, the gun lying by him, and a drink on the table. Dr. Lion said to let Don sleep it off, get rid of the pills and the gun, and then have him come to the office when he was recovered. Don slept for about twelve more hours. He was lucky to be alive.

After this incident, Don wanted to get sober again and worked his way back with the help of Dr. Lion, but he hadn't yet faced his alcoholism.

With the combination of Don's personality and his drinking, bizarre events in his life were not the exception, they were the norm. A particularly bizarre event occurred at Guy Haines' cabin. Guy frequently had Don, Ronnie Schell, and other friends up to his cabin on the Russian River. One time, Don gave Ronnie sailing lessons. After Ronnie sailed right over Guy's dog, Rocky, Don told his listeners, "Ladies and gentlemen, I want you to know that this is the only person who ever ran over a dog in a sailboat!"

This time, Don was up there alone with Guy and his wife, Bev. The men had been lying in the sun drinking beer all day, martinis before dinner, and a gallon of wine with and after dinner. Their drunken "conversation" about Guy's father-in-law, the great deer hunter, became heated.

"You bastard! There's no defense for killing a poor innocent animal!" Don was getting argumentative.

"Hey, I'm just saying you've gotta thin the herd. Has to be done, you know! A bullet's painless compared to starving them to death."

"Painless, my ass! How d'ya like me to shoot you and put you out of your misery?" Don was picking up momentum. "You're gonna die one day. Wanna get it over with? Or hey, better yet, big guy, we've got too many people on this earth. Wanna thin them out? Yeah, what say we put *them* out of their misery! You're the big white hunter!"

"We're talking animals here!" Guy really didn't want to have this pros and cons argument—again. "Hunting's old as the earth. What d'ya think you're eatin' when you dig into those juicy steaks you love so much? You don't object to them killing that cow for you!"

"I'm *eating* what they killed." Don's voice was now low and even. "There's a difference, ol' buddy. *You're* hanging the damn head as a trophy, and the rest lies rotting somewhere. The point is . . . it's not a fair fight. You've got a rifle, what's that animal got?"

"Four fast hooves, that's what it's got! And they run like hell, let me tell ya." Guy was pacing around the room. "They know their turf inside and out. You play hell ever catching them. That's the whole sport of it!"

"Well, let me think a minute," Don said slowly, taking another drink. "So in other words, it's fair because if they're quick enough and smart enough, they'll get away. If not, they deserve to die."

"Oh Christ, will you get off it!" Guy moaned.

"No, this is important." Don was slurring his words,

nodding his head, boring his eyes into Guy's. "I'll tell you what—" He pulled out his .45 automatic out faster than Billy the Kid. "Why don't you get a big kitchen knife. I'll hunt you. Let's see how fair it is."

"You're on!"

As far as Guy was concerned, the whole thing was turning into a huge joke, but Bev, who had been watching the argument heat up, jumped over and grabbed Don's gun.

Guy ran into the bedroom and came back with his .38 automatic. "Here, this is even better." He handed Don the gun. "You can't miss with this."

Before Bev could do anything further, the two men grabbed their glasses, now filled with vodka, and left— Rocky, the dog, hot on their heels.

The night was silent and eerie, the fog low over the water. They downed their vodka and tossed the glasses over the dam.

"Okay, you've got to give me a head start, y'know," Guy told Don.

Don leaned his forehead against a tree. "One . . . two . . ."

Guy took off with Rocky—the dog's chains and tags tinkling like church bells—and headed for the main road, then off into the meadow.

Two shots rang out.

Guy kept running until he nearly fell over a hollowed out log. He crawled into it and lay there—listening. His heart was pounding.

Another shot.

Oh shit, he thought, some poor guy was walking his dog down the road, and Don's killed him! That was his last thought before he passed out.

Don headed toward the beach, shooting at every can he saw. Bev heard the shots from the cabin. Before she could decide whether or not she should call the police, Don burst through the doorway with the smoking gun in his hand.

"Where's Guy?" she asked, ever so hesitantly.

"He's dead," Don said matter-of-factly. He pointed the gun at her. "Now take off your clothes—we're going to make love!"

Bev had no way of knowing if Don was lying. She figured her best chance was to play along. "I'll tell you what, Don, why don't you go to the bedroom. I'll be right in. I'll just turn out the lights."

Don stumbled into the bedroom, and Bev locked herself in the bathroom. When she didn't hear any more noise, she came out and found Don passed out on the bed. She slid the gun from his hand.

Now—where was Guy? What were those shots?

At four in the morning Guy woke up, stiff as hell and freezing, and climbed out of the log. When he got home, he found Bev half-crazed.

"The next day we laughed about it and carried on," Guy says. "This was Don's idea of an entertaining evening when he was drinking."

A few mornings later, Don was back on KSFO, no one the wiser, with not a second thought about any of it. He always owned a gun, though he didn't always carry it. It was common for him to get serious threats and to be harassed.

Ronnie Schell remembers many times when he and Guy, Russ Coughlan, or Vernon Alley would have to get the gun away from Don. "He'd keep darting up and getting another drink! We'd have to wait until he passed out to finally get it out of his hand."

These shenanigans were Don's idea of a good time.

By the winter of 1960, Don moved into a more serious phase. He once again announced that he was quitting television for good. He told William Steif of the *San Francisco News*: "I'm all used up, all through. It's a need on my part to lead a more normal life. TV is an abnormal life—narcissistic. You're constantly being reminded of yourself. I'm divorcing my life from this ego feed, not that the business and the public haven't treated me well. I have no gripes at all. San Francisco is probably the only city in the country that would have accepted me and all my foibles. This is an area that has a particular affection for rascals.

"I'm taking all the scrapbooks, the striped sweater, the trophies, and all the rest, and I'm going to lock them in an old Chinese cedar chest I have, which is reminiscent of a casket . . . Maybe I'll look [at them] years from now. For a while, I thought I'd save the world, but I've given up."

In keeping with this state of mind, Don talked of writing a book called "Figs in Winter," based on a quote from Epictetus. Gone was the Rolls, and in its place was a green Rambler and a much simpler life—part of his path to greater balance. "I am paying," he said, "for those figs in winter."

The Races

Don plunged into an all-around cleaner, healthier life, eating wheat germ and yogurt, taking vitamins, exercising, and, for the most part, staying on the wagon.

"He would go on health kicks for about a month at a time," Ronnie Schell says. "He was on one when I first met him. Three of us went on it —Hugh Heller, myself, and Don. Like everything else, Don gave it up after a month. He drank so much, I'd say to him, 'I don't know how you can look so good.' He'd say it was because of these health kicks and that his body could take this stuff."

In January of the new year, 1961, Don—feeling charged up—demanded a rematch of the previous year's sulky race at Bay Meadows with Herb Caen.

In June of 1960, Herb Caen had written, "Will Sherwood never learn? Last year, brimming with yogurt, wheat germ, and false pride, he challenged me to a bowling duel —and I'm pleased to recall that it took me only five Scotches and half a pack of cigarettes to clobber him." In 1961 Herb announced the rematch.

> Today, he [Don] has challenged me to a sulky race at Bay Meadows, and I feel just sulky enough to beat him. If I can get the horse to stop at the quarter poles

181

for a Scotch, I'm in. Square shooters, particularly when they're as square as Sherwood, never win.

Don's sulky easily and handily trounced Herb. This time the headline in the *San Francisco Chronicle* read, "FAST WRITER, SLOW NAG." Don finished the race ten lengths ahead of Herb and happily grabbed the prize, a one-hundred dollar gift certificate to a men's store. He'd worn a hole in the seat of his pants while "fidgeting about in the sulky." "Next time," he said, "I'll stand up like Ben Hur!" Herb took his medicine like a good sport:

> Clean Living, as personified by Don Sherwood (that's a laugh right there), triumphed over the Dirty Guys—that's me—at Bay Meadows Saturday. Due perhaps to the fact that I'd overtrained a bit on Scotch the night before, Mr. Sherwood, brimming with yogurt and braggadocio, beat me several lengths in the second of our match harness races—but I would like to say, in appreciation, that the crowd was with me all the way (all the world loves a loser) and that Mr. Sherwood's head immediately expanded right through his plastic helmet. The luck of the draw beat me before the race even began. Mr. Sherwood drew a horse named Scotch Kate, who'd obviously been lapping up the Dewar's for months, and I knew there'd be no beating a lass like that. Besides, I had a horse and a half running against me—Mr. Sherwood is half-man, half-horse, you know—and I can only apologize to my fellow Scotch-drinkers. Ol' Wheat Germ is ahead at the moment, but wait till the NEXT race. Meanwhile, back to the bar . . .

Within days, Herb couldn't resist adding the following:

> Square shooters always win (in the end): Don Sherwood might've beaten me at Bay Meadows in our harness race last Saturday, but who was in bed with the flu yesterday? Not old Scotch-on-the-rocks, I'll tellya. Old yogurt-and-wheat-germ, that's who . . .

Harness racing was not enough to satisfy Don's gnawing competitive drive. Next he challenged KSFO colleague Jim Lange, who had come to the station in 1960 to replace Bob Colvig and do the afternoon show.

"I got half in the jug one afternoon and called Jim from a bar," Don said. "I said to him, 'You think you're some kind of big shot. Let's have a contest of strength and health. I'll whup you, boy.' He said, 'How about a race?' and I talked it up to a marathon! About the furthest I'd moved was from a bar stool to a taxi cab and to the apartment! Jim took me up on it, and we got started."

Don's "training" for the big day meant giving up drinking for one day and walking back and forth in his living room about ten times. His "trainer" was Giants' sportscaster Russ Hodges; Jim Lange's was Lon Simmons.

The *San Francisco Chronicle* described the race at the starting line:

> Exactly 14 minutes after sunrise on Sunday morning, cheered by some 200 supporters shivering on Stinson's sandy slopes, the two jockeys jogged off on the long, hard route to San Francisco—23.8 miles away.

"It started as a minimal challenge," Jim says. "I thought, knowing him, that in some way he would cheat. I figured he'd walk to Sausalito and take a boat to San Francisco! We started out at seven in the morning, hundreds of people lining the road, and he said, 'Why don't we just walk together?' We got about two miles into the trip, and I had to go to the bathroom. By the time I came back, he was a mile ahead, and it really became a race."

Don took a rest—and a drink or two—in Sausalito. Jim caught up.

"I kept going, and halfway across the Golden Gate Bridge, I saw the lineup of people on the Marina! Hundreds of people. Lon reported to me that Don was still walking. I got to the finish line, and about twenty minutes later Don came through. We had a big celebration. I got the trophy, and we both made speeches to the crowd. I always appreciated Don doing this. He didn't need to do something like that, and it was a break for me."

The Stinson Beach Race, as it would later be called, turned out to be one of the biggest promotions ever. "There were hundreds of thousands of people. Nothing else was going on. It was a beautiful day, and people got caught up in it," Don told the press." A while into it, I knew it was a big big mistake! . . . I came in third in a two-man race, but I finished, and that surprised everyone. I got up on the wagon at the finish line, and the people applauded. They were having a ball. I raised my hand, took the microphone, and told them I was hereby announcing my candidacy for mayor of this fine city. The roar of the crowd! I felt like Caesar must have felt—that's intoxicating."

Aaron Edwards remembers, "There were no stations between Marin and San Francisco, no bathrooms! Don waited till Lombard Street. He was in trouble, poor guy! The next day, totally unexpectedly, he showed up for work. No one thought he'd come in. He would have been in less pain if he'd broken both legs. He walked like a wind-up toy!"

This was not the last time that there would be talk, in jest or otherwise, of Don running for political office. His wacky ideas were intriguing, and Don, more than anyone else, could unite people. Think of all that might have happened to San Francisco under an elected Don Sherwood. . . . When Don was presented with a shiny Key to the City by Mayor Shelley, Ronnie Schell screamed, "Change the locks!"

KSFO held almost weekly station events all over San Francisco. They were very successful and added to the station's already dominant presence in the city.

The key person responsible for these promotions was "the wild Armenian," Louise Jorjorian, director of promotions. She had been the publicity person at KGO when Don was doing his television show, was subsequently hired by Westinghouse, and then grabbed by KSFO. Now she and Don were once again working closely together.

She was in charge of promotion and outside activities, sales promotion, sales merchandising, and publicity—as

well as promotion and merchandising for the Giants and
the Forty-Niners. Everyone remembers Don talking about
Louise, but no one could imagine the enormous job she
did. She was everywhere all day, operating at the speed of
light, and winning awards that distinguished her in the industry.

"Any time you win an award, it's with the effort and
support of many people," Louise says. "I never even took
or wanted time for vacation! How many people can say
that every day they just want to get to work? I did! We
were one happy family, and working for Bill Shaw was
wonderful.

"This one month, I remember, there were about five
promotions going on, in addition to sales ad campaigns
and deejay promotions. I was also president of the American Women in Radio and Television, and was getting
ready to go to the national convention in New York. I was
up to my ears in everything! The night before I left for New
York, Don threw me a surprise party at his place. He never
invited people to his place, so it was really special. 'See Jorjorian,' he kept saying, 'you think no one loves you!' "

KSFO promotions included remote broadcasts done in
every imaginable arena. One of the best-known remotes
was "Man on the Street," which Don did with the late Jack
Carney. Jack played the interviewer. He'd say, "As you
know, nine out of ten residents of San Francisco listen to
KSFO . . ." He chatted with "residents" at random, all of
whom were played by Don—anyone from a boxer leaving
the gym, to an old lady at Candlestick Park, looking for the
bathroom. Don's spontaneous off-the-wall responses sent
Jack into convulsions. They laughed so hard when they
were doing the promo, they had to do as many as twenty-
six takes and use a horn to cover what Don called the
"shame, shame" words.

KSFO broadcast from the San Leandro ferry on its last
run, on "Monty Bandaar's Sailing Ship," and from the
window of the Roos Atkins store, among other places. One
of the most elaborate and well-loved annual promotions
was "KSFO Under Glass." "The promotion got so big and

so successful over the years that we had to hire an architect to build a portable glass studio that we set up in the center of Union Square," Louise says.

Louise worked with Don every day. "When I first worked with Don, I was a young, straight-laced girl from Boston who had never heard of anyone getting married more than once. I couldn't even understand his dirty jokes at first!

"You wanted to work with Don because you knew it would be a huge success. He always listened to ideas. Even when he'd say, 'That's a crappy idea!' a moment later he'd say, 'You could do it this way.' Then it was his idea, and you were off and running. He wanted to keep things alive."

In 1957 Bill Shaw had come to KSFO with a vision. He had allowed Don his head and then built the station around him. Each new person added to the station brought more than individual talent—each increased the team talent. Shaw's management philosophy emphasized a team effort.

Louise had made some valentines for a previous promotion. They were being given to certain station sponsors. Later, when deejay Al Collins came to KSFO, he convinced Louise that they were too beautiful to keep from the listeners. This gave birth to the "KSFO LOVES YOU" bumper stickers, a campaign subsequently copied in New York and all major cities. The stickers led to contests and, eventually, the memorable KSFO Loves You annual cruises to Hawaii.

Small wonder KSFO was riding high.

Superfrog

Every person in the KSFO lineup was original and creative. The newest to join the staff was Carter Blakemore Smith, Charlie "Max" Smith's nephew. He became part of KSFO's news team in 1962, coming from KRE in Berkeley. Carter B. had been talking to KSFO for many months.

Aaron Edwards had a falling out with management and subsequently switched to the afternoon show. Don gradually pulled Carter B. into the morning show.

CARTER B.:

At first I was very cautious of Don because he was a superstar, and I was just a punk kid working as a newsman. His viciousness was legendary, and he could be ruthless on the air and off.

Once I got to know him better, this turned out to be to my advantage because I didn't worry about it and could hold my own. He liked and respected that. I would bring material to him, and he started to work me into the show doing little bits. I did a gardening bit, a doctor bit, all in fun but with a serious side to it. He'd casually say on the air, "So, you gonna come in here?" The other news director took over, and I went into the booth.

Whatever Don wanted, he got, even if that meant crip-

CARTER...

pling the news department. I liked that because I didn't want to stay in news, I wanted to be a disc jockey. This was a chance to get the training, to watch and learn from Sherwood. There's a lot about radio that you can't know unless you are right there with someone, seeing it—little techniques that most people never think about. Sherwood had a reputation for being disorganized, but in the studio, he was totally organized. He knew exactly what he was doing every second. His brilliance was that, what came across as crazy and spontaneous, was highly structured. In the studio, he had masterful self-control.

He intimidated people, but I wasn't intimidated by him. I never made any money off of him; I got paid the same whether I did his show in the morning or not. Occasionally I'd say, "Hey, this isn't working out," and then I wouldn't go in there. He'd say on the air, "Carter must be really mad now 'cause he's not coming in here anymore." Or I might say on the air, "I'm not coming in here anymore, because you put me down, and I don't need that." He'd tease you on the air, saying things like "You have a horrible zit on your nose today!" We had ups and downs, but if you came back at him in a loving way and not antagonistic, it was okay.

Don talked on different levels, and you could never tell from what he was saying which level he was on. There were things he wouldn't reveal very often or ever. He did what he did for the joy of it. When he was working, and working right, it was great.

With Don it was like an art, and an artist must paint, or compose, or write, or whatever. When Don was doing his show, he was full of joy. He had more natural talent than anybody on the air that I've ever known.

When he knew he wasn't going to be good, he just didn't show up. I wish we all had that luxury. If he wasn't happy, he didn't pretend to be. That's a fraud anyway. No one is happy or up all the time. And because he had power, he could get away with it. Before

CARTER...

he had those ratings, he got fired, but once he had the ratings, he could do what he wanted.

Bill Shaw had the patience to allow Sherwood to develop on the air. Don had a keen ear, and he was a good salesman. Shaw genuinely liked Don, and he was a very good manager. He wasn't Santa Claus, but we had a happy ship because it was totally successful. I've never been on a station since that was so successful, and so much fun. And that's our business, to have fun. The harder you have to work, the tougher it gets.

When Don and I worked together, we were very close, on and off the air. He was generous, warm, and honest, though he could hurt you, like honest people can.

HERB CAEN:

Disc jockey Carter Smith failed to make his morning show last Sunday, so his place was taken by a glib young man who called himself Ted Parnell. Several listeners phoned in to register approval: "The guy's good, keep him on." A Carson City radio station exec called to offer Parnell $100 a week. However, more seasoned KSFO listeners, who dug immediately that Ted Parnell was actually Don Sherwood, jumped nervously out of bed thinking it was Monday.

Jeff Skov moved into the news department as Carter B. shifted to deejay. "I was interested in news, and Don did not screw around with the news like he had before," Jeff says. "We did a more serious thing. We'd talk about it, in a more provocative way, especially during the half-hour headlines. Once I'd been there a while and Don knew what I could do, we worked well together. I didn't want to become a deejay, so I didn't represent any kind of threat to him.

"The one thing he said to me, as this young eager beaver, was 'Hey kid, Gene Autry ain't coming to your funeral —slow down.' That stuck with me."

HERB CAEN:

Don Sherwood said, "Winners don't knock and knockers don't win" once too often on KSFO. Jeff Skov introduced him the other morn as "the man with the biggest knockers in town."

Lon Simmons comments, "A lot of us felt that we had a pretty good sense of humor, but when you were with Don, you'd back off because he could make you feel like you had none at all! He came up with such great lines. Of course, if you were going out with Frank Sinatra, you probably wouldn't sing very much.

"Certain people are overpowering in the things they do, and Don was one of them. With his brilliant mind and humor, any insecurities he had came out with a little stinger on them, so that he could handle situations he wasn't comfortable in."

Bill Shaw had prepared a written "design" for KSFO, which every staff person had. It was a concise outline of radio: how it works, when it works, what's expected:

Radio has a priceless ingredient, it's the only method of communication yet devised which can let all the people know, wherever they are, about any event within minutes. This alone makes radio a necessity. Radio has a wonderful ability to entertain, to interest, to comfort, to influence. Radio's matchless ability to inform—and to inform with high interest, excitement and color—is just beginning to be truly understood.

San Francisco is different. The character of our community dictates a very important part of our general approach. Our listeners are people with an unusually strong affection for and a fierce pride in the area in which they live. It's an area of tradition and honor. San Francisco is a happy city, an exciting city, a colorful city, a city with 'the light touch': a substantial city with muscle as well as heart. On the other hand, it is the least patient with the trite, the banal, the uninspired. We cannot afford to be heavy-handed. Above all, San Francisco demands good taste.

Shaw summarized KSFO's job as being (1) to *inform* by delivering the brightest, fastest, most accurate news coverage available, with emphasis on local happenings; (2) to *entertain* with the right kind of music, properly paced and showcased with "personality," and with the finest in sports coverage; and (3) to *serve the public* with an honest and continuing attempt to live up to their licensed right to broadcast.

He stressed knowing and addressing the audience, playing the music the listeners wanted to hear, not what the deejay liked to hear. He emphasized that if a disc jockey didn't have anything pertinent to say, "don't say anything—play a record."

The way Bill Shaw saw radio it was a people business, not a mechanical business. He reminded everyone to reflect the kinds of traits that were likable: honesty, sincerity, warmth, friendliness, naturalness, and enthusiasm. The traits listed to avoid were cynicism, sarcasm, condescension, ennui, and carelessness.

Don Sherwood was the only one who could get away with borrowing from the "bad" list occasionally. As Bill Shaw often said, "Don Sherwood at his worst is better than anyone else!"

HERB CAEN:

When Don Sherwood fails to show up for his 6 – 9 a.m. KSFO show, his aide, Carter Smith, phones and asks gently: "Flu?" "Flu," groans Don. Spelled "Flew," as in flying around town the night before.

Don and Carter B. developed a "soap opera" called "SUPERFROG—Champion of the Oppressed, Scourge of the Scurrilous!" It ran for years and remains a favorite. The setup was: "Masquerading as a mild-mannered dress designer, Peter Le Fauvre, yet with his model companion, Polliwog, when called upon by law enforcement officers, with a single 'ree deep' turns into the croaker of crime— Superfrog!"

Trumpets provided a dramatic opening to this ongoing serial about Superfrog, Polliwog, and the Inspector. Don, of course, provided all the voices except Superfrog, or "Sup," which was Carter B. As with all of Don's bits, the story was spontaneous and unscripted. Charlie Smith provided his usual, hilarious sound effects, such as the "frog copter."

Don had a real thing for frogs. One of his memorable statements was, "A woman is just a woman, but a frog is a friend forever."

Peck's Bad Boy—
Behind the Mask

The media was, by turns, friend and foe to Don, not only reporting his comings and goings, but simultaneously helping to create a public image of him. That image was womanizer, legendary drinker, prankster, rebel—in short, Peck's Bad Boy.

When it came to his womanizing, his fans seemed amused by his lack of responsibility and Don Juan exploits. If he appeared to be too stable, the media soon asked, What's happened to Peck's Bad Boy? They gave him a license to misbehave; an excuse. They liked to think of him as a ladies' man, and his actions appeared to support the assumption. It was not completely true and definitely not that simple.

Lon Simmons remembers a trip that he and Don took with the Forty-Niners to Minneapolis. "For all his public image, he was sort of naive about things. Outside of San Francisco, he wasn't at all a 'bar sophisticate.'

"When we were in the hotel bar, it was packed with available women, and Don said to me, 'Well, you guys are more experienced at this. You know how to meet ladies.' At home in San Francisco, he didn't have to initiate anything. Away from his own turf, he was uncomfortable and couldn't make a move. I went over to a lady and brought her back to our table, for Don, but before we ever got to dinner, he'd insulted her so much with his sarcasm, she left!"

"He had long-term friendships with guys," Marilyn Walker says, "because he could go out and drink or play with them and then not see them for six months. He didn't have to get involved.

"Whenever we were on the outs, he'd quote to me, 'Why can't a woman be more like a man?' Then when he wanted to contact me, he'd play songs on the radio like "I've Grown Accustomed to Her Face" or "Lady Is a Tramp"! That's when the romantic side of him would come out. Wherever I was, I'd call him, as if he were Svengali."

When he and Marilyn first met and she was living in Los Angeles, he sent her an autographed picture signed:

> M is for Marilyn
> M is for My Love
> M is for Magic.
>   Don

She was dating Gordon Scott, one of the movie Tarzans, at the time. Don sent her a a massive arrangement of gladioli and carnations, and signed the card Don "Tarzan" Sherwood. In spite of the fact that he was jealous of 'Tarzan,' he didn't stop to think that Marilyn might feel the same way about his dating Caryl Paul, whom he had not stopped seeing. Sentiment and romance were one thing: commitment and exclusivity were another.

One of Don and Marilyn's typical separations came about when Don asked her if she would like to go to Hawaii.

"Great! That would be nice," she answered cheerily.

"Well, I can't get away just now, but you go. Sam Sanford and his wife will take good care of you, and I'll try to join you later."

Off Marilyn went, only to find herself very lonely on the Big Island. After a few days she called Don.

"Hello?" a woman with a German accent answered.

Marilyn remembered Don telling her about a German woman he'd met on his trip to Europe.

"Oh, hello . . . is Don there?"

"No, he isn't, who's calling?"

"Would you mind telling him that Marilyn from Hawaii called? . . . And by the way, how long are you staying?" She was leaving hours before Marilyn was due to arrive back in San Francisco.

After Marilyn hung up, Sam Sanford came by, and for the next several hours, she poured out her heart and her rage over Mai Tais. When she got up to go back to her hotel room, she felt as if "someone had sawed off my legs!"

The next morning, Don called. "Hi. I got a message from you. I can explain everything! . . . Why don't you get the next plane back?"

She knew all too well what loving Don meant. She flew home to patch things up, and their life together resumed.

Every morning Marilyn would go to KSFO with Don, and after his show, they'd go for breakfast. "His morning show was more intense than anything most other people ever do, including other entertainers who have a shorter show, scripted and with breaks," Marilyn says. "For Don, there was no break. It was three solid, intense hours regardless of how he felt."

The rest of the day, they would go scuba diving, snorkeling, water-skiing, boating, or to the movies. Don also did a lot of reading, and he loved to play the piano.

"We'd usually have to go to bed at about nine, so he could get up early the next morning," Marilyn continues. "But sometimes we'd go to the opera, or there would be a special on television that he didn't want to miss. A lot of times he lied the next morning about why he was out late, saying he was at some party or other, because he thought the public would be more receptive to that than if he said, 'I was at the opera.' "

Don did other things anonymously that few people knew about, like making recordings for the blind. He had a young blind friend who had told him that such recordings were the only way he could keep up with current affairs.

Don also visited the inmates at San Quentin, before it was popular to do so. He was fascinated by the criminal mind, as he was with the violent aspects of society. He had specific views on capital punishment: "If we kill the murderers and the rapists, they won't be there for us to study. There'll be no way to learn about the workings of the criminal mind." Don's psychiatrist, Dr. Lion, had told Don that if he had not had the creative outlet of radio, he would have been in prison. He had all the symptoms of a sociopath.

There were many messages in Don's actions, reflecting his erratic and contradictory private world. The public, far removed, was entertained by it all. Don, in his own confusion, alternately played to the public image and rebelled against it.

The listeners freely voiced their opinions when he did something they thought was too serious, "out of character." Through the bags of mail that were hauled into his studio every morning, they let him know exactly how they felt about his every move. One example of this was the following letter, which Don received and read on the air:

Dear Don Sherwood:
   Over a week has passed. Every morning from 7 to 8, I have patiently endured your newly instituted patriotic nonsense. What gives?
   If this new addition to an otherwise highly entertaining and unpredictable program were combined with some intelligent analysis, one might conclude that it had some value. As it is, those of us who are rather square, not cool, but who simply make it on our own steam or experience are experiencing an over-powering sensation of nausea, which becomes increasingly difficult to control. To put it bluntly, friend, the whole business puts you to shame. If you could

only listen to yourself one morning, feebly muttering about the Communist threat marching gallantly to the strains of Yankee Doodle, I'm convinced you, too, would be obliged to get sick.

There are, one assumes, two possible explanations: 1) The whole business might be your idea of a fine joke. Let me assure you, it falls flat on its face. 2) You've been subjected to some subtle pressure from the powers that be and have therefore no choice but to solemnly and ridiculously declare your full-blooded and All-American intentions. In either case, may I assure you that you're in the process of losing a good portion of your listeners. Please cut it before you really mess yourself up.

A Friend

Don was compelled to reply to the letter on the air:

This guy writes an intelligent letter. He's a pretty sharp cat. I'm not a newscaster, I'm a disc jockey. However, I've had the pleasure of being on television, or the displeasure. I've met a lot of interesting people who have told me a lot of interesting things.

When I talk about being glad you're American, the boss didn't tell me to. I was over in Europe, and I talked to people from East Germany. I turned on faucets where no water came out, and I saw poverty. I came back and couldn't help it, my chest expanded about four inches. A lot of people don't realize it. They take it all for granted. I'm reminding you who you are, that's all. And I'm going to declare my "ridiculous full-blooded All-American intentions" every cotton-pickin' morning when I feel like it, and you can't do anything about it!

Not to turn this into a political rally or anything, but let me pose a question to you. It's a question that a man asked me the other day: If you took a man from anywhere in the world, any country, and you put two plane tickets in his hand—one to the Soviet Union and one to the United States of America—which one do you think he would pick up and use?

This was the kind of response that snapped everyone back to attention, reminding them that there was more to Don than a media character sketch.

Parkey Sharkey
and the Law

Parkey Sharkey, the cab driver, was a self-made "character" of a different sort. A former amateur middleweight champion, he made a name for himself locally by bombarding newspaper editors with long "missiles" on everything that bothered him.

In 1939, Parkey owned a parking lot in Palo Alto. One of his customers was Ty Cobb, the baseball player.

After parking in the lot one day, Ty refused to pay the fifteen cents parking fee. Parkey sued him in small claims court and won, getting his fifteen cents and court costs of a dollar-and-a-half.

This was Don's kind of guy. He couldn't resist bringing him onto his KTVU-TV show. Parkey responded like an overgrown kid in a candy store and quickly became the Peninsula's most celebrated unemployed cab driver. He didn't waste any time publicizing his first book, *The Inebriated Cab Driver*, and due to overwhelming public demand, raised the price of his second book, *Whiskey Road*, to a dollar a copy. The Bay Area claimed Parkey as its own, while Don and Herb Caen became his "custodians."

HERB CAEN:

Parkey Sharkey, the gabby cabby, was stimulated to bring out his treasure, a 112-year-old Canadian ha'-penny. Don Sherwood auctioned it off for $7.50, says Parkey, and an hour later a coin collector phoned to say it was worth $3500 . . . "I'm sick," reports Parkey. "I am staying out of the dumps drinking mountain wine. My middle name is 'Stupid!' "

Poor Parkey Sharkey. Nobody seems interested in him but me, and occasionally Don Sherwood. Parkey recently broke pretty decisively with Paul Coates, the Los Angeles columnist, and declared himself my exclusive problem. Sample: "Disaster has struck me. My '47 Chevy taxi has fallen apart, no low gear, no second gear, and no third gear. The motor runs, but what good is it? If I don't get a job it's the poorhouse for Parkey Sharkey. I have got to have a car, sos, sos. Think I better get a jug and go to tortilly flats or back on relief —Parkey."

The responsibility was too much for Herb alone, so Don had to pull his weight. Parkey devised a plan for 1962 that would get the job done: during the year, he would save $2,000, with Don as his financial caretaker. This would buy him two taxicabs and two drivers, and in turn, enable him to retire in a cabin in La Honda "to enjoy the fruits of absentee ownership."

"To heck with worrying about Parkey's cab license," Herb responded. "I want to see Sherwood's *banking* license!"

HERB CAEN:

In our last chapter, you'll recall, Sherwood had been named president of Parkey Sharkey's cab company, after having saved Parkey's small change for him so he could buy a taxi permit. Now, alas, disaster has struck again. "Now that I have my taxi license back I need a taxi to go with it. My taxi trip to Monterey ruined my

clutch, low gear shot now, had to buy another tire today, three tires in two weeks. What am I going to tell
Sherwood?" (How about, "Mr. President, it is time for
another look at the budget . . .")

As if things weren't tough enough, Parkey got pulled
over for drunk driving; he was handed a stiff $300 fine plus
thirty days in Sheriff Earl Whitmore's jail.

A communiqué arrived for Herb Caen:

> I just got out of jail. I had money for a room, but I
> had just sent it to Sherwood toward my $2000 goal . . .
> I went home and had a fight with my wife. She kicked
> me out in the cold at 1 a.m. There was still snow on the
> ground . . . I had no money for a room, so I went to the
> Whitmore Hotel—jail in Redwood City. I said, "Can I
> have a room for the night, my wife kicked me out
> again." They said "Sure, Mr. Sharkey, we've seen you
> on TV and heard you on Sherwood's radio show." The
> cops were nice to me, but I did not get a private room.
> I had to sleep in the drunk tank. The drunks knew me,
> one of them used to be a good customer of mine . . . I
> am recuperating now at a friend's house. It was a hor-
> rible night for me. I am sending Sherwood $2 more to-
> ward my goal.

Things went well for a time with Don saving Parkey's
money. Then Parkey got a job at the Auto Bargain Center
in Redwood City. "I sold a car today and made twenty dollars commission. Don Sherwood can now go jump in the
nearest lake."

HERB CAEN:

> Parkey is always getting mad at Sherwood, who in
> our last chapter was the custodian of Parkey's savings.
> When he is not getting mad at Sherwood, he is getting
> mad at me and Paul Coates. I think it's his real career.

PARKEY SHARKEY:

> I have told my friends Dick Nolan and Don Sher-
> wood to jump in a lake. Skip me on your column. I am

doing okay and you and Sherwood can jump in a lake. I don't make a buck off of either of you.

HERB CAEN:

Times is tough, Parkey. Sherwood is down to $48.65 a week take-home from radio AND television, and my poverty is proverbial, hevvin knows. May I recommend Prescott Sullivan and Doug Pledger?

But it was not that easy. Parkey made up with both Don and Herb, and assigned them the task of stepping up their efforts to plug his one-dollar book.

Following a stroke that summer, Parkey wisely chose to concentrate on getting more R & R. Being fairly famous was great, but that wasn't exactly what he'd been after— something his pal Don could relate to.

Both men had survived rough, fragmented childhoods. Parkey ended up going from reform school to boxing, Don from dropout to the Merchant Marine. Parkey was a vocal rebel in his own life, in his own way, and that was something Don admired and understood. The Parkey Sharkeys of the world were important to Don, and although it was used in a wonderfully amusing way, Parkey's life was a constant reminder to Don of an infinitely less-than-perfect, less-than-fair society. Even though they may have lost touch, hearsay has it that when Parkey died, Don anonymously paid for the funeral.

In the tradition of Parkey, Don soon paid a visit to a "Whitmore Hotel." With Christmas glitter and holiday jubilation draped throughout the city, as 1962 came to a close, Don characteristically avoided the good cheer of it all. He skipped the KSFO Christmas party and took Marilyn to a favorite haunt of his: the piano bar on Geary that he had owned.

He and Marilyn were sitting in the bar, minding their own business, when a cop burst through the door. To his absolute surprise, since he was sober, Don found himself under arrest on an "811," which the officer defined as "drunk and disorderly." Don didn't take the arresting officer seriously and made a joke of the whole thing. The next thing he knew, he really was under arrest.

During the short ride to the police station, Don had time to think about his arrest and became very upset. He refused bail and proceeded to force the issue to a full-blown trial.

The trial provided Don with an opportunity to make a statement about policemen's overzealous behavior. "I fought the charge," he said, "because this could happen to anybody, and I've got the time to fight it. Just think what a man . . . an officer . . . can do to kids."

At one point, Don was questioned by the deputy district attorney as to whether he was antisocial. "Yes, I am, as a matter of fact," he said. "But, 'antisocial' puts it on the pathological level. I am *asocial*." When questioned about how much he'd been drinking, Don said he'd had a couple of beers and maybe a brandy. He told the court that he didn't drink much, "maybe an occasional glass of wine." While this wasn't exactly what those close to him would have said, it was true that he had not been drinking heavily that particular night.

The jury acquitted him after "the longest and driest drunk trial on record." In a later interview, Don said, "I thought going to court would be a good thing. Show people I've changed, that I want to build up a good name, that I was willing to go out on a limb to do it. I spent ten years playing Peck's Bad Boy, and no one's going to let me forget it!"

Without regard for the consequences, Don had once again gone to bat for what he believed in. As usual, he won.

Hugh Heller agrees. "At that time, drinking was a *moral* issue. We didn't know what we know today about alcoholism."

HERB CAEN:

Don "Purer Than the Driven Snow" Sherwood, who talked himself *into* a drunk trial, almost talked himself right back into the soup after his acquittal Thursday. To celebrate the jury's decision, Sherwood and his lawyer Harry Wainwright, walked into the Harrison House bar, where the Great Man found himself standing next to Art Schaffer, the Dep. Dist. Atty. who had just prosecuted him. "Double bourbon!" hollered Sherwood to the bartender. "That's all I ever drink." After Schaffer had done a satisfactory double-take, and Wainwright had fallen to the floor in a fake faint, our hero switched to beer. (Laughter).

Musings of a
Bad Father on a
Good Day

Don consistently made noises to the effect that he abhorred the responsibility of family. If he'd had it to do over again, chances are he would have chosen not to have children. It wasn't until he was in his mid-thirties that he even began to examine and appreciate what fatherhood meant. Even then, he had no idea where to start.

As he grew older, and as his children grew older, the situation became more complicated. He found himself at a complete loss when he was faced with the normal problems of parenting. His decisions were arbitrary and inconsistent. Everything was black and white; there were no gray areas when it came to dealing with them.

Don frequently made reference to children, parenting, and family during his radio show, through stories or jokes that people sent to him or that he found in the course of his own reading. His private life was reflected in the articles, comments, and anecdotes. One morning he read the following piece:

MUSINGS OF A GOOD FATHER ON A BAD DAY

There is nothing sadder than a childless couple. It breaks your heart to see them out relaxing around the swimming pools in Florida, sitting all suntanned and miserable on the decks of their boats, trotting off to Europe. It's an empty life. There's nothing but more money to spend, more time to enjoy and a whole lot less to worry about.

The childless couples get so selfish and wrapped up in their own concerns that I have to feel sorry for them. They don't fight over the child's discipline, they don't blame each other for the child's most nauseous characteristics, and they miss all the fun of doing without things for the child's sake. They go along in their dull way, doing what they want, buying what they want, fulfilling each other. It's a pretty pathetic picture.

Everyone should have children. No one should be allowed to escape the wonderful experience attached to each stage of development of the young. The happy memories of the baby days, the alert nights, the coughing spells, debts, diapers, "dipso" baby sitters, saturated mattresses, spilled foods, tantrums, emergencies and the never-ending crisis.

Then comes the real fulfillment as the child grows like a little acorn and becomes a real nut. The wonder of watching the overweight ballerina making a fool of herself in a leotard. The warm smile of the small lad with the sun glittering on 500 bucks worth of braces ruined by peanut brittle. The rollicking, merry and carefree voices of hordes of hysterical kiddies stampeding at a birthday party.

I pity the couple without children to brighten the cocktail hour by brushing the martini from the shaking hand, massaging the potato chips into the rug and wrestling for the olives. How dismally vacant is the peaceful home without the constant childish problems that make for a well-rounded adult life and an early breakdown—the tender, thoughtful discussions when the report card reveals the prodigy to be one step below a half-wit; the close-knit family gatherings around the fireplace to roast hot dogs (and the cat if he isn't fast on his feet) and the end of the day reunions with all the joyful day's happenings related like well-placed blows to the stomach.

The feeling of reward the first time you took the boy hunting. He didn't mean to shoot you in the leg. The boy was excited. Remember how he cried? How sorry he was? How disappointed that you weren't a deer? Those are the times with a growing son that a man treasures, those poignant moments, captured forever and hidden in the heart, and the permanent limp.

Think back to the night of romantic adventure when your budding, beautiful daughter eloped with the village idiot. What childless couple ever share in the stark reality of that drama? Aren't you a better man for having lived richly, fully—acquiring that tic by your left eye? Could a woman without children touch the strength of heroism of your wife as she tried to fling herself out of the bedroom window? It takes a father to attain the stature of standing by ready and resolute—to jump after her. The climax came when you two became really close in the realization that, after all, your baby girl was a woman with the mind of a pygmy.

The childless couple lives in a vacuum. They live their long lonely days with golf, trips, dinner dates, civic affairs, tranquility, leisure and money. They contribute no addition to the human race—which is a satisfaction in itself. There is a terrifying emptiness without children and the childless couple is too comfortable to know it. You just have to look at them and see what the years have done. He looks boyish, unlined, rested. She is slim, well-groomed, youthful. It isn't natural—if they had kids, they'd look like the rest of us; tired, gray, wrinkled and sagging—in other words, NORMAL.

He liked giving his listeners food for thought, but the real motivation behind his selections was to clarify his own thinking. It was an ongoing dialogue with himself.

He did not communicate well with his children. He talked *at* them, and played *with* them, but he had no idea that children were real people. He was, in essence, a week-end father to Greg and Robin, even though he had almost daily contact with them. Diane hardly saw him.

When Hugh Heller was in Los Angeles doing the George Gobel show, he was also producing the pilot for "Leave It to Beaver." He called Don one day because he was having a problem finding the actor to play opposite Beaver. He suggested Greg for the part.

"What about your daughters?" Don asked Hugh. "What are you doing with them?"

"I'm not putting them in any shows!" Hugh answered.

"Well, that's the answer to your question," Don replied. He was not about to have Greg involved in show business and subject him to the child-star life. It did not occur to him to consult Greg about *his* feelings in the matter.

Don had been the special guest at a father's night meeting of the Fiesta Gardens PTA, where he was presented with a "Father of the Year" award. He surely knew the honor was ill-deserved. An interesting observation was made in the papers that Don sat drinking one night with a couple of radio executives at the Fairmont. As he listened to the others talking about their kids, he became sober and misty-eyed. They had inadvertently hit a nerve.

SHIRLEY SHERWOOD:

Don had a lot of free time and didn't have a home, though he always had his apartment. Our home became his home. He came for dinner, like the "father of the house," helping the children with homework, supervising their discipline and activities. But it was spontaneous; you never knew when he'd show up.

I was dating at that time, so Don always knew who I was dating and had some wonderful remarks to make! "At least you could have found someone as good. We know you'll never find anyone better, but at least you

SHIRLEY...

could find someone half as good!" No one was good enough to date his ex-wife, and absolutely no one was good enough to be around his kids. He made me feel like a teenager whose father was giving her first beau the third degree.

Even though we were divorced, he still had a family. It was his house. He had a woman who was not his wife but whom he controlled. He didn't want anyone else in my life.

Shirley had remarried. After her blowup with Don over Bob Newhart, she eloped with a successful realtor. "I managed to make his life miserable for two years," she says. Don was very disappointed and upset when she remarried, and it took him a long time to forgive her.

ROBIN SHERWOOD COHELAN:

When Mom remarried and we moved to Hillsborough, I was in the third grade. That was when the father wars started. One week one of them gave me a piano, the next week the other one gave me an organ. Both my stepfather and Dad had money and were competitive. It was fun, and I milked it for a while, though I was never nice to my stepfather.

Later, when I talked to Dad about why he divorced my mother, he explained that as long as the door was open, and he wasn't married to the woman he was living with, he could relax. But as soon as he was married, the door shut, and he had to get out. I inherited that from him.

SHIRLEY :

Don was a product of his environment, but I don't think it was as bad as he said. Inga was not a warm, loving person—a hugger and kisser. She was cold. But deep

SHIRLEY...

down they were so much alike, like Don and Robin. He'd call me in the middle of the night, all the time, and we'd talk for hours about how we should have stayed together. At that moment he meant it. I would weep after he'd call me.

He was the love of my life, always part of it—even now. I'd think, if I could only fall *out* of love with this man! The only man I ever dated that I think Don halfway approved of was George Cerruti, the bandleader from his television days. If I'd been capable of marrying the right man, it would have been George.

Don's problems affected every member of the family. His effect was so strong that they have found it almost impossible to sustain long-lasting relationships with anyone else.

Growing Up

Whenever any man got too close to his children, Don overreacted. "He couldn't bear the thought of Greg and I loving another man," Robin says. "He wanted to encompass your whole being. He was fed for so many years by the masses."

As each child was granted intermittent, private time with Dad, their independent relationships with him developed.

Of the three children, nine-year-old Greg was spending the most intensive time with Don. "It was a weird scene to be hanging out with him in clubs and bars, Greg says." Dad started referring to me as his forty-year-old son. "I always felt like I was the parent."

GREG :

One night, he decided at midnight that we should go to *Sam's* Restaurant in Tiburon and have a drink. It was pitch-black, and we were driving the boat about thirty miles an hour, when we hit a pole that was floating in the water. The boat flew out of the water, bow up, miraculously coming down intact. I said, "You know, Dad, we could be home, right now, watching TV."

His response was "Hey, we're having *fun!*" He always

GREG...

thought we were having such fun! But it was *his* fun, not mine particularly. Not fun *kid* things. They were things he wanted to do, and you could come along. We'd go diving and body surfing, water-skiing, or to the zoo and the football games, which he loved, although I didn't.

The guys at *Scoma's* Restaurant would call me, or I'd call them, and they'd say, "Yeah, he's here." I'd go there, and Dad would have "one more, one last vodka tonic." Then I'd take him home.

Dad and I went to *Bimbo's 365 Club* one night, a nightclub with topless showgirls. There was an incredible fishbowl as you came in that showed a tiny naked woman swimming inside it. We went downstairs during her break to meet her. She sat there, practically naked, smoking with Dad and hitting on him. And there I sat, fascinated with the mechanism of this turntable and mirrors and the optical illusion created of her swimming in space!

Another night we went to *Bop City* in the Fillmore district. Dad was totally wasted, and we were sitting at the bar in this all-black, after-hours club at three in the morning, listening to a band playing. We were the only white people in there. I thought we were going to get killed. At eight or nine, I knew this was *not* where we were supposed to be. I sat there with my Coke while Dad went to the bathroom—he was getting sick—and I felt like I was in a movie. I dragged him out of the bathroom and got someone to help us get a cab. I was very glad to be out of there.

We spent a lot of time in bars and went to brothels together. I had no idea that he was a celebrity, so I wondered why everyone seemed to know him. They all called him by name. I thought he was just an incredibly friendly guy.

When I went to other kids' houses from the private school I went to, I thought it was weird—all suit and ties

GREG...

for dinner, the mother with a little bell to ring, and maids. I was surprised to see a father around.

I remember thinking other kids' lives were boring. They had to be in early, and I didn't have any hours. You only have your own context, so as a child you don't think, "Now, what I need is a good family."

Later, when I was about twelve and we flew to Mexico, we went into a Mexican whorehouse. He couldn't speak Spanish, so I "procured" a woman for him. That was one of his spontaneous trips, just for three days, which was tops for him. It was always a matter of how long it would take for him to say, "I hate it here!"

Sometimes this happened as soon as you got there, sometimes a few days later. If he hated it, you hated it. The trick was to hate it just as much and at just the same time!

He didn't have conversations with you like normal people or chat about little things, little pleasantries and such. No, Dad was obsessed with big things like, "Why is everything happening the way it is?" He'd pontificate on the meaning of life.

He could take the smallest amount of information, read one quote from someone, and from that, extrapolate a whole theory of life. He was always looking for a one-sentence answer for why he felt the way he did, why we behave the way we do, why what is acceptable is acceptable, what is 'normal?' He was looking for the world view all the time, which is what he was doing on the radio, on the air.

MARILYN WALKER:

I really sympathize with any person who has to be a weekend parent. It is very difficult to come into a situation where you have to discipline a child you haven't seen—when it's off and on, off and on.

Don felt really guilty not "knowing" how to be a par-

MARILYN...

ent, not knowing how to deal with situations that came up. He wanted his kids to grow up strong and independent, to be assertive and not intimidated by anyone.

One time he took Greg and some other guys with their sons up to Rio Vista to water-ski. Greg was at the awkward stage and had a hard time expressing himself to Don, who intimidated him. When it was time to get something to eat, Don asked Greg if he wanted anything.

"Uh-huh."

"Want a hamburger?" Don asked.

"Uh-huh."

"Want a milk shake?"

"Uh-huh."

When Don came back with everyone's food, there was nothing for Greg. "It's a funny thing," he told Greg. "When the lady asked if I wanted anything to drink, I said, 'uh-huh.' She said, 'If you can't say, "Yes, please" and "thank you," I can't serve you.'"

Greg didn't get anything to eat all day. By the time they came home, Don was overwhelmed with guilt, but he didn't know how else to make Greg understand why he had to speak up for himself.

Don was constantly filled with dreams and plans for finding a happier, more peaceful life together, with him as the philosopher-king. He fantasized a world, on a ship or a caravan or something equally exotic, where he, his family and friends could all live together. His fantasies were based on escaping from this imperfect world, on creating a utopia to share with friends. This went way back to when he was five and living in the worlds of Tom Swift and Winnie-the-Pooh.

"If there was a Rosebud in his life, like there was in *Citizen Cane*, you'll find it in the hundred-acre wood in Winnie-the-Pooh," Greg says. "The last book of the series talks about Christopher Robin growing up, saying, 'They're making me do it'—they, the grownups."

Peter Pan . . . Christopher Robin . . . Don Sherwood.

The writing was on the wall. "They" were "making him do it," too. It was time to grow up.

"Mr. San Francisco Radio"

When Don's contract with KSFO was up in 1963, he didn't renew it—at least not right away. He was again focused on the disc jockey dilemma: how to be taken seriously?

Now thirty-seven years old, his interests and insatiable curiosities compelled him toward a nonentertainment, educational program. "I told the station I would do a show interviewing intellectuals, for free if necessary. I mightn't talk well, but I talk good. Get me?" he told Lisa Hobbs of the *San Francisco Examiner*. "I can get through to people, and I thought that I could translate their ideas for the general public. The program manager looked at me incredulously and said, 'Do you think these men would give their thoughts to a *disc jockey?*' "

Gerald Nachman of the *San Francisco Chronicle* wrote: "Don Sherwood is suffering from Acute Embarrassment At Being A Comedian, a malady which sooner or later overtakes all comics. His is the old story of the buffoon who wants to play Hamlet, the cartoonist who wants to paint like Grandma Moses, the clown who wants to become a trapeze artist . . . a clown trying his fling at mental-acrobatics.

"One of the occupational hazards of being a comic seems to be that pretty soon . . . you begin thinking, 'Hmmmm, maybe I'm a half-wit instead of a wit.' This often results in a maybe-I-can-serve-Mankind-better-if-I-were-a-great-thinker complex, which seems to be Sherwood's ailment."

In an astute observation about Don, Charles Einstein of the *San Francisco Examiner* quoted Charles Philips's remark about Napoleon: "Wrapped in the solitude of his own originality."

Don's fans laughed with him as well as at him, but he was becoming defensive. He said to Lisa Hobbs, "I'm a disc jockey. Does that make me so shallow I can't get hurt?"

While Don was still deliberating about his KSFO contract, KGO-TV stepped in and offered him Les Crane's television show. Crane was leaving for New York, and the spot was Don's, if he wanted it. Don took the offer, and Jack Carney stepped into the morning show on KSFO.

KSFO left the usual candle burning in the window.

This was fortunate because Don was back by November of the same year, following President John F. Kennedy's death. Ronnie Schell remembers that this news sent Don straight back to the bottle after a long dry period.

HERB CAEN:

Biggest shake-up yet in the works at KSFO. Don Sherwood returns to his familiar 6-9 a.m. slot on Monday, Jack Carney takes over the afternoon hours, and Del Courtney goes off the payroll after nine years as a KSFO-gey.

In the interim, Hugh Heller had hired a New York talent for KSFO by the name of Al "Jazzbo" Collins.

AL COLLINS:

When I walked in, Don said, "So, you're the big deal from New York, huh? You know, you'll come on after

AL...

me . . . I could play the National Anthem and sign off . . ." I said, "Don't do that to me, I'll just play it again and sign back on!" As I was leaving, I said, "It's all over for you, man. Just remember that."

I came in early one morning to pull my music. When Don saw me, he walked past saying, "You've got it!" I didn't know what he meant, until I realized he'd just left for the day forty minutes early and given me his show to complete before my own! It was like what he'd done to Aaron Edwards.

Then there was the time he went out on remote with a crew, and he was supposed to call in to me with reports. I waited and waited, but there was no call. Don had told the crew to go down Highway 101 to the San Francisco Airport. Then he got on a plane and flew off who knows where!

He was a power to behold. I was used to having plenty of it, and I was amazed. I didn't lock horns with him, being a peaceful guy. We left it with a working "Hello, how ya doing" and didn't socialize together outside of the station PAL—Police Athletic League—games, bowling team, or other activities.

The PAL games, organized to benefit the Police Athletic League, were said to offer an example of "Bad Bad Softball"—the team's theme song. Louise Jorjorian cooked it all up. It started as a little game at Funston Park, growing to the point where it packed the Cow Palace. Both teams were seriously competitive, always bringing in ringers.

KSFO's PAL lineup at various times, included Jack Carney, Al Collins, Aaron Edwards, Carter B. Smith, Stu Smith, Jim Lange, Al Newman, Chet Casselman, Pete Scott, Lon Simmons, Russ Hodges, John Brodie, and Chub Feeney, and all of those who were at KSFO at each year's game, including Promotion Director Louise Jorjorian as the team nurse.

RENO'S—Reno Barsocchini's team—had a star-studded lineup including Herb Caen, Frank Dill, Joe Di-Maggio, Jake Erlich, Lefty Gomez, Carl Hubble, Rick Berry, Jack Christiansen, Big Ben Davidson, Lefty O'Doul, Art Rosenbaum, Bob Strenger, Bob St. Clair, Bucky Walters and other who rotated in and out.

HERB CAEN:

Don Sherwood, browsing through the Blue Cross Newsletter, like a good hypochondriac should, ran across this: "A tiny structure in the brain—the ras—gives us our ability to think, learn and act." He was all set to tell his radio audience the next morning that "not enough of you people are using your ras" but cooler heads prevailed.

Fan: I think things are loosening up a little on the air, don't you?

Don: Well, I don't know, but I sure want to be around when they do!

This, from a guy who regularly announced, "Today's the day I'm gonna say the 'F' word." Everyone who worked with Don was waiting for the day his mike would accidentally be on while he spoke in his natural vernacular —he'd never have worked in radio again!

Speaking of obscenities, the Lenny Bruce obscenity trials taking place in Chicago cost DJ Dan Sorkin his job. "I was fired in Chicago after testifying as a character witness in the Lenny Bruce obscenity trials," Dan says. "KSFO had been offering me a position for a couple of years but I'd always said no because I had plenty of money and was having a lot of fun in Chicago. Now it was time."

DAN SORKIN:

I always admired Don. He was one of the naturally most creative radio personalities I'd ever heard. His re-

DAN...

motes from Monty Bandaar's ship, his gags with Carter
B., and his characters, were all fantastic.

Every station puts together the promotional spots for
their personalities and forms a team family. At KSFO we
never had a problem forming that team family because
we were truly the best there was, the best stable of talent
that I'd ever been associated with. Don, Carter, Al Collins, Jack Carney . . . we really liked each other, which
made it easy to do the promotional spots. We'd get together in the studio, start with an idea, let the tape roll,
and have a party for four or five hours—getting 60 to 70
spots. With this group of people, led by Don, it was
easy, fun, simple. We never wanted to leave these sessions.

Don was a giant in the industry because he was an individual. He was an audio painter, painting a canvas on
the radio.

As KSFO continued solidifying its position, other stations in the city scrambled to compete.

Jim Dunbar was brought out from Chicago to be program director at KGO radio, not an enviable position in
light of the task! Jim listened to Don's program for a few
weeks, pondering the options, and came up with a format
which has since become a mainstay in the marketplace:
talk radio. "There was no way to compete straight on with
Sherwood," Jim says.

Don and Jim Dunbar first met when Lenny Bruce, one
of Don's favorite people, was playing off Broadway. "It so
happened that my wife and I were seated right next to
him. Don didn't know who I was, but he noticed my
pretty, young wife. After introducing himself, he said to
us, 'You look happy.' I've never forgotten that."

KNBR brought Frank Dill out from New York to be
their morning man. Dill became and remains a major San
Francisco radio personality.

"I remember going to the Cow Palace for an annual celebrity PAL softball tournament where Don was playing on the KSFO NO STARS team," Frank says. "I was on RENO'S VIPs. When Don's name was announced, he came out to the most incredible cheer from the whole audience. I felt an envious twinge, naturally.

"Years later, when Don was no longer on radio, I organized a KNBR parade on the air, in my own honor, for fun. We had a big parade in Pleasanton with one hundred thousand people, and a two-hundred-sixty-person marching unit. That day, as I made my way down the main street, through the cheering crowds, I thought, Don, I now know what it's like!

"Don was one of the magic things that happen only once in a while. He was the perfect radio personality for his time in his city. He matched the era and the city perfectly."

Don was so popular that San Francisco State College students lined up outside the studio to watch the morning show through the window. His schedule was jammed with celebrity activities—bowling tournaments, star basketball, speaking engagements, and Press Club functions. It was anyone's guess what his topic would be—the Junior Ad Club was treated to his "Mackeral in the Moonlight Glitters but It Stinks" speech.

As Don's thirty-ninth birthday approached, Hugh Heller returned to L.A. to work for Gene Autry—owner of KSFO. Hugh was there to help boost the ratings of stations in other major cities. In San Francisco, Al Newman was promoted to Program Director.

Al Newman coordinated a fun-filled birthday morning show that included calls from celebrities as well as a flood of birthday greetings from his fans. One anonymous well-wisher forewarned, "Old deejays never die; they just look that way."

"Hello Daddy!"

One morning the bags of mail were dragged into Don's studio and dumped with the remainder of the letters and packages from the day before. Don had already cut off all the phone lines that were lit up. He puffed on his Lucky Strike, sipped his coffee, and propped his feet up. Reaching into the stack of mail, Don grabbed a gift-wrapped I. Magnin package with a bright yellow bow on it. A doll? he thought. What the hell . . .?

The card attached read: "HELLO DADDY!"

Barbara Butterfield of Mountain View, a clerk in a department store, filed a paternity suit against Don just days before her baby was due. She was demanding $300 monthly support plus all medical expenses.

The court proceedings dragged along at the normal turtle's pace, beginning with a change of venue from Santa Clara County to San Francisco. Nineteen months later the testimony started.

Harry Wainwright and a solemn Don marched into court and denied all charges.

Ms. Butterfield said she'd contacted Don about a film idea after sending him repeated letters promoting his possible involvement in the project. She arrived at KSFO studios one day and went to breakfast with Don and entourage. She claimed that, after breakfast, Don invited her to his place on Hyde Street for "some serious conversation about the theatre." She further claimed to have spent a "head-twirling six hours" at his place, where he made love to her.

After a subsequent argument, she continued to write him letters, including a final one informing him that he was about to become a father.

"At the same time there was a similar suit against Governor Rockefeller by a woman who had set things up to look like they'd been together," Marilyn says. "Don had a lot to lose."

Ronnie Schell and Guy Haines were key witnesses. "After breakfast," Ronnie testified, "Don gave me his car keys and said he'd meet me at noon. He did. We spent the whole afternoon and evening together, except for the time he spent without me at Cookie Piccetti's."

Ronnie had dropped him off at Piccetti's bar so that Cookie could be his baby-sitter for a few hours. This was the bar that Don had once driven his motorcycle into when he grew tired of looking for a parking spot. Cookie, known as San Francisco's legendary barkeep, knew Don well.

Don claimed Ms. Butterfield was a "disturbed" fan, who had previously claimed fictional, fantasy encounters with other entertainers and who "bombarded" him with "approximately three times the correspondence George Bernard Shaw once directed to Ellen Terry."

"This woman was totally out of her mind!" Guy Haines says. "She'd stand on the dock where his boat was and wave this baby at Don as he was pulling out of the berth."

Harry Wainwright, Don's attorney, questioned Ms. Butterfield: "You say that Don and you made love in his apartment on the front room floor at midday. Correct?"

"Yes, that's right."

"I take it you both had your clothes off?"

"Yes."

"And did you engage in any other variations of love-making, such as oral sex?"

"Yes, we did."

"Then will you tell the court, is Don circumcised?"

"I don't know."

"I rest my case. . . ."

The court case was heard without jury. The judge ruled that Ms. Butterfield had not provided sufficient evidence to establish that Don was the father of her child.

Don walked out of court with Harry Wainwright, his integrity intact, wondering how often he was going to have to defend himself to the public, the courts, and the world.

The society editor of the *San Francisco Examiner*, Joan Woods, went on vacation soon thereafter, and Don was asked to write a column in her place on the subject of women.

HER INTELLECTUALITY NEEDS UNCHAINING

Women . . . have played a subordinate role to men for years, and their emergence today to prominent roles in business, government, medicine and the arts is causing a great deal of confusion—for them and for society.

Today's woman is torn between the way grandma used to do it, and the way she herself feels . . . A woman has to have worthwhile projects to satisfy her creativity and drive. I think it must be deadly to do the same dishes, vacuum the same corners of the same room, day in and year out, without an outlet. This would drive me insane. It would be worse than prison.

The male would have a much more valuable companion if the woman had intellectual stimulation. There would not be that rapid growth by him away from her, which results in the age-old cry: "She was great when I married her!"

The surveys show a great deal of unrest on the home front, and that's a serious problem. Maybe what we really need first is a revival of old-fashioned respect for the homemaker who views creating a gracious home and rearing happy children as a profession in itself, instead of a confinement.

During the early years a child requires unconditional love . . . Mama can go to work later, but those first five years she should be occupied full time by the young child. I've always been fascinated by the Eskimos, who have practically no mental illness or crime, as we know it. For the first three years a child is never allowed to cry . . . What happens when a child isn't loved? Prisons, accidents, greed, envy, jealousy . . . hate.

There aren't enough psychiatrists to put Humpty Dumpty together again, and we haven't enough agencies to mend all the lives broken by the confusion and doubts which spring from lack of love or a broken home. Only the ability to love should qualify a couple for parenthood . . . although unfortunately there's no way society can either control or judge that quality before two people sign up to marry.

I think BOTH men and women have two roles . . . to create a home atmosphere to springboard healthy well-adjusted offspring into life, and to work out their individual goals to satisfy the inner creative urgings of their personalities.

Me? I'm a weekend daddy, walking around with two cement sacks of guilt on my shoulders. The more I realize the effects of a broken home, the guiltier I feel about the example I set for my kids. . . .

"I think he hated women, although he was fascinated by them and they all loved him," Ronnie Schell adds. "One of the things he told me was that through his psychotherapy he had lost his ability with women. He said, 'When I was sick—I like the *when*—I'd go into a bar, and I had an electricity about me. Any woman equally neurotic or sick would come to me like a magnet. Now I've lost that. I go in a bar and get nothing. They don't see the vulnerability. I'm too much in control.'"

"In theory, Don probably would have been at the forefront of the women's rights movement," Marilyn comments, "but because of his relationship with his mother, it was difficult for him to have any kind of equal relationship with a woman. He could go get a whore, or he could sleep with someone who meant nothing to him, but when he cared about a woman, it was all very difficult for him."

Though Don and Marilyn were still "together"—off and on—they were living apart. Their communication was frequently by letter. The name he chose in signing the letter reflected his mood and message.

Dear Mar;
    Got home, drunk, and realized you are right: I love—but probably not supermarket style.

Bless you,
Fred

The year 1964 had started with this letter from Don:

Dear Marilyn,
    I felt a relationship that had gone on as long as this needed just a bit more explanation for its demise.
    You've heard stories, I'm sure, of the amputee who continually gets pains in the severed limb. In the section that no longer exists. This then, might give you some idea of the terrible gnawing that accompanied my being with you.
    Now I can understand a lonely feeling when you are far away, but why, why, when you were right there?
    As we have discussed on many an occasion, we seem chemically, emotionally and socially bent on not only destruction of ourselves, but also each other. This is manifested in so many obvious ways. Along with some that are beautiful in their subtlety.
    I am, and I think you are as well, a creature terribly caught up in the habit syndrome, i.e. cigarettes, liquor, religion, places, people, etc. This, I understand, comes from a feeling of loss in childhood.
    Our relationship has degenerated into a miasma of "Who's on first . . ." so, with much regret, because I remember a few things (and will always remember them) that made our relationship quite exciting and warm . . .

You must remember, *I* was very frightened, extremely cynical, and quite screwed up mentally in regards to marriage and related unions. SO look, next time, a little more carefully before you set about to capture, enchant, and whatever else you do.

Forever fondly,

One letter tried to convince Marilyn to come back and live with him.

Dear Ms. Walker;

Two weeks ago the subject arose of your coming to work for this firm. We discussed the subject covering the general duties involved and also the benefits that could be derived by you. At our second get-together, I felt you were beginning to warm up to the proposition. Is that true?

When anyone in as important a position as that which you would hold is faced with an untoward situation, they should have the necessary initiative and company fidelity to carry out any duties without being constantly directed. This position is one of extreme variance in scope. It takes a person of good intelligence, high character, and as mentioned, fidelity, keeping the demands of the job uppermost in your mind at all times.

Because you have evidenced many of these qualities, I feel you would also be reticent to accept the position if you yourself felt any inadequacy.

I would like to hear from you on this matter. Hoping all is well with you and those close to you. May I remain with best regards,

D. S. Cohelan

Marilyn wanted very much to accept the "position." Unfortunately, she had not yet decided if she was willing to forego her own dreams and opportunities in order to share Don's.

That was always the choice.

They had talked of marriage; Marilyn still has the engagement ring Don gave her. They even got in the car to drive to Las Vegas a few times. But something always happened to convince them to hold off, something silly, like Don getting a speeding ticket.

Without accepting the "full-time position," Marilyn agreed to go with Don to the New York World's Fair. There was no way to say goodbye . . . yet.

Lessons

Ronnie Schell moved to Hollywood for the Gomer Pyle show. He and Don started to correspond, a series of letters flowed back and forth. Don began to read Ronnie's letters on the air, omitting, of course, those portions which would endanger the station's FCC license.

A typical letter from "R. S." to "D. S." combined information with gossip, insult with flattery:

SUNDAY MOURN

(A personal letter follows in a few days, my love)

D. S.:
R. S. here from Hollywood. How are you, pal? I thought it was about time that I dropped you a line to give you all the latest scoops from one who has made it big. (Somehow, that sounds vulgar.) After all, Don, as you know, show business is my life, my life is show business.

First of all, with "Good Morning, World" about to go down the drain, I have moved back to "Gomer Pyle," resuming my unheralded, yet rather innocuous role of "Duke." We are currently filming our tenth show for the coming season, and I must admit it is a great relief to be working on a top rated series again. As you know, the ratings on "Good Morning, World" weren't too good. In fact, I think we ended up two points below "And now, our National Anthem." Anyway, I'm Gomer's buddy again, and I've had so few lines thus far in the first ten shows, I may be in constant danger next season of being arrested for loitering in front of a television camera . . .

You'll be happy to hear that last month I broke into my largest piggy bank, molded after a girl I once dated in Houston, and purchased a four hundred dollar set of golf clubs. (true!) Since that time, I have been taking three golf lessons a week . . . My teacher says I'll become an excellent golfer. He repeated it twice during my nineteenth lesson, entitled, "Approaching The Tee."

Well, D. S., I must memorize my script for next week (Pg. 14, line 6). I plan a trip to the Bay Area next month and will see you without fail. (Or, if you prefer, I'll bring him with me.)

Your pal,
R.S.

In early 1965 a surprising thing happened in the San Francisco radio polls: "Mr. San Francisco Radio" had held onto first place for the eighth year in a row, but there was a strong contender—the KYA "Emperor" Gene Nelson.

The *San Mateo Times* reported, "Newcomer Gene Nelson of KYA has caused the biggest stir in local radio since Sherwood first hit the scene. Nelson's vote came closer to Sherwood than anybody has in years."

Gene Nelson was a star from Buffalo and Cincinnati who had come to KYA in 1962. "Sherwood was the big morning man. I was young, cocky, and stupid enough to try to beat him! My cross to bear was people coming up and saying, 'Ah, you're in radio. What time are ya on?' I'd say, 'Six to nine in the morning . . .' and they'd say, 'Oh, same time as Sherwood.'

"He knew about me and never paid any attention, until I started to gain on him. Then I beat him in one ratings book, and suddenly he recognized me, or the fact that I might have some talent. When I was on KYA, I pulled twenty percent when he pulled thirty percent, and I felt the impact. That's a monstrous share of the pie. Today, the number one station is ten percent of the market. He mentioned my name on the air and said a couple of nice things about me.

"I was in the Mark Hopkins Hotel, and he was in the Fairmont, so we were next door to each other. He would send guys over to borrow records he wanted to play, like I was there for his convenience!"

Don sustained his lead but was forced to share ratings and recognition with other talented deejays who remained top names in San Francisco radio. Gene Nelson was a name Don would not be allowed to forget.

In the meantime, Al Newman, the program director and friend of Don's, came up with an idea for a movie. He and Don decided to write a script together. "We'd work on it for hours every day after leaving the station and having breakfast, writing and talking and developing it," Al remembers. "We hired a secretary to type it. It was a fabulous story. We finished it, then a producer took it, and other people got involved, and the whole thing fell apart. Next thing we knew *Escape from New York* came out . . . our story. That was the end of that."

Enrico Banducci remembers Don telling him all about it. He agrees it was a very good script and that it kept Don focussed, stimulated, and on a track for a while.

Don was godfather to Al's son, Daniel, but typically refused to accept any responsibility for the child. "He taught my kids to play craps," Al says, "and never gave them their money back."

Al and Don's relationship was inevitably stormy, as all of Don's friendships were. But after a fight there was usually an early morning call from a sad, often drunk Don, apologizing and trying to make things right again. For those who rode the pied piper's magic roller coaster, Don's "Hey, I love you, man" went a long way.

Don wasn't teaching his own child Diane anything— not even how to shoot craps. She was in high school now and having a tough time. Her mother, Sally, had remarried, so Don spent very little time with either of them.

"We had a good relationship," Sally says, "but he didn't have much to do with Diane's life. During her last high school years, though, he started to be there for her."

DIANE :

He never did many kid things because he always expected you to behave on a more sophisticated level. I remember the one thing we did that he got a kick out of—taking Greg and me out on his boat over to Red Rock Island. We'd crawl around the caves while he scared us half to death, telling us we would fall into the mine shaft. When we asked him for a flashlight, he said, "Oh, Christ! Just like your mother!"

My mother was remarried, to a man who was a problem for me. She married him when I was ten years old. He couldn't deal with my growing-up stage. His solution was to stop speaking to me, to pretend I wasn't there. It was oppressive, and I had to get away, but I needed encouragement to be independent.

My mother called Dad and said, "Your daughter's a basket case. You'd better do something." He taught me to play tennis, to write a check—normal things. Then how to drive—this from a man terrified of driving!

We drove from San Jose to San Francisco in his old, green Rambler station wagon. He had his fingers dug into the dash the whole way. But he was so proud when he took me to the DMV. I think it's the first thing he'd ever started with me and actually finished.

Two days after I got my license, he was going to New York for the weekend, so he loaned me the Rambler. The first thing I did was wash the car, because it had all this sea gull shit on it. I used an SOS pad . . . Everything came off all right, along with the paint! I got hysterical. Mom tried to calm me down by sending me to the store for ice cream. She should have sent me to get another seagull!

DIANE...

I'd never learned to park in angled spaces, so I pulled in, backed out, pulled in closer, back and forth, until I was door handle to door handle with the car next to me. Now I was stuck—couldn't go forward or back without scraping the car next to me. I called Mom. She came down and called someone who came with a crane. They lifted the car up and moved it over, hooking right into the frame of the Rambler. So now the frame was bent, the side of the car was all messed up, and it had SOS circles all over it. It was one battered car that I drove home!

When Dad got back, I drove the car to his place. "Hi, Dad . . . about your car . . ." I said. He looked out the window, then went out on the balcony, looking down thirty-one stories and said, "I don't see any problems."

He took it very well, but he did buy me a car of my own. He also got me out of my mother's house into an apartment of my own, where I lived until I graduated high school. I really began to blossom under his help and influence.

Don couldn't win when it came to lending out cars. Hap Harper remembers the time Don loaned him his T-bird for a weekend. Hap drove him to the airport.

"Everything was fine, I didn't have any problems," Hap says. "When it came time to put gas in and return it to him, I thought I would do him a favor and put in aviation fuel, which I thought would give it all kinds of extra zip. . . . I picked him up at the airport. The car was running fine. Then he dropped me off and headed up to San Francisco. When he came to the first stoplight, the car died. He started it, and it died at the next light . . . and every light. He drove it like that for two or three days. I called him to say 'Hey Don, I haven't heard anything about how great your car is running.' He said, 'Why, what did you do to it?' I told him, and he said, 'I'll kill you, you son of a bitch!' "

Diane and Don spent a lot of time together during her

junior and senior years in high school. In addition to teaching her things, he persuaded her to see Dr. Lion.

"I transferred my energy from trying to deal with my stepfather to 'now Dad will look after me.' He was hardly the one to look after anyone. You were at the mercy of his whim.

"Dr. Lion was not necessarily a good man," Diane adds. "He told me the 'rules' the way he saw it, but he didn't help me work out what I should do. Dad really relied on Dr. Lion, who once told him he would never learn to love and should stop sleeping with women because he was violating them. I think he worked with Dad because Dad was so entertaining."

While Diane was growing under her father's tutelage, life was about to give Don a lesson. He began to have some tests, as Herb Caen noted, "to find out why he can't climb a flight of stairs without falling to the floor, gasping."

The diagnosis was emphysema.

Stockton with Palm Trees

Shocked by the diagnosis of emphysema, Don debated what to do next. An opportunist named Bob Sherman promptly offered him part-ownership and the morning show at a Honolulu radio station.

Don's KSFO contract stipulated that if he left, he could do radio everywhere except in the eleven Western states. Hawaii was not yet a state. As far as Bay Area radio was concerned, it was forbidden territory for him for ten years.

Don opted for Hawaii.

He left his *$500/day* job at KSFO—which still meant $200 on the day's he didn't show and was docked $300—and flew away with $35,000 a year coming to him from KSFO under the contract stipulation of paying him to not to go to competing stations.

HERB CAEN:

Among those who were surprised to find Don Sherwood off the air yesterday morning was Don Sherwood. This was to have been his final week on KSFO—after 14 years—but at the last minute his bosses told him NOT to mention the fact that he is leaving for Hawaii. "You mean you want me to be on the air 15 hours

without once saying goodbye? Forget it!" he exploded.
And so . . . he was gone, fwhoosh, without so much as
a farewell . . .

Jim Lange stepped in on very short notice, after rear-
ranging his schedule, which now included being TV host
for "Oh My Word" and "The Dating Game" in Los Angeles, plus doing weekends at KSFO in San Francisco. He began to commute for the L.A. tapings. When asked where
he lived, he replied, "On PSA!"

Carter B., asked if Don's sudden departure took him
by surprise, said, "The only thing Don could do to surprise
me would be if he had a sex-change operation."

Bill Shaw says, "I made a mental bet that it wouldn't
last thirteen weeks."

Don kept his Russian Hill apartment, "so I won't feel
I'm really leaving San Francisco for good. I'll fly back every
other weekend till the money runs out." By Easter, he was
in Honolulu setting up house in a new Diamond Head
apartment. Greg and Robin flew over to spend the holiday
with him.

Bob Sherman, owner of radio station KHAI, presold
Sherwood to all the advertising agencies. Then he left
town on a fast horse. KHAI's Bob Bowen says, "I was station manager because nobody else wanted the job. Bob
Sherman was a real con man who'd built too many radio
stations. We had a nice address at the Royal Hawaiian Hotel, on a trade basis. The station was started with Ray
Sweeney, Dick Cook, Sam Sanford, myself, and no
money. We were broke.

"I had to change the studios for Don, since he wanted
his own engineer. He, of course, missed his first two
shows! Three Mai Tais crippled him. 'I never go to work
with a hangover,' he said. The third day he showed up
and marched into my office. He was already starting to
figure out that his deal wasn't what he thought it was.
Spreading his big, long fingers out on my desk, he leaned
forward and said, 'Bowen, you are the biggest fucking asshole.'

"He didn't like me, to say the least, but we were all holding the bag. Some of the creditors were calling Don, wanting him to pay the bills. He was drawing $2,000 a month, and I ran around collecting the money to pay him. The agreement was that if he stayed one year and pumped up the station, he'd get a twenty-five percent interest. But as he uncovered the debts, it was clear that was meaningless!"

HERB CAEN:

Don Sherwood, reporting from his new airquarters at KHAI, Honolulu: "Oh, there are so many things to do here! Take about a day and a half . . . the sea, snorkeling, scuba, surfing, floating, drinking and watching . . . four hours a day. That only leaves 20 hours for boredom . . . 10:30 am, time for cocktails. Bye." I miss him, too.

John Farrington, the KHAI afternoon man, knew Don was *the* broadcast person on the West Coast.

JOHN FARRINGTON:

I remember the day he came in, I did a bit on him on my show. I knew he'd drunk his way across the Pacific, and that Bowen was about to pick him up at the airport. I timed it to when I thought he'd be on the road, and said, "Now Don Sherwood's coming in, and he'll be on the air tomorrow morning, a great star from San Francisco, and I know you'll enjoy him. Unfortunately, Don has a drinking problem, and I know that at this moment, he's at a gas station looking for the key to the men's room." Then I played a record and went on. Don heard it all. By the time he got to the station, he'd decided I was going to work with him on the morning show. I was

JOHN...

ordered to report to him at the bar of the Royal Hawaiian.

I went, scared to death and irritated. I sat down, and Don said, "John, I like your style. I'm going to give you a great choice—work with me for one thousand dollars on the morning show, or not work here at all." Then he was supposed to work with me in the afternoon, a two-for-one deal.

I tried to get out of it, but couldn't. It was very difficult to be up and organized at that time of the morning, and I didn't click with Don at all. I did the news and was supposed to be his foil, but I was not in his league, and I was used to working alone. He was very nice to me even though things didn't work out.

I tried to find women for him to date, but that didn't work out either. He liked to tell me that the Porsche I'd busted my butt to get was nothing more than an extension of my penis and that I should give the car up and get a jeep.

Ray Sweeney, who also worked the morning show, remembers, "I was to do the engineering, and Dick Cook would do the news, but Don couldn't deal with Dick Cook. I was to be the foil, but I didn't put out the way Don wanted, and I didn't fall apart laughing at his antics.

"When I first had lunch with him, he spent the rest of the day drinking. When I went to pick him up the next morning, Greg met me at the door and said, 'Pop can't make it.' I said, 'Give me a break.' Greg checked with Don again, came back, and said, 'Donnie-boy says *you're* a trooper; do it yourself.' From then on, I'd do the show about once a week.

"When I came to Hawaii as sales manager, I was also told I'd have a piece of the station. In fact, all put together, we had a total of about two hundred percent interest!"

Jerry Bundsen, Herb Caen's assistant, was in Hawaii visiting and remembers the day he was a guest on Dick

Cook's program. "While I was being interviewed, Don called Dick, on the air, and said, 'When you finish your show today, you're through. When I get there, I don't want to see you.' Dick was dumbfounded, naturally, and I didn't know what to say or do. At first we thought Don was kidding. I felt terrible for Dick. Don really did fire him that day."

Don was finally in a position of true authority, and he ruthlessly used it to let Dick Cook know once and for all that he didn't like him.

HERB CAEN:

> Don Sherwood, reporting from KHAI: "I find it difficult to work for a company whose ownership I don't like. This station has only two owners, and I can't stand Bob Sherman OR me."

> Don Sherwood flew back from Honolulu (he's in a local hospital) because it was feared he had suffered a coronary to go along with his emphysema. However, his heart checked out okay and he returns this weekend to what he calls "Stockton with palm trees."

Joe Quigg was another one who'd been wooed to KHAI along with Don. He was in sales. "Sherman wanted to be another Gene Autry. To do that he needed Sherwood," Joe says. "My first meeting with Don, in the bar of the Royal Hawaiian, wasn't a good one. We both had a woman with us and he started to use bad language. When I told him to watch it, he fired me. I didn't care because I wasn't in awe of him. He called me later that day and said, 'I need you.' "

Joe went back, but he knew the situation was hopeless. And it was. Shortly thereafter, Don called it quits and returned to San Francisco.

HERB CAEN:

As you've probably heard by now, radio fans, Don Sherwood is returning to KSFO (stop that dancing in the streets). Starting October 9, at a salary of repulsive proportions, he'll be back in the old 6 to 9 a.m. slot, give or take an hour or two, and his psychoanalyst has already been alerted to stand by (he has a portable couch and makes house calls). The loser in this case is Jim Lange, crestfallen but brave . . .

Jim Lange was not upset. "Every time my contract was about to run out, Don would leave again! It didn't really bother me; they kept me on the payroll."

"Don hated it in Hawaii and was feeling awful with his emphysema," Joe Quigg says. "He told me he had to get out and was sorry to leave me holding the bag. I faced the sponsors and made sure they knew that Don and I were not responsible for the goings-on. The station went straight to hell. Finally I left, too, and San Francisco won the toss of the coin."

The Short Straw

Hawaii Joe Quigg became Don's house guest in the Green Street "penthouse" for the fall. By now they were friends, so Don immediately tackled the first order of business—get Joe a job. KFOG radio hired him.

"Not only did he help get me a job and put me up when I came here, with less than a hundred bucks on me," Joe says, "he'd do a few commercials for a company, free, so that I could get the advertising account. He was incredibly generous, at least to me."

Within a short time of Joe's arrival, and after nearly a decade of bachelorhood—Marilyn, by now, was no longer in the picture—Don fell hard for a woman named Nancy Brown.

He told the press about his latest theory on marriage: "When you meet someone you think is Miss Right, you must spend four seasons together. After that, if you're still getting along, it's time to think of marriage."

Before his Four-Seasons theory could be tested, Don and Nancy Brown were engaged and announcing a fall 1968 wedding. As if to prove his theory true, however, Ms. Brown called it off and returned the ring before the autumn leaves hit the ground.

While wedding bells didn't ring for Don, they did for Hawaii Joe—

JOE QUIGG:

Don met a Pan Am stewardess and introduced her to me. It seemed right that he should be my best man. Rehearsal was scheduled for 7 p.m. We waited and waited, but Don didn't show. The priest agreed to wait when we told him it was Sherwood.

Finally, Don came stumbling in from the side fire-exit, drunker than hell, with a hooker on his arm! I couldn't believe it.

Then on my wedding day, he was supposed to help get me dressed and didn't show again. A friend and I found him passed out on his couch. We poured vodka down him, got him dressed, and dragged him to the church. We kept pouring more vodka down him all the way. Thank God, he pulled it together.

It was a high mass, Roman Catholic ceremony. After a while Don got fidgety. I remembered Carter B. telling me if Sherwood was in any kind of shape at all, not to let him crack me up. Don started whispering things to me about the altar boy picking his nose and stuff like that, but I refused to get sucked into it.

When it came time for Don to take the rings off the pillow and put them in the Holy water, he couldn't get the rings untied! He finally jerked them off, ripping the pillow and sending the stuffing all over the place. He threw the rings in the gold dish, then leaned over to me, cursed my mother, and swore to kill whoever had tied those rings.

That finally got me. I couldn't help myself. Even the priest had a hard time serving communion because he was shaking with laughter, too.

But as the days passed, show after show, Don became increasingly contemplative and moody. In retrospect, the following letter, which he read on the air, foreshadowed his next move:

AN OPEN LETTER TO A
DISCOURAGED YOUNGSTER

Today you came to me for a job. From the look of your shoulders as you walked out, I suspect you've been turned down before, and maybe you believe by now that kids out of high school can't find work.

But I hired a teenager today. You saw him. He was the one with polished shoes and a necktie. What was so special about him? Not experience, neither of you had any. It was his attitude that put him on the payroll instead of you. Attitude, son. A-T-T-I-T-U-D-E. He wanted that job badly enough to shuck the leather jacket, get a haircut, and look in the phone book to find out what this company makes. He did his best to impress me. That's where he edged you out.

You see, kid, people who hire people aren't "with" a lot of things. We know more about Bing than Ringo, and we have Stone-Age ideas about who owes whom a living. Maybe that makes us prehistoric, but there's nothing wrong with the checks we sign.

What I need is someone who'll go out in the plant, keep his eyes open, and work for me like he'd work for *himself*. If you have even the vaguest idea of what I'm trying to say, let it show the next time you ask for a job. You'll be head and shoulders over the rest.

You know, kid, men have always had to get a job like you get a girl: Case the situation, wear a clean shirt, and try to appear reasonably willing. Maybe jobs aren't as plentiful right now, but a lot of us can remember when master craftsmen walked the streets. By comparison, you don't know the meaning of "scarce."

For both our sakes, get eager, will you?

The Boss

When all his thinking was done, and nothing had changed his mind, Don informed Bill Shaw, "Papa Bear," that he was leaving. It was clear that he meant it.

Gene Nelson—Don's competitor from across the street

—had come over from KYA to join the team. "When Sherwood made it clear he was going to quit, KSFO hired Terry McGovern out of Pittsburgh to come in as the heir apparent," Gene says. "Sherwood must have had an inkling of this. Even though he was quitting, and it was his own idea, he couldn't stand the idea that someone was going to take his place and that maybe this guy might even be successful. He'd close the show every morning saying, 'Well, that's it for me. Stay tuned for Terry McGovern, whoever the heck he is.' One day he said, 'KSFO now leaves the air and will resume broadcasting at 6 a.m. tomorrow.' "

"Don and I were in the men's room and I said to him, 'Hey, Don. I hear you're leaving.' " Terry McGovern says. "He said, 'Yeah, well kid, I hope they treat you better here than they did me. Watch out you don't pull the short straw.' "

TERRY McGOVERN:

It would never have occurred to me that I would ever follow in and take his show. I had learned that you never follow "The Guy"—you try to replace the guy who followed The Guy. If you follow a Don Sherwood or any success like that, you're just cannon fodder.

Well, I pulled the short straw. They put me in his morning show for fifteen long months. I worked, sweated, and became neurotic. Finally, they brought in Jim Lange. My ratings were good, so I kept my job there, but got off the morning show.

GENE NELSON:

Sherwood and I saw each other socially sometimes, and he was instrumental in getting me the job at KSFO. After I had approached KSFO, he went to bat for me. The all-night show was not what I wanted, but that's what opened up, so I took it.

Once I got there, of course, Don's attitude towards me changed. As soon as anyone got close to him and he be-

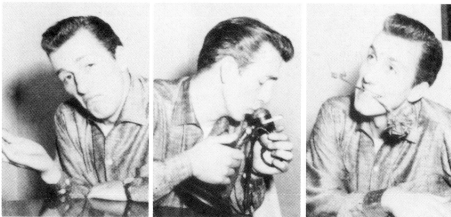

The many faces of Don. "What do I think? . . . What day is it?" *(Courtesy of the San Francisco News)*

Don's early ventures into television include the popular KGO-TV "POP CLUB" show, a music program orchestrated around a soda fountain theme. On this particular show, Don demonstrates the amazing boxing talent of Tom Rooney's pet kangaroo, Sydney. *(Courtesy of the Sherwood family collection/ Photographer: Ray De Aragon)*

With guests Ronnie Schell ("America's slowest rising young comedian") and Bill Dana (Jose Jimenez) on Don's KTVU evening variety show, it promises to be very entertaining, and as always, a free-for-all. *(Courtesy of Ronnie Schell)*

Don "Tarzan" Sherwood, strutting his stuff for Marilyn. Trying to find the right angle for this photo wasn't easy! *(Courtesy of Marilyn Walker-Vollmer)*

"The World's Greatest Disc Jockey"— party animal extraordinaire— in action at the KSFO studio. Bill Stroebel of the *Oakland Tribune* notes that Don apparently combs his hair with an electric fan. *(Courtesy of Oakland Tribune Photographer: Keith Dennison)*

Marilyn Walker and Don, hugging after Don's acquittal from a drunk driving charge, 1962. *(Courtesy of San Francisco Chronicle/Photographer: Peter Breinig)*

While not always ready for the rigors of a competitive P.A.L. baseball game, Don is at least present in body. *(Courtesy of Jim Lange/ Photographer: Jim Marshall)*

It's no surprise to anyone that Jim Lange is the first to cross the finish line at the Stinson Beach/Ferry building race; what is a surprise is that Don crosses it at all. The 23.8-mile race brings over ten thousand fans out to cheer them on and hear the speeches. *(Courtesy of Jim Lange/ Photographer: Gene Wright)*

THE SHERWOOD FAMILY PORTRAIT

SEATED left to right: KSFO's Steve Brown, Chet Casselman, Mike Powell, Steve "Deadstick" Crowley, Jeff Skov. STANDING left to right: Parkey Sharkey, Carter Blakemore Smith, MORNING MAN, Charles Homer Smith, Lonesome Marcelle and Just Plain Rosita. HANGING: Allan Murray Newman, P.D.

KSFO family portrait: a lineup of talent that dominates the market. *(Courtesy of KSFO)*

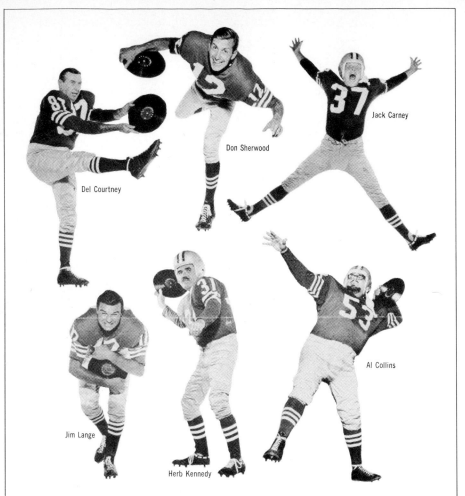

Del Courtney

Don Sherwood

Jack Carney

Jim Lange

Herb Kennedy

Al Collins

WHEN IN DOUBT...PUNT!

But for scatback entertainment, a powerhouse line and music reception that never misses...kick off with Sherwood every morning and run with the greatest team of personalities on Radio today...560 is the number of the play...KSFO is the signal...So hike that dial to.... The World's Greatest Radio Station... KSFO!

KSFO family in later years, drawing talent from all over the country to continue its reign over San Francisco. *(Courtesy of KSFO)*

Don proudly escorts his daugher, Diane, to Allen Chase's "Over-Forty" party in Los Angeles. *(Courtesy of the Sherwood family collection)*

Don's self-portrait, drawn in 1970. *(Courtesy of the Sherwood family collection)*

Don, at fifty-eight, retreats to Sausalito. His face, his eyes, his smile, tell of a man who has weathered a full, stormy life. *(Courtesy San Francisco Chronicle/Photographer: Peter Breinig)*

The man who has owned the town now sits back to observe it from a new distance. *(Courtesy of the Sherwood family collection)*

GENE...

came your friend, he'd turn on you. Sherwood and Jack
Carney were close, then all of a sudden there was a
falling out—I think, when Sherwood took off for Hawaii
and Carney got the morning show. The kiss of death for
Carney was when Sherwood came back, and Carney
was bumped. Suddenly he was chopped liver.

That's how KSFO did it—you're good enough unless
Sherwood's available, and then you're not good enough.
In, out, in, out, always second best. That's hard to put
up with.

Sherwood said to me, "You know KSFO is like South
America. You've got the very rich and the very poor,
and there ain't no middle class. I'm the very rich."

We went to breakfast one morning, after his show—
seven or eight of us in his entourage, including some ad
agency people. Sherwood said to them, "You may remember Gene, he used to work for KYA . . . had a pretty
good following over there. We hired him over here on
KSFO and stuck his ass in the middle of the all-night
show. We buried him. You ever hear of him now?"

He just looked at me. It was a joke, but it wasn't a
very good one. I think that's exactly how he saw it. The
station didn't bury me, they had cautioned me about going from the morning spot to an all-night spot, but I'd
said I was willing to pay my dues.

Each morning when 6 a.m. came around, my show
would be wrapping up. One morning Don didn't get
there to do his show until seven-thirty, and by then I'd
been on for seven-and-a-half hours! I took some shots at
him on the air, and he was offended by that, so I got on
his bad side. Eventually, I got the nine to midnight shift,
and Don and I didn't see much of each other.

Don had this thing in his head that February was a
bad month for him, that everything bad in his life had
happened to him in February. He couldn't face it and
would be gone that month every year. Carter B. once
took the ratings for a period and estimated that *he'd* done

GENE...

forty percent of the shows that were in that time period, but *he* sure didn't get forty percent of the salary. He made dirt wages and carried a big part of the load.

What was so frustrating for me competing with Sherwood is that while I believed I could compete—*on the air*—I couldn't compete with the fact that when he was *off the air*, he got just as much attention. He was a walking billboard for himself and for the station, always on the front page of the paper.

KSFO had been number one for many consecutive years—in good measure thanks to Don, Mr. San Francisco Radio. Now radio was changing and there was a new format in the wind at the station. Don wanted no part of it.

Walkout

With no more energy or drive to carry on, Don left KSFO in October 1969. "They've been fat for so long, nothing is happening here," he said, having been there for the better part of sixteen years. "Once you've been really flat, living in a basement, expecting a kid and making twenty-five dollars a week hauling oil drums—which I did back in the beginning—you realize losing a job isn't the end of the world," he added. "I don't have the world all figured out, but I'm leaving to get more out of a day. You add up all the days you let slip by, and it adds up to a lot of unsatisfying months."

Don reminded everyone that his first walkout ever had been in kindergarten, when he didn't like the teacher. Not much had changed.

He took off to Mexico for rest and rejuvenation. By December he was back in San Francisco, and Joe Quigg, separated from his wife, was once again staying with him.

"In December my wife was having our child, and Don came to Childrens' Hospital with me for moral support," Joe remembers. "He ran out and came back with champagne which he passed out to all the unwed, expectant mothers there in the hospital, singing Christmas carols to them. He was a big hit that night!"

JOE QUIGG:

I learned a lot about people living with him, watching how he addressed problems. He could be a real lint-picker, on the one hand, but then he'd turn around and be a complete slob. He was total extremes, except that he always had a thing about personal hygiene.

I remember, at one point, he took all the furniture out of the place and put in a pool table, a regular-size table that took up the whole room. Now this was the "penthouse," surrounded by plate glass. In the time I lived with him, they had to replace nine panels of glass! He also drilled a hole in the balcony ceiling, thirty-one floors up, to put in a punching bag—one of those fast bags. You could hear that thing way down at the *Washington Bar & Grill*! I'm sure he did it just to annoy people.

There was a threat on his life while I was living with him. It happened all the time. I took one of the calls, so I know the threats were real. Bill Buchalter was his constant bodyguard and packed a gun at all times. I took Don to the police range and taught him how to shoot a Colt .45 automatic he'd been given. He'd change his phone number every thirty or forty days because of all the crazy calls.

One night Don and I went drinking, which was not a constant thing, since he and I were not usually in sync— he'd be on the wagon when I wasn't, and vice versa. We went out and picked up a couple of girls, went back to their place, and ended up the next morning not knowing where we were. We were both supposed to be at work. Don didn't care, but I did! We didn't even know the names of the girls, so Don told me to go out and read the street sign, so we could call a cab. I went out in my underwear with a beer in my hand, but had forgotten my glasses, so I couldn't read anything. It was a security building, and the door slammed shut behind me—I'm locked out, freezing my butt off, and don't know what button to push, since I don't know any names and I

JOE...

know Don won't answer, anyway, in case it's one of the girl's boyfriends.

People thought I was crazy and called the police. I yelled until Don heard me and let me in. We finally thought to go through the girls' mail to get their address, and called a cab. Don had found the vodka by then, and we were both in terrible shape.

Our cars had been towed, so we ended up getting a cab to Fisherman's Wharf and continuing on with what became a four-day tear, ending up in Reno, gambling until we could sign no more markers. My banker had to wire us money to get home.

Temporarily unemployed but hardly out of funds, Don occupied himself seeing his friends and playing hard.

"Don called me one night, as we were sitting down to dinner," Guy Haines recalls. "He said we had to get over there *right away*. A friend and I went over to his place on Green. When we walked in, there was a woman lying on the living room floor, naked. Don says, "Hey, grab a wet towel—give her a few cracks. She loves it!' I'm serious! I say, 'No way!' It turns out this woman he called Lily of the Valley was a minister's wife from Modesto who came to San Francisco once a month to see Don and 'let loose.'

You never knew what you were going to find when Don called to say, 'You better get over here right away.' "

While Don was fooling around, and generally being hedonistic, a new television station came calling. KBHK-44 wanted Don to do a video deejay show weekday mornings from 6 to 9, another version of Russ Coughlan's earlier idea. This time, however, it was exactly like doing his KSFO show except it was on television, and Don would get a cut from the commercials, plus salary.

By contract, Don still wasn't allowed to do competing radio in the Bay Area.

This was a way to get around that.

During the entire show, the viewers would see noth-

ing but an old-style 1930s radio on the screen. The viewers
would *hear* Don, exactly as they had when he was on the
radio.

Don told Dwight Newton, "You can just listen; you
don't have to watch. If I did a visual entertainment show at
that hour, I would drive them up the walls. I now reach
about a million people on the radio, some seventy percent
listen at home. If you're a dyed-in-the-wool fan, you'll get
me coming out of your television as easily as coming out of
your radio. You could get me coming out of your toastmas-
ter, for all the difference it would make."

It promised to be a show of questionable success.

Jim Dunbar was doing the "A.M. San Francisco" show
on KGO-TV. He recalls the day the "zodiac killer" was
supposed to turn himself in to Jim and Melvin Belli on
Jim's show. "That day, Don said on his television program, 'You people shouldn't be watching me, it's the
wrong station. Switch to Channel 7, Jim Dunbar is with the
zodiac killer.'

"The killer never showed, and it all fell apart, but I
never forgot Don saying that. He was incredibly honest.
His show was in trouble, and he still said that."

Ronnie Schell was keeping tabs on Don's progress.

TUESDAY

Dear D. S.:

R. S. here from the big network. How are you, pal?
Just a belated note from the entire Ronnie Schell family to
wish you all the luck in the world in your new venture as
America's very first video disc jockey. (Do you think Del
Courtney and Les Malloy will sue?) And three cheers for
the Kaiser Company for hiring you. Don, I hope you last
longer than their liberty ships did . . .

I've been awfully busy the past week working on my
successful television series and completing the first draft of
my autobiography. The book itself will feature the high-
lights of my life in show business. I've tentatively entitled
it "YAWN."

Not much else is new down here, Don. Saturday night

my wife and I attended a big private Hollywood party which was dull to say the least. The high point of the evening was throwing the coats on the bed.

Again, pal, best of luck in your new job and keep in mind that I will be holding January open to be available to attend your first annual "Farewell to Videodiscjockeying" party.

Your pal,
R.S.

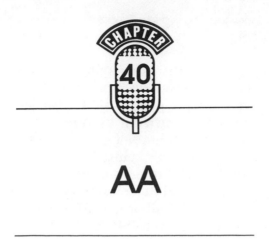

AA

Not surprisingly, the KBHK-44 video DJ show did not last long. Don's attention was increasingly focused inward. Without the demands and distractions of his KSFO show, he was beginning to re-evaluate his life.

His smoking addiction was clearly worsening his chances of retarding the emphysema, but he wasn't ready to deal with it yet. He did, however, make a major decision: he joined Alcoholics Anonymous.

"I'm the AA's most un-anonymous member," he told Bob MacKenzie of the *Oakland Tribune*. "It is a great organization, and it rescued me. Like everybody else, I thought it was for helpless types. Then I went to a meeting and found guys every bit as smart and successful as I was, standing up and admitting they can't handle it. I was the typical guy who says to himself, nobody as smart as I am can be an alcoholic. Next thing you know, you're in a rubber room.

"For years I got away with not showing up for my show just because I could get away with it—I was a character. Everybody would chuckle and say, Donny-babe, you're such a devil. I was always given artistic license, which was really just a license to be a baby. At AA they don't call me a devil. They call me a drunk."

Shirley, intimately familiar with Don's battle, says,

"He was obsessed with his drinking and was one of the first public figures to admit his alcoholism."

"Dad made it more complicated because he admitted his alcoholism and abstracted it from himself," Greg adds. "He saw it as apart from himself and, at the same time, admitted it was intrinsic to his being."

Don's behavior all throughout his adult life closely followed the patterns of Adult Children of Alcoholics (ACA). Claudia Black's role definitions of ACA parents, outlined in her book, "IT WILL NEVER HAPPEN TO ME", pinpoint Don's role as being the "acting out child": "They are the delinquents, the early offenders. These children are the ones with low self-esteem. If they live to be adults, they never learn to feel good about themselves. They are unable to interact with others in ways that are acceptable."

These same traits are evident in children of what psychologists call dysfunctional families. Don had already spent years with his psychiatrist, Dr. Lion, examining his childhood and his relationship with "Big Inga." Now, after years of therapy, he began a different, but equally obsessive, study of himself.

Inconsistency was still his only constant, but for the first time he was considering all of the possibilities. Perhaps he *could* change the patterns in his life. His family and friends were thrilled, although experience dictated a wait-and-see approach.

Trust was an issue too hot to touch.

Living on his houseboat in Sausalito, having again cleared away most of his worldly possessions, Don withdrew from his kingdom—San Francisco—to observe it from across the bay. His reputation and notoriety followed him, in ways and for reasons Don never quite understood. Incredibly, he continued to win polls long after leaving radio.

Don left an indelible mark on many of his fans. One fan, Marty Rojas, listened to Don from the early fifties on. "As I went through adolescence, he was a constant in my life. Every morning, or almost every morning, he was there. Adolescence was *awful* for me—one of the most painful times of my life, and Sherwood was often the only person who could make me laugh. When my friends were listening to rock and roll, I was listening to Don. He opened the doors to adult humor for me. But most of all, he was *there*, and I can never forget that."

Don's frame of mind now, though was such that he was not seeking or feasting on the attention of the masses. Ironically, he frequented the *No Name Bar*—on and off the wagon. Because he had no phone on his boat, the *No-Name* became one of the few ways of contacting him. All mail was sent to his mother Inga's in Fairfax.

The new decade of the seventies also marked the beginning of growth for Don and his children, now adults. They were no longer little people incapable of response, but rather, intelligent human beings with whom Don could communicate.

HERB CAEN:

> Don Sherwood is indeed a man of the peepul: he doesn't own a tux. So he's renting one for Allen Chase's wildly publicized party for aging swingers in L.A. tomorrow night. Don is taking a 21-year old beauty with him—his daughter, Diane.

When Don got a call from Portland notifying him that Diane had been in a terrible car accident and was in the college infirmary, he flew up to see her immediately.

"Dad called me from the airport and told me to get a cab to the hotel and we'd have dinner!" Diane says, shaking her head. "I tried to explain that I was in bed with lots of holes in me, but he insisted that we have dinner together. He picked me up and took me out to dinner. He made me sit in this fancy restaurant in the Portland Hilton, with people around us getting up and asking to be moved because I was all scrunched up and couldn't even close my mouth. Everyone was horrified, but Dad sat there and looked right at me, eating dinner like nothing was wrong. We had a great time. It was probably the right thing to do, because it helped me regain my confidence."

Don's way of dealing with Dan Sorkin's serious motorcycle accident had been equally bizarre. "He came to see me in the hospital after my leg had been sawed off and I was trying to figure out what had happened to me," Dan says. "He said, 'By the way, when you get your new leg, what color are you going to have it?' We discussed color schemes! That's the kind of guy he was."

Don could not be counted on to have a "normal" rsponse to things because he had no sense of what was normal. His response was strictly reactive.

About this time, his other daughter Robin developed a crush on Pete Scott, the Asst. Program Director at KSFO.

ROBIN :

As I entered my teens, communication with my father improved, but we still couldn't relax with each other. Peter and I had an easy rapport, we'd laugh and flirt, but he was no fool; he kept me at arm's length. Then Dad ended his friendship with Peter, with no explanation given. Looking back, I suspect my infatuation was partially to blame. I think it was painful for Dad to see me so comfortable with another man.

I remember when Dad got pneumonia and ended up in the hospital. I went to visit him. He immediately started to put Peter down, and wanted me to agree with him, but I couldn't lie. Ever so gently I said, "Oh Dad, Peter's not that bad." He exploded. Pointing toward the door, he screamed, "Well I hope the two of you will be very happy together, now get the fuck out of here!"

Weeks later I received a package from my father. It contained every photograph he had of me. I had been disowned.

Pete Scott was stung in the battle and Don's insecurities once again cost him a valuable friendship—and almost a daughter.

GREG :

Dad had persisted for years in a redundant pattern of misery, and there's only one way to look at that—nothing ever got through to him. The love of other people for him never got through, and the offshoot was a frightening, almost unloving, yet humorous honesty. Most people can't be that honest, wouldn't be that honest. Normal human beings aren't that open. Of course, Dad's perception of the world allowed him that honesty —sharp, clear, enhanced by total lack of desire to make things right for other people.

Robin is our best example of Dad. She is the seed of him that goes on. She has the same, uncluttered way of looking at the world. She's not one to say, 'I wonder what people think of me.'

ROBIN :

He could really pull the wool over your eyes. He'd say something and you'd think, *he's nuts*. But he had such conviction and he had a thing about honesty—his honesty.

GREG :

His humor was inherent in his 'angst.' He could be charming and diplomatic, and would do that when he deemed it appropriate.

He was a rare example of what you get looking at people of the arts, writers and others—uncompromising. And usually very self-destructive.

He thought he had to be an expert at everything. For so many years, he couldn't relate to Robin, as a father or as a human being, so he decided he didn't have a daughter. "She's a back stabber, a woman," he'd say. He'd rationalize it so that he didn't need them.

I accommodated him, knowing when not to ask for something. As Carter B. once said, he'd give you

GREG...

everything for free if you were there, because you were so enjoyable. He'd help solve every problem in your life, but once he got the sense that you *needed* something from him, it was all over. He was a giving person in certain ways, but once he felt responsibility or obligation, the tables turned.

He was very adolescent. He relished that vacuum, that bubble that success created.

There were brief periods in my life when I'd walk away and say, "I'm not getting anything from you, so you may be the most popular person in the world, my father, but I can't and won't compromise myself." But by and large, I decided, on balance, to try to stay with it. I suffered the consequences by choice, and I also got the benefits. He was incredibly bright and I built a relationship around that. The cost was to lose a sense of myself. To deal with a person like this you have to sublimate yourself thoroughly, right down to the merest, most arbitrary wish or desire, because doing otherwise can create a flash of violent conflict—or the end, the severing of the relationship.

It became the one thought in my life, that one false move and everything could stop.

End of an Era

San Francisco was coming of age. The small-town flavor was being replaced by a more cosmopolitan atmosphere. The Mom-and-Pop shops were disappearing; franchises were taking over. The hippies and flower children were being pushed out by an emerging "yuppie" class.

There was a sad inevitability to what was happening, and those who had been part of the city's heyday could only sit by and watch. Some of them responded with bitterness; others, like Enrico Banducci, welcomed the color and diversity of the new era.

Enrico was one of Don's closest and oldest friends. Throughout the years, *Enrico's* had been one of Don's haunts. Now that he was basically retired, it became his home away from home.

Enrico's was a European restaurant, small and intimate, with sidewalk tables facing Broadway. Everyone congregated there to meet old friends and new, to see and to be seen while sipping wine and watching San Francisco pass by: punk rockers and motorcycle mamas, artists, musicians, dancers, writers, hookers and pimps, together with men and women from the Financial District.

At the sidewalk tables you might bask in the sun or have to bundle up against the wind. Moving inside to wait for a table in the narrow bar area, you'd see the first bar stool by the door had a little brass plaque that read DON SHERWOOD.

Whatever else you might be doing, you'd be seen at *Enrico's* where, as Enrico says, "Sables or sandals were equally welcome."

Sitting in the restaurant one day, Don urged Enrico, "Let's do something *right* in the city, for God's sake, and bring some splendor to it! . . . You're Marshall Naify's friend. Let's tell him to dig up an old film for us. We'll go to his house, I'll rent a limousine, and we'll dress in tails."

ENRICO :

We told Marshall the name of the film we wanted to see, picked the night, and rented our tuxes. Three or four of us went to dinner and then to Marshall's on Vallejo—he owned United Artist and had a big place with a studio.

We all sat down to have some cognac like the big shots do, you know, acting all uppity and talking like "gentlemen." Finally, we said to the guy running the projector, "We're ready for the film now." After all this, the film comes on, and Marshall had gotten the wrong one!

Don started yelling, "What the fuck? I come to this place all spruced up, rent the limo. . . ." I started laughing, while Don kept on with "How dare he!" We couldn't be ritzy anymore. Marshall told us to come back the next week, and he'd get the right one, but that wouldn't do. We got back in the limo, and Don dropped me at *Enrico's*, still bitching that it cost him five hundred dollars! We looked like silly idiots, but we laughed all the way home.

One day I saw Don sitting there in the restaurant with a book. "Don't bother me, I'm reading," he said. He was reading *MY LIFE AND LOVES*, three volumes by Frank Harris—a porno writer—and I said, "What are you do-

ENRICO...

ing reading that dirty book?" He looked at me and said, "You see it as dirty, I see it as adventure! This guy really *had* it!" Harris always had a sexual thing going on, and everyone was reading that book back in the thirties. I told Don I'd read it when I was twelve. "That's why you're stunted!" he said. Sometimes he had philosophy books or whatever with him. You couldn't always see what he was reading. Often he'd sit reading for four or five hours in the corner.

I came in once, and Don yelled, "Hey, Ric come here! Guess what? I quit smoking today, and I quit drinking a week ago."

I was so happy. I sat there telling him how good he was going to feel. He rolled those eyes of his, with a devil's stare, while I went on and on. I patted him on the back, and when I came back ten minutes later he was at the bar having a cigarette! "Hey, Ric, you bastard, you got me smoking again!"

I'd have him over for Thanksgiving dinner, and he loved that. He always came in by himself. People might meet him there, but he always came in alone.

People would come to interview him, but by the time he'd had a few glasses of wine, they were likely to run out—tail between their legs. You couldn't be a weakling and interview Don! He would laugh and say, "*He's* going to write my story! Look at that. He can't even listen to me!"

He'd stick it to me all the time, never missing an opportunity to tell me what a pain in the ass I was. "You're a pseudo–intellectual," he'd say. "Get away from me, I don't want to talk to you anymore." So I'd say, "Fine! I'm not talking to you anymore either," and go away. Five minutes later, he'd call me over again, and I'd remind him, "I'm not talking to you anymore." "Hey, that was five minutes ago!" he'd whine.

He and Herb Caen would have their spats. Don would

ENRICO...

tell me about it, referring to Herb as "that guy that goes rat-a-tat-tat," imitating the typewriter. "Herb Caen, you mean?" I'd say. "Yeah, that bastard, look what he said about me. . . ." Next day they'd be having lunch, friends again.

I loved Don. He so loved life; he loved seeing people doing what they were doing.

Enrico's closed in 1988, but Enrico continues to live in San Francisco, pursuing related business interests. The *hungry i* had already closed its doors in 1970, by which time Don had been essentially out of the public eye for two years. Because he had left so abruptly—and stayed away— his fans were left with a lingering question: whatever happened to Sherwood?

Gene Nelson was still doing the night show on KSFO. In December of 1972, he convinced Don to do a radio interview.

GENE :

Don wouldn't come to the station because he hated KSFO and everyone there, we did the taping at my house.

He said he was glad to be out of radio and that he should never have gotten into it because it was the wrong thing for him. He had decided he should have gone into the navy and been a sailor—he couldn't handle radio without drinking. It was always one with the other. He didn't believe he could be successful without the drinking. Now he was in AA and hadn't had a drink in four years. Part of the AA program is for the person to go back and make peace with everyone he's dumped on, so Don did this in the interview.

I broadcast that interview twice. There was a tremen-

GENE...

dous response. The papers were full of Sherwood again, so after that he looked on me as a friend.

At forty-seven, after divorcing himself from his old life, the Pied Piper was convinced he had learned to play a new tune.

In truth, he had put away his flute.

Inner Journey

Having played to an audience of over a million people, Don now played to a handful, with his children front row center. His roles ranged from Lucifer to God, but they were all memorable performances.

When Diane invited him to play Father at her wedding to the fisherman she had fallen in love with, his RSVP was a note that read, "Have a nice life." The wedding came off, as planned, and Diane and her groom happily went off to live on a fishing boat in Eureka.

"He stopped talking to me, and that became mutual," Diane says. "He thought the only legitimate reason to get married was to have children, and I was getting married to go fishing. He didn't like any expression of romanticism."

This was quite a contradiction in the sense that Don was, according to Greg, "an incurable romantic," and that there was a new lady in Don's life, Sandy Utter.

Diane dropped out of sight, and Robin followed suit. After graduating, Robin moved to Thailand with her math teacher, without her father's knowledge or consent. They were still not on speaking terms, not only because of the blowup over Pete Scott, but because much of Don's rage against life had been directed at Robin. He saw too much of himself in her. It was easier to avoid her than to face the reflection.

ROBIN :

Sandy told me that, when I was in Thailand, Dad would play this song about a love being gone and get all moody over me! When I came back, he sent me to Humboldt State. This was the beginning of me realizing that maybe he did like me.

We began to get closer, and I started to see real love from him. He'd still turn around and bite me, but I was starting to understand him, and I was beginning to get into psychology myself, so I could relate to him through that. We'd sit at *Enrico's*, and he'd say, "I did this because . . . you've got to understand. . . ." He could be so lucid about why he'd hurt all of us. He had told me I was shit for so long—and if your father tells you you're shit, you live like you are. I responded to his early rejection of me much like he did to his mother's and developed an "I don't care about you" attitude. As a child, I'd refuse to cry when he yelled at me with that voice that seemed to threaten my very existence.

But now there was a new beginning for us.

Dr. Lion had told him that he was a classic example of a psychopath, but that because of his *gift*, he was able to make enough money to never get desperate. I think the reason I'm walking and talking today is that Dad was becoming a psychologist.

His favorite line was "We are all victims of victims." When we went over and over why he did what he did, he based everything on the fact that he was an abused child, which forced him to use all of his resources. He existed only in other people's eyes, with no sense of self. He needed the big arena because alone, he didn't exist.

His mother, Inga, never wanted him and was never able to give him even the most basic sense of self-worth. His Aunt Marie kept asking him why he continued to try to get through to his mother. He wanted to let go and accept the injustice, but he couldn't. He was bitter until the end.

Dad had a theory about the heart. He saw it as a cup

ROBIN...

that is open to love when we're young. As we grow, a lid forms over it, and no more love can get in. If we got very little, we're screwed for life. He felt crippled, yet his capacity to give and receive love did expand. And as he changed, my life changed.

Don was no longer playing a game of mental gymnastics. His attempt to make his life meaningful was an inner journey that promised to be permanent. His new perspective was not only long overdue for his own growth, it was also essential to his children's eventual ability to overcome the emotional handicaps that he had created in them—

GREG :

At a young age I was trying to figure out why he was the way he was. It was a major preoccupation of mine.

He played such a heavy role in my life as a parent and as a person. I was always dealing with the friction. This human being, so fraught with all these problems and complications, was not giving me what other people were getting from their parent. How was I to relate to what I got? The perspective I needed was not born of him extending himself—being Fitzgerald reading about Fitzgerald. It does fixate you unless you have a great deal of personal time and power to become better. But if you are essentially a paranoid, hypersensitive person, like he was, why take the chance? When in doubt, do what everybody loves.

ROBIN :

When I was little, he would make me pee in my pants from fear, he had such power. But when he liked you, when he was shining his light on you—or rather on himself via you—you'd bask in it. His self-love was contagious.

ROBIN...

He could fake you out, short term, and seduce you into thinking he was interested in you, but he couldn't maintain it. His needs overrode the impulse to give selflessly. It's the curse of egotism, I guess. All the adulation in the world never healed him, his self-hate had the last word. He said that his IQ was in battle with his EQ—his emotional quotient. His emotional side crippled him and prevented him from utilizing his high IQ. He would go from thinking he was shit to knowing he was the answer to life—the narcissistic swing. He could pontificate with absolute conviction, but if you disagreed with him, he'd recoil. He needed his version of reality supported totally, or there was trouble.

This was as frightening a time for Don as it was for his children; opening wounds to examine them, opening himself up for the first time to scrutiny and judgment. But he was battling an almighty trigger within him that could fire at any moment.

It was a time to back up and catch those people whom he had lost along the way, including himself.

The previous year he had discovered the Sea of Cortez. "I've found beauty and a place where a man can be a man," Don told everyone. "I'm taking the houseboat, and that's where I'm going to live for the rest of my life. I've thrown away all of my press clippings."

Don had found "paradise" before.

John Wasserman of the *San Francisco Examiner* had interviewed Don and wrote:

> Dan Cohelan is on his way to paradise. At 4 p.m. Saturday, or thereabouts, he and his houseboat are scheduled to leave by truck for somewhere in Southern California, the better to be launched in quiet waters. The former $2500-a-week disc jockey, now a $250-a-week itinerant voyager on the seas of earth and mind, has left for the waters of Baja, California, there to join

battle with Demon Nicotine, the final barrier between Dan Cohelan and the truth.

We sat last week in Denny's coffee shop and talked with Don. At first I thought he did protest too much. A man who has truly got himself together doesn't spend all his time announcing that fact. Doesn't have to. I thought of the endless employment of quotations—B. F. Skinner, the Greeks, the Chinese, Sandburg, Shakespeare—often the mark not of an educated man, but the reverse.

I thought of the cliches which dot his conversation: "I was programmed," "I hired people to love me," "I got courage out of a bottle," "I was lucky." Yet if these be pretensions, they are innocent enough. The joy of discovery. The thrill of a new toy. The fearlessness of a Court Fool, confident in his special invulnerability.

Talk with anyone who has discovered a misspent life, then opened a new account; Synanon people, Scientologists, alcoholics on the wagon. Same thing. Same child-like freshness, same evangelical tedium. But Dan Cohelan is different on two counts. One, he is always entertaining. Two, his perceptions are remanded to his own custody, not imposed on an unwaiting world. He tells the truth and nothing but the truth. He tries to live the truth. Only the truth presently escapes him.

"Be honest with yourself. Do what YOU want to do; not what is dictated by others," he says. As philosophy, there's less there that meets the eye. As a personal creed, it is his liberation. "I am, finally, my own best friend," Don says.

Don lasted a week in "paradise" before he was back looking for an apartment.

"What most people don't understand," Don's friend Russ Coughlan says, "is what it's like to have a whole city pretending to be your buddy, everyone saying they know you—saying, 'Don and I were sitting around in the bar'— yeah, yeah! Everywhere he went it was that way, which made him disregard people. He'd say, 'Who am I? A nothing—so why kiss my ass?' "

Each step Don took, out into the world that he now chose to face head-on with no celebrity status, no crutches, and no protection, called upon a courage that was very different from that of a rebel.

The courage had to come from his very core. In order to reach it, he had to open himself up and face all the pain he had been anesthetizing. He couldn't do it all at once. He started drinking again. It had been too difficult, too soon.

Coming Back

Isolated with his thoughts and increasingly aware of the pain inherent in the process he had started, it became easier each day for Don to listen to the voice within him that said, Maybe you should go back to what you know, while you still can. Another voice added, A year–and–a–half after you leave your show, you walk down the street, and no one knows you.

He could see himself down that road—an unknown, alcoholic old man, eating at the counter of *Mannings* coffee shop, a sweat-marked, beaten-up hat set to the side as he ate his roast beef sandwich and mashed potatoes.

He had to do something, and do it now!

Elma Greer, KSFO records librarian, had kept in touch after he left the station. They had gone out to dinner a few times and to a couple of concerts and football games. In May of 1974, she was told in confidence that Don was talking to the station about coming back.

ELMA GREER:

I started to sneak out music to him, so he could get caught up. You should have heard his comments about the music!

KSFO was having their annual KSFO LOVES YOU promotion trip to Hawaii. At Don's insistence, I pre-

ELMA...

tended to be sick, and everyone else went off. But before he and I could get to work, Don called me and said *he* was sick. I had stayed home for nothing!

Don wanted to come back as program manager and have me be the program director. I didn't think his life with KSFO was going to last because of his history and his health. I told him I would be of more help to him in the library working with the deejays. He made his assistant, Sharon Meyers program director and gave her a terrible time.

Once he was back, life was hell. I worked eighteen hours a day, and he kept changing his mind about everything. We worked Saturdays and Sundays, along with Sandy, who worked right by him. He kept saying, "I want the *sound*, the sound!" I cried a lot.

Sandy was great, a very funny lady. Their relationship was an up and down thing, but she was good for him. She was stable. Being Sherwood's lady was not easy. All his ladies had to cater to him—come in and bring his coffee, come into the library and get his records—and Sandy did all that. I thought, How would you like to have to wipe his ass every morning? We went through hell, trying to get what was in his brain on the air.

Bill Moen, a long-time, familiar voice on San Francisco's KABL, had suffered in earlier years, listening to Don "do everything I wanted to do" as morning man. "For many years, it was station policy at KABL that we couldn't say our names—ever—which was like being a ghost," says Bill. "Don had all the freedom, and I envied him.

"When he left in 1969, I thought, Thank God he retired! Now the rest of us have a chance. When he came back, my sales manager, Bill Clark, came in and announced: 'It's all over. Sherwood's back. The inmates are in charge of the asylum!' "

"Sherwood and I had kind of patched up our differences from before by the time he came back," Gene Nelson says. "But I got myself in trouble again."

GENE NELSON:

I was doing the 9 to noon shift. Sherwood called me in and asked me what I thought about the station. I gave him my input. Then he called me in and asked if I was happy on my shift. I said, "Yes and no—it isn't where I want to be all my life. . . ." He asked what my preference was, and I said the morning show, although I didn't mean "I want your job." I could see the light go out of his eyes, and it was all over.

Every day I'd come in and find letters from listeners with their critical comments underlined, lying on my desk. What a way to start my day. It was insidious. I finally went to Sherwood and said, "I understand the critical letters and you sharing them with me, but why not share the good letters too? I think's that only fair." He said, "We don't get any good letters."

"We had just returned from Hawaii when we were all informed that Don was back," Jim Lange says. "I had been at KSFO quite a while by then. I got tossed out of the morning slot again when Don decided he was the morning man. This time it hurt more than the previous times."

A lot of people were let go, including Al Newman, Don's very good friend—causing a wound that would never heal. Don also tried to move Jim Lange to the afternoon, but that was in conflict with Jim's television show.

"Don was trying to do too much. His rule was to play a tremendous amount of music, yet he was not giving us that example in his morning show," Jim adds. "I left after a while, although, again, my contract said 'morning show,' so I continued to get paid."

Bill Shaw, Don's father image, friend, and former general manager, who had been vital to Don's success, comments: "Coming back as program manager was not a good idea. Don didn't have the patience to work with other people. It's like a very good baseball player not being a good manager because he's not patient with others who are not as good as he is."

"As far as I'm concerned, Don was the best deejay in the whole country," Russ "the Moose" Syracuse says. Russ is a popular San Francisco radio personality now on KFRC. "I was at KSFO back in 1969 before Don left, doing a bit called 'Love Line.' Don would call in, disguising his voice, pretending to be a neurotic, lovesick guy who needed to talk to someone. I'd guess it was Don, eventually.

"I was working the all-night shift when Don came back. The first thing he did was cut my exhausting schedule from six nights a week to five. He's the only P.D. who *ever* did anything for an all-night guy. We were fellow philosophers, so simpatico."

Gary Mora, who would later become a well-known KSFO deejay and creator of the Gary Mora Road Show productions, was then a kid in his early twenties, working as a producer/engineer and technician with Don.

"The night before he went back on the air, he was so nervous," Gary remembers. "He said, 'They're expecting fireworks, and it won't happen.' There had been a lot of media coverage leading up to his return. He wasn't in good shape, so short of breath that he couldn't get through reading a commercial without using his atomizer.

"I remember him coming to me after he saw me bringing in my sleeping bag for between shifts, saying, 'Mora, you're crazy! Take it easy.'

"Sandy was with him all the time, even though they fought a lot. She loved him so much, and he depended on her. She'd say, 'Oh, he's so soft,' and get all teary-eyed. I remember when my son was born with a deformity, Don was very compassionate."

The fans wanted their old Don back on the airwaves—though many people were justifiably skeptical. Ronnie Schell threw in his two-cents' worth—

D. S.:

R. S. here from glamorous Hollywood, the city you never conquered. How are you, big fella? I heard from the grapevine that you were coming out of retirement again. Well, congratulations and welcome back to show-biz. This news is most welcome, and I understand that everyone is discussing your return.

I understand you are going back to your 6-9 show sometime this week and are going to devote your first program to discussing all the exciting and adventurous things you've done the past five years. I think it's a great beginning, Don, but tell me, what will you talk about the rest of the 2 hours and 56 minutes?? And of course you realize that getting back into the public eye again will require you to do a lot of things you never really enjoyed doing. You know, dating girls: oh, and naturally, you'll have to have a whole set of new 8 x 10 glossy photographs. Is it true that you will also serve as program director, in charge of the music played on the station? If so, what great news for people like Kay Kyser, Hilo Hattie, and the Chordettes.

I guess the only negative aspect of this letter, Don, is to have to inform you that in the time you've been gone, I have moved far, far ahead of you in the B.T.S.B. (big time show biz). In fact, the last time I looked at the list of popular Bay Area personalities, I had moved up to #27, just ahead of George Cerruti and his entire accordion, while you were down to #88, just below Marjorie Trumbull, but tied with Al "Papagayo" Williams' dead parrot.

Well, D. S., as one of your three closest friends, (or have you sold those two big mirrors?), I can only say that I am sincerely happy you are back on the air. I must sign off for now but will drop a line or two later with all the news from the big time. And as I've so often told you, keep in constant touch . . . there's so little time.

Your friend,
R. S.

D. S.:

R. S. here from Hollywood. First of all, I was sent a copy of the article Mary Stanyan did on you in the Examiner a couple weeks back. For the most part I thought she did a fine job. For those of us who know you well, it was possible to detect a few minor errors . . . You erred when you said that in the old days, you never dated funny women. Surely you'll recall that close friends who knew you intimately used to laugh loudly *whenever* they saw you with a girl. And Don, it never was the audiences that drove you crazy at the movies. You hated going because they always made you check your overcoat and hat at the candy counter. Incidentally, if there's still only "fair communication" with your son, try calling him Greg instead of Gary. However, one should excuse you for that. I understand that the mind often boggles at the mid-century mark. I think the best part of the article dealt with your feelings about sobriety. Not that you were ever really a bad drinker in the old days, D. S. . . . it's just that you never knew when to quit and it often mixed up your mind a bit, like one of the several times that you visited me at Lake Tahoe when I was playing Harrah's and I would come into the gambling casino early in the morning and find you with yet another drink in your hand, reeling in front of the slot machine yelling "Hit me! Hit me!" (needless to say, many patrons volunteered). And the casino guard would finally politely lead you out of the place, letting you stop briefly at the 21 table to attempt a yank at the dealer's handle.

I must leave you for now, pal.

See you next month,
old timer,
R. S.

To Everything
There Is
a Season

"**B**etween the years 1962 and 1964 alone, you could become an old-fashioned person," Terry McGovern comments. "In 1962 no one knew who the Beatles were—by 1964 no one didn't know who they were. So much was going on, the whole world changed.

"Don was not a part of the Beatles, the hippie movement, the Kent State ordeal, all the movements going on in San Francisco and across the country. He was a postwar San Francisco man from the past already, a man from the era that said men were those who drank and smoked and had lots of women. By the seventies, when he came back to radio, there was no way he could step into the current market."

"When rock and roll came in, stations began to program by computer," Jim Lange says. "A few stations had success with the younger demographics, age twelve to twenty-five, with kids who just wanted music, not personalities. FM radio came in about the same time, with better quality, so the big thing was to play three songs in a row, then five, then up to twelve in a row. The original "personality" concept of radio was gone—having someone on radio who is your friend."

Dave McElhatton comments: "Broadcasting was no longer driven by intuitive people like Bill Shaw, but rather by people saying, 'I haven't got the foggiest notion of what to do, so I'll hire a consultant, get a focus group together, and they'll tell me what to do.' That way, they can say, 'I didn't do it.'

"Bill Shaw was one of the last great gamblers, and Don was an innovator. Beyond all the laughing and scratching, he had things he really believed in. That's why his old show was the single most exciting thing going on in Bay Area radio in the sixties. Now, it was a new ball-game."

Chet Casselman makes an interesting observation, saying that the approach went from "We're *different*" to "They've got X, we've got X"—the attempt to be alike, with nothing to distinguish anything in the market. "Bright, young people became afraid to make a choice that was different, for fear that they would be criticized."

"When stations started grabbing people's attention with the 'more music' idea, their ratings forced the MOR—middle-of-the-road—stations to think they should be doing the same thing, Bob Hamilton, today program director at KSFO, says. "Everything in radio follows the ratings." Ratings are the significant source of information that we program by. Only three thousand people decide those ratings in the San Francisco market."

"The thing about radio is that the public constantly makes a choice. Ken Dennis, KSFO's present general manager, adds." They vote by the push of a button! If you don't like something anymore, you push a button. The public makes clear what they want from a radio station, and those ratings dictate everything."

In Don's day as King of Radio, he received so much fan mail, he never had to wonder what people were thinking. "Letter writing is a thing of the past," Bob Hamilton says. "Everything is 'instant'—it's all phones and fax machines. No one writes a letter, and you can hardly get them to send in a postcard. It's all too time-consuming. By the mid–sixties, communications had advanced, and competition had increased. Everyone's understanding of the radio medium grew. So, of course radio changed."

"Today, people listen for twenty or thirty minutes at a time! You don't have people tuning in for many hours at a time like they did twenty years ago. You developed a *personality* over those hours. People still want that personality, but they want it in ten minutes!" Ken Dennis comments. "Radio in the fifties and sixties was based on people taking the *time* to enjoy hours of listening. Just like today, they promoted music geared to their audience likes and dislikes."

"One day Don called the record promoters in and told them that he didn't want them to bring him any more records," Terry McGovern says, sounding incredulous even after all these years. " 'And nothing with a guitar!' Don specified. When he said that, one guy stood up and asked him, 'If this was thirty years ago, would you have said that about the piano?' We were all embarrassed for Don. He said he was going to play Frank Sinatra. It was a death knoll."

"Because Don was the king in the early sixties, he commanded the market—everyone followed him," Ken Dennis says. "But when he left, he lost that hold, and coming back six years later, he couldn't start off with whatever he wanted, since there were other established leaders by then. If he had come back ready to work with a program director in place, who was familiar with the market, ready to work together, to gradually get back into it, he may have been able to rise to the top again."

GENE NELSON:

Sherwood, as program manager, was very aloof. He'd sit back like the king. Decisions were made, and bodies would fall, all behind closed doors. I had seen the other

GENE...

side of him—the charming and supportive side—but like most drunks, he had a mean side, and this was it.

The skids were being greased for me. I knew I was going to be fired, that he had it planned. But as it turned out, he was gone before I was.

ELMA GREER:

People thought he was behind the times, but in fact, he was always early with his ideas, ahead of his time. With the internal pressure from sales and other areas, no one could understand what he wanted to do. He called in all kinds of people to help, but it didn't work. He rushed into it. We were working on the programming, and all of a sudden, he put himself on the air as well, instead of waiting. He didn't have the energy to do both. Being morning man and program manager are both full-time jobs. If he'd given us six months to get the music the way he wanted, sat in for someone once in a while, and then gone on the air, it might have worked.

Jack Carney, Jim Lange, and Terry McGovern were on the air. Jack finally said, "I could have the number one ratings in this town, but there's only one number one person in this town—Sherwood. I have to be number one." He went to St. Louis, where he became the biggest thing that had ever happened there.

Don wasn't as good on the air as he had always been, maybe because the emphysema was getting worse, and he didn't have Charlie Smith to throw the wild tracks at him. Charlie and Don had had a misunderstanding a while before this, and Sherwood had gotten upset, so Charlie left him and went into the engineering dept. Bob Texeira became Don's engineer. He worked well with Don but without the wild tracks. And Aaron wasn't there anymore. Don resorted to reading out of the *Readers Digest*. The spontaneity and creativity weren't there. He was bored.

ELMA...

Still the listeners were loyal. We threw everything at them, and they hung in there. They were excited that Don was back, but I can't say they felt the same once he was on the air. We stopped getting the feedback.

When Don finally left the station, he claimed it was my fault that he was not successful. I never heard from him again.

As many times as he had said he would never become a has-been, never overstay his success, Don had been sucked in. In May 1975, when he finally accepted the fact that his return had been a mistake, he said goodbye to the place where he had spent most of the mornings of his life.

There were no bets on his return.

On April 30, 1976, Don and Sandy were married in Las Vegas. Each of his wives' names had started with "S": Svetlana, Sally, Shirley, Suzie. It defied coincidence and invited interpretation. Now there was Sandy. Maybe, just maybe, it could work this fifth time around.

Don told Mary Stanyan of the *San Francisco Examiner* that Sandy was ". . . not a career girl: she's a homebody with two children. And funny. She breaks me up, and I break her up, which is good for my ego. But if ten years ago you had told me I'd go for a girl who was amusing, I'd have said *that* was the funniest remark I ever heard."

Don was fifty-one and feeling his mortality. Sandy had been the woman in his life for several years. Everyone close to him was glad they were together . . . but the marriage did not survive.

"Don called me after he and Sandy separated," Marilyn Walker says. "He remembered that when we were first together, all those years ago, Gavin Arthur's horoscopes for us had predicted that we would have 'a beautiful melting of the minds' when Don was 52 years old. I had never stopped loving him, but I knew if I got close to him again, it would start all over. I dared not go to San Francisco. I had already chosen *my* life over our life together, and moved forward. So I didn't go to see him, and I didn't tell him I was getting a divorce at that time, too. While I couldn't be with Don, I never regretted a single moment of our past."

Alone again, Don went through a mental process of elimination. Who were the most important people in his life? There were three who could provide him with his raison d'être: Diane, Greg, and Robin.

Atonement

Don began a process of reconciliation with his children. The complexity of this maneuver, in light of all that he had to make amends for, demanded that he tackle one child at a time.

Diane and her husband of three years happened to have their fishing boat hauled out in the boat yard in Sausalito, near Don's boat. "Dad would walk by every day, but ever since my wedding, we hadn't talked. My husband said, 'Go and talk to him, tell him we're here, show him the boat and what you're doing.' So one day I went up to him and said, 'Hi Dad, it's me!' He got really defensive and acted strange. I asked him to come and see our boat, and he said, 'Well, maybe I'll stop by one of these days.' Then someone he knew came up to us, and he introduced me by saying, 'Hey, this is one of my kids . . . ah . . . ah . . . Diane.' I left and didn't talk to him again for two years."

He'd have to come back to her later.

Don began to see Robin more often and to write letters to her. Al Newman aptly describes Robin as "Don in drag." Jack Erdmann, Don's AA partner and close personal friend, describes Don and Robin as "identical minds clashing." Both descriptions define and explain the dynamics of their ever-impassioned battle.

There is no clearer expression of Don's heart and mind

than the series of letters he wrote to Robin over the nine-year period following his farewell to public life. As he searched intensely for *the* answers to his lifelong questions, he felt compelled to impart his thoughts and beliefs to this particular daughter—his alter ego.

What began as a few notes soon expanded into a chronicling of events, tantamount to a journal.

Dearest Robin,
   Most important to any seeker after truth is to listen closely to the opposition. The truth (or near truth, if you will) will definitely stand the test of time.
   Because, understandably, the world overwhelms them, most people want desperately for magic things to be true.
                                   My love,

                                   Dad

★ ★ ★

My dearest Robin,
   Once upon a time, a friend of my Mama's said, "That boy should have an education! At least he should finish high school!" So this dear friend of my mother's ponied up the necessary moolah and off I went to a private school.
   I had quit three high schools up until that time. It should have been obvious to everyone concerned that I *really* wasn't cut out for formal education.
   I went to the Bates school over on Sacramento Street, with all the rich-bitch failures, had the English teacher try to stick his wee-wee up my young well-formed bung, listened to hours of droning, dull, rhetorical redundancy, and one afternoon about a month before graduation, I walked down the steps, never to return. I don't know if I ever really regretted it. "There are some things some animals can't do," Dr. Seuss says.
   All of this by way of saying to you that your college attendance, your curriculum, your employment plans and ideas for the future—none of these are etched in stone! Baby doll, if you sit down one day and quietly say to yourself that it ain't what you thought it would be and you

don't like it and you'd rather live in Philadelphia, so what? Whatever you do, feel or are, I support you one hundred percent.

I had an interesting thought about romantic love. Without *hope*, the human animal is a pretty dismal creature. Could it be that the only thing that gives us true Hope is when we are in the throes of a mad a-building love affair, knowing full well the eventual consequences must have a debilitating effect on our subconscious? So it might not be love, per se, but rather a hope for the future that is involved in our rather continuous search. Would it not be more rewarding to put Romantic Love where it belongs and replace it with goals of *several* different sorts? Maybe even one or two that might be achieved?

Love,

In the midst of this progressive trend, things suddenly reversed. Inexplicably, the letters stopped and communications went dead. Robin, accepting this as par for the course, continued to work at her menial job and live in "some little hovel." She was twenty-five.

In 1978, Don had a very bad emphysema attack that landed him in the hospital. Diane came to see him once he got home and was off medication.

"He apologized to me for being such a strange father, and from then on, we didn't have any more real disagreements. I could talk to him and tell him exactly what I thought. He said, 'You know, I really think you might be a real human being! You really do feel things, maybe you do love me.' Then, of course, he'd turn around and say, 'I can always count on you to talk too much, to take over.' But he was a balance for me, telling me things like 'Don't end up like your mother. Stop saying the word *safe*. Leave that out of your life.' "

The cold war with Robin also began to dissolve—

"One day Dad called, out of the blue. He'd decided he wanted 'to be a father again,' " Robin says. "We went to *Enrico's*, and he asked what he could do for me, since I was such a mess. Going to India was the most important thing to me—I'd been studying Hinduism since 1973. 'You got it!' he said. I was overjoyed! We got drunk together, and I went back to work and told everyone I was quitting and going to India. The next day Dad called and said, 'Hey, listen, I was really drunk. I just can't do this India thing. I'm sorry, Hon.' I said, 'Oh, okay.' I didn't want to give him any attitude about it. He imagined enough without my help.

"Then a few months later, he came around again. By February of the next year, I was on my way to India, with an around-the-world ticket and two thousand dollars. We had a bon voyage party, and he came to the airport to see me off. Mom wrote me that after I got on the plane, Dad burst into tears, at 6 a.m. and totally sober! It blew my mind to think of him feeling that way for me. It was rare for him to show such vulnerability."

[To Robin in India]

March, 1979

Dearest daughter,

Your letters are like pearls. Even though you may not hear from me or anyone back here, keep writing. I don't really know if this will reach you.

In spite of homesickness and colds, you still sound full of adventure and love of what you're doing. Keep it up. There are answers to questions out there—don't even consider giving up until you can reasonably and intellectually stand behind your decision to do so.

The only problem I feel from you is your goddamned adherence to what I consider the worst possible diet for a hyperactive human, which you are . . . I am currently living proof that the chicken is man's most noble friend. That and the exclusion of milk and wheat. Your father (Father of the Century) is so on top of things it is becoming frightening to friends and relatives.

If things continue to improve, health-wise, I have the inkling of an idea I might be up to coming over to Greece and meeting you for a week. I think I'm good for a week—maybe four days. Maybe lunch on the piazza?

Greg has gotten his baby self a job with "FOCUS" magazine. He sells space in the mag and helps with the advertising designs. We'll see.

Keep sending those marvelous letters and cards and stay well—try a chicken and know that I LOVE you very much.

Dad

★ ★ ★

[To Robin, back from India]

Rob,

I just know you'll either give me a call or send me a nice note, saying "Thank you, Dad, for the money and the typewriter." I just know you will. And it won't be a snide or unforgiving "Thank You" either. It'll be from a sense of appreciation.

Won't it?

Dad

★ ★ ★

December 1979

Dearest Rob,

Out of the mud grows the Lotus. Out of your sense of loss and feelings of loneliness, that pendulum has started to swing. Now the problem is to get it to swing both ways, between work and pleasure, steadily and not in great sweeps.

A friend of mine stays with his lined and wrinkled, ill-tempered, fat, old wife because he learned as a child, by osmosis, that is what one does. His parents stuck together no matter what. I know, I was there. His wife sticks with him because her parents lived on a farm where the answer to life was to have eight kids and hold on, through thick and thin, forever. They had that kind of lifestyle as a template.

They are not smarter than you or me—nor do they have bigger goddamned hearts! They learned a certain set of reactions when they were cubs.

What did you learn when you were a cub?

You grew up with a whole different set of rules of conduct. Leopards are very uncomfortable sitting in a damp bog and croaking. Very few frogs bite impalas on the neck.

The unseen force you call "God" and I call "That's-The-Way-Things-Are" will always be a factor in the study time of your life. However, it might be worth your while to research all the books you can find on the subject of love. Talk to some successful marrieds if you can find some.

Old Maid—dedicated to her work—sounds romantic but it won't work. As Jacob Bronowski said, "The human animal is unique among all animals, he is both solitary and social." As you have a super intelligence, putting some of your energies in this direction will bear fruit.

I am feeling better than I have ever felt in all my born days. Ran across a book by a Dr. Abrahamson—*"Body, Mind & Sugar"*—changed my whole goddamned habits, and I'm beginning to reap the rewards. It is truly phenomenal.

We are truly alike, and this has done some truly funky things to my brain pan. I have been alone but not lonely. I have been constructively busy, and comparatively speaking, affirmative beyond my wildest hopes. Maybe everything isn't chemical, but a hell of a lot IS.

Come over and let me fix good food for you. We will sit on the boat and be a part of the water and the sea birds and the mountain, and we shall talk of cabbages and kings and I will make a valiant effort not to pontificate.

Love you,

★ ★ ★

October 1980

Dearest Daughter,

As my hero "Kojak" would say, "Who loves ya Baby?"
Be not in dismay at any lack of communication. You sound
very busy, either working or being very confused. I have
been out of town, now and then, trying to find a local
Shangri-La, with no success.

Did Brother Buzz turn you on to the Sept. issue of
Psychology Today—an article titled "Schlemiel Children?"
Marvelous!! An in-depth study done on the "class clown/
funny grown-up" syndrome. I got a great deal from it, one
thing being why Dr. Lion, working as long and hard as he
did with me, didn't get very far.

I have become proficient at salad making and would love
it if you could get over my way and partake of greens and
brilliant exchange. I would always drive you home. Do call.

Love,

Don was now living part-time in the Bay Area and the
other part of the year in Palm Springs. His health went up
and down, getting better and then worsening. In Palm
Springs he met a woman, Vera, whom none of Don's family or friends ever met. All that is known is that Vera was
very devoted to Don and took care of his every need.

★ ★ ★

Dear Rob,

I got a call, after four months, from Sandette Marie. She
simply stated it—"I can get laid better, I can go more places,
I don't have to wonder what is coming next, but by God,
Sherwood, nobody talks like you do!" Another blow for
high intelligence (or high bullshit). At least Sandy and I can
be friends, and I truly enjoy rapping with her.

My growth, both physical and mental, is steady and
satisfying. In fact, I have the answer to life!! The answer to
life is the continual search for the answer to life. How's
that?

I do love you and it is so gratifying to be able to be a part of your most apparent growth and joy. Keep it up, watch your health, and *be* Robin Sherwood Cohelan at all times, because Robin Sherwood Cohelan is ONE of a kind. Unique . . . and so very dear to me.

Love,

Dad

★ ★ ★

Transformation

"**Y**ou transform people by love, and Dad started doing that," Robin says. "He started to see that he could live through me. I was like him, a self-styled philosopher, unable to stick with a straight job for long. I inherited his restlessness. He was incredibly tolerant of me constantly changing jobs and plans. He said that he, too, was a 'late bloomer.' What a gift that understanding was to me!"

Don and Robin had passed the test of honesty, and trust was making excellent progress.

[From Palm Springs]

February 1981

Dearest Robin,

I am so distressed to hear of your illnesses. You have come from unbalanced people, perhaps, but both yo' mama and me have the resiliency of alley cats. So should thee.

My day is like this:

7-8 AM:	Sit and meditate, or what passes for it
8-8:30:	Walk the 4th fairway of Palm Springs golf course
8:30-9:	Breakfast/Cold meat balls, mustard, lettuce and mayo, apricots (no sugar)
9-10:	Digest the above while writing letters or

	doing foolish things with paper and pen— budget, stock market, etc.
10-11:	Maintenance: shopping, cleaning, errands
11-11:30:	Walk the fairway again
11:30-12:30:	Lunch on the sun-drenched patio. Chicken salad.
12:30-1:30:	Nap while digesting
1:30-3:	Swim—ever so slowly but beautifully
3-4:30:	Practice piano lessons!
4:30-5:30:	Read the paper
5:30-6:	Walk the fairway
6 PM:	Turn on "MASH" and eat dinner
7 PM:	TV, shower, talk with Vera-deara
9:30/10 PM:	Bed

Most days I don't have enough time to do everything.
Please be well.

> My love goes North
> to you,

★ ★ ★

March 1981

Dearest Daughter, Mystic of the Mission —

This will be my last communication from Shangri-La for this year. I shall be coastbound the first of April.

Vera-deara and I shall spend a week overlooking the Pacific Ocean at Laguna Beach—great little studio with dos beds and a kitchen, and a chance to breathe some ocean air, which because of the current temp of 85, seems rather a good idea.

I shall be in the Bay Area on the 7th of April for six days. I hope we can lunch it or dinner, and tell each other of our plans and adventures, OK? I will call you until I get you. I rectum I shall be spending those days on the boat in Sausalito—the air is good and the price is right.

Then—are you ready for this? I plan to take off for an exploration of the whole Pacific coast, all the way to Victoria, B.C. This with an eye toward finding a possible summer retreat. Neat little plan—Winter in Palm Springs,

Summer on the coast. Plan B—off to London town for the year. There I can explore the streets, research the Adrenal Gland in the great medical libraries, write to you, play the piano, and take side trips to Lisbon, Crete, the Rhine . . . Amazing, isn't it, what a judicious adherence to one's correct chemical intake can produce?

Much love,

★ ★ ★

June 1981

Dearest daughter,

So you are bad—so what? Almost anyone who has known me for a week or so will reiterate that I'm as mean as cat shit on a pump handle! . . . and yo' mama wasn't any rose either!

Difficult as this time might be, did it ever strike you that those people and the job that you offended might possibly have no place in your life anymore? The only real problem is CHANGE. We humans still have that residual prehistoric dislike for *change*.

Whenever, if ever, you come and visit me, I have ten pages of a marvelous allergy book that you must read. It simply substantiates what I have suspicioned for two years. And it's not a fad, kook book. It finally has been recognized by even the conservative Medical profession that there are mood swing factors in diet.

Know that your summer job is about as pleasant a look ahead as a big boil on the behind, but think of it this way— every day you go in to a job that doesn't please or reward you—remember that you have those two years ahead chock full of options and variables to make damn sure that you don't end up having to do this mundane bullshit for the rest of your life or until you sell your ass to some guy out of pure desperation! You, my bright beauty, are going to find exactly what suits you . . . I know these things because I am close to the source. (The force)

I think your decision is gutsy and very wise.

All hail the academic life!

All hail the thinking life!

If you are in need of conversation, dinner, a bit of fatherly advice, or anything at all, just dial HELLO-TA—believe it or not, that's my new telephone number.

I love you so much,

[signature]

★ ★ ★

July 1981

Dearest Daughter,

Vera-deara has left the premises. This was by mutual agreement. I am on the road to facing life without all the doping support systems and find that Vera did not meet certain standards, or vice versa.

I have developed a hypothesis: If one tends to change from a prince to a frog, and then change back again, and again . . . it makes it very difficult for semi-normal people to know what the hell is going on! Plus the fact that when you meet someone as a frog and you change back to the prince, the prince doesn't like the person who liked the frog in the first place—if you get what I mean.

I think I was a prince when I met Sandy. I had not had a drink in better than a year. I stayed prince-like for another two years.

Then, in April, 1974, I changed into a frog with the help of my favorite all-time drug, alcohol. The frog has a tendency to cry a lot, throw up, and screw around with whores.

Despite my attempts to convince Sandy of the beauty of my multiplicity, she couldn't buy it. She had loved the prince and kissing the frog made her puke.

On the other hand, when I met Vera, I was the frog in full croaking bloom. I was just the weak-kneed, bullshit filled, little ball-less boy that pleased her. During the past few months there has been a fear in Vera's heart that some kind of heinous change was taking place. Every time I would reach a point where the green skin would start to fade and some of the beauty of the prince would begin to show through, Vera would puke. She digs frogs.

I have now decided that as tough as it may be, I choose to end my days as a prince. I want to look at everything without dope. I may well end up killing myself having to face up to the fact that I *think* the world owes me a living, and the world doesn't! But it will be more satisfying than burbling along like a frog.

I love you,

★ ★ ★

My dearest daughter,

Thank you very much for the thoughtful letter. I'm sure that your meeting with the psychic ladies must have struck a ding-dong in your memory bank that caused a reflection of some of the things that Dear Departed Dr. Lion must have covered. I know he did with me and we are so much the same—by blood and by background.

My father deserted me and never came back, and my mother found her role too taxing and overwhelming so she vacillated between smothering me as her own little living doll and castigating me when I was other than a little doll. I developed the same problem you have. I don't trust ANYBODY, and therefore I must continually test them. Then I pick people who will fail me, thereby reinforcing my beliefs that "People are no damn good!" This allows me to stay in a nice, comfortable, effortless, static position in life. To be vulnerable (and lose *control* of a relationship or situation) frightens me beyond my capability to EVER be such.

If I do get the love, service and friendship of someone, at least now I will try to treat it with more delicacy and understanding. Vera is no longer a "goddamn fool for loving me," that just happens to be the way Vera is. I will never love her. I can't. But remember, maybe you can't return their love, but you can be kind.

I remember and think back to our first confrontation of note. . . Obviously, you were already distrustful of people —even your own father, and so you tested me. Wrong move! I was so goddamn self-deprecatory that I figured in your youth (2 or 3 years old) you must be still wise enough, and not clouded by the world, to be able to look deep and see who I really was—a BAD CAT. Can you believe a man in his thirties thinking that kind of weak-kneed drivel? Had I been self-assured, I would have realized that the years spent with yo' mama and yo' grandma had confused you, and that you needed my love and help more than anything in the world. It has taken a long time for me to figure that one out! It is never too late.

Former Frightened Father

Dearest Daughter,

Talking to you thru print is one of my favorite pastimes. Verbal bullshit sometimes comes too easily to me, and does not mean as much as this business of having to think a bit first. (Plus the fact that you can always say, "But you said, Daddy . . .")

You write: "I've been on this path for a long time, but it has taken me a while." For years I used the tag line to an old joke—"It doesn't take me long to look at a horseshoe." Now I find that I have been blowing smoke up my own ass —it really does take me a long while to look at a horseshoe or anything else.

I believe it has to do with the Think/Feel syndrome. Not only are you and I allergic to almost everything in the goddamn world, but here, in a nutshell is what else you have to fight. Dr. Heinz Kohut, considered the "new Freud," viewed emotional problems as stemming from early injuries to the child's developing sense of "self," and focused on narcissism. He believed that without warm relationships and unconditional acceptance early on, children cannot feel worthwhile when they reach adulthood. Lonely and understimulated, they'll spend their lives in pursuit of attention, admiration, unrealistic goals and insatiable ambitions. Their shaky self-esteem and inability to form satisfying relationships with others will lead to delinquency, depressions, alcoholism, addictions,

perversions and dangerous risk taking. Does this sound like
anyone you know?

You write, "Do I deserve this?" You deserve everything
good that happens to you. Anything bad is just the result of
poor management, either yours or God's. First check to see
if you blew it, if not, then get on God's case. . . .

Take it one step at a time, dear heart. And *think*—that's
what we do best. You're doing the best you can with your
mama, and if you have to send me a "Fuck You" letter,
send ahead, because I know, just as I have finally
understood the Queen of Fairfax, so too will you
understand me. She did the best she could, as I am doing.

Love you,

Dad

★ ★ ★

November 1981

Dearest Daughter,

Discoveries whilst gaining energy thru correct diet,
practically no smoking, perfect living conditions: I must
learn to accept three things which have always been an
anathema to me; boredom, bullshit, and bad health. I am
the cause of all three. I can try to eliminate them from my
life but it will never be 100% successful so I must learn to
bite the bullet.

Sometimes I think it would be better to go to the store
and get a pack of Lucky Strikes and then go to the nearest
Italian joint for a big plate of spaghetti and wash it down
with a beer. At least then I would be so sick I wouldn't care.

Please don't let this happen to you. Break your buns to
find a work that will continue until the day you die. God, I
wish I could come up with something like that for me.
Money or no money, if a person is not motivated in his
latter days, he is sca-rewed. The world does not dance or
sparkle enough to keep an active mind interested. You have
to have something to invest *in* the world. I have always
been so passive except when I had to get off my butt and
make a buck. So I made a buck. When I quit, I didn't have a
meaningful backup. No interests that made sense. The boat

and sailing the seven seas would have been the perfect combination for me, but when you get out of breath combing your hair, you cannot sail the seven seas. So here I am, living the life of an Arab potentate in the most beautiful of surroundings, peaceful, and it ain't enough!

I repeat: Do not let this happen to you. If it is teaching, counseling, doctoring, researching—whatever—find it now and go for it. Children grow up and live their own lives, husbands and wives grow apart—*your work*, you always have.

You mention your fears upon addressing the typewriter machine preparatory to composing something. I've seen enough people with half your talent make it, based on one thing—persistence. There are people in your father's racket who could not hold a candle to me and yet are now doing famously—Jim Lange, Terry McGovern, Pete Scott, Gene Nelson, etc. Why? They were persistent! They had the Hutzpah, they hung in there, they didn't bother their asses about perfection, editing, or the fact they must be funny, funny all the time. They also did not burn themselves out at 44 years of age.

So sit down and write. Let the cream rise to the top and don't be afraid, because *you've got it*!

I have pet hummingbirds: John Wayne, Joaquin Murrietta, and Della Orange. They are not enough. I discovered a town down a lonely, dirt road about 80 miles from here, it gave me goose-pimples! It was out of the Twilight Zone—we must go there. *It is not enough.*

I will keep you apprised of my search. Meanwhile, keep going with yours.

> I love you very much,
>
> *Dad*

Don was back in the Bay Area for Christmas 1981, restless, frustrated, and lonely. The holiday only made it worse for him. He didn't like obligatory gift giving or false sentiments, nor did he like the commercialization of holidays. He rarely gave Christmas presents, although he had once given Guy Haines' son a dented ping-pong ball.

Bob Lanci, one of the bartenders at *Enrico's* and a

friend to Don, was sitting at home paying bills that Christmas Day. The phone rang. "Hey, Bobby, it's Don. How about coming with me on a ride around the city?"

"I thought it was a great idea," Bob says. "Don had no plans for Christmas, and I wasn't doing anything. We drove around the city in a limo, stopping at various bars and having a great time together. He, as always, wanted to hear all about my sexual exploits. So I told him, with great exaggeration! He only told me one of his, saying he had sex with five women in one day, starting in Los Angeles, then San Francisco, then Honolulu! That was his big story."

After dropping Bob back home again, Don went on and ended up happily having dinner with the limo chauffeur's family, whom he had never met. He was out enjoying people—"people doing what they're doing"—and that was good medicine even if the alcohol was not.

Revelations

Don's rare form of emphysema, known as alpha one antitrypsin, was affecting every area of his life. He had already had four pulmonary seizures. "I'm missing an anti–enzyme," Don told Jerry Carroll of the *San Francisco Chronicle* in 1982. "When my body is not devouring protein, it's devouring me. It's centered in my lungs. Christ, I don't know why they couldn't be devouring the cheeks of my ass instead!"

He was forced to study nutrition in order to figure out what foods were conducive to his survival. His body became his primary occupation—his whole world. "He kept detailed charts of everything he ate, as well as of his mood swings," Robin says. But, clearly, Don's illness was terminal; his only hope was to learn enough about it to extend his life as long as possible. No one knew how long he had to live.

The correspondence between Don and Robin continued. They shared their struggles and their victories, big and small. Don focussed largely on his physical battle, Robin on her education. With her father's help and encouragement, she completed her undergraduate degree and graduated magna cum laude.

Jan. 15, 1982

Dear Sweet Scholar:

I have just gone thru some changes that I truly believe will finally bear fruit. I had quit drinking, and then smoking —all under the aegis of "No Crutches, No Crotches, No Crosses"—then, the wheels came off. I got very clear and as a result very angry at what I saw in myself and the world around me. I decided at this late stage of the game it would be better for me to "lighten up" and try to achieve a balance of a little vin and a couple of cig fixes in the evening. Otherwise I was going to separate again from Vera-deara and who knows what else.

Within six days I knew the truth about myself to the degree that I cannot abide by "normalcy." It seemed as though nothing was being achieved. I was surviving, yes, but growing and finding out things, no. My curiosity has won out over my need to comfortably survive. I have quit drinking again and am down to 6-9 cigs a day, and never any coffee. My diet is perfection for the skin tone and breathing and mental attitude. Very, very slowly I am going to wean myself from the final use of cigs—in spite of the professional opinion that I am basically too angry to do such a thing.

I look back over the 56 years. High/low, high/low, in and out, up and down, here and there—most of it a simple matter of dancing so they wouldn't put me in the truck. The folks gave me their template and their criteria and because I didn't want to feel such a terrible outcast I went along with it. The time has come, me wee sweetie, to face up to what I *can* do as against what I cannot do. Un-doped.

I may not even be able to get out of bed. Wish me the best of luck. I shall keep you informed.

Much love,

★ ★ ★

February 1982

My dearest daughter,

First and foremost may I offer the most sincere of congratulations on your achieving the Dean's list! Good for you!

As to your solitude, go with the self-examination and go in very good company. As the great French philosopher, Montaigne, said, "The more I frequent and know myself, the more my deformity astonishes me, and the less I understand myself." Self-appraisal was his occupation in life. "All contradictions may be found in me . . . bashful, insolent, chaste, lascivious, talkative, taciturn, tough, delicate, clever, stupid, surly, lying, truthful, learned, ignorant, liberal, miserly and prodigal . . ." There, my darling daughter, is a man of my own heart.

A word of caution: Be very careful about how much of yourself, your youthful self, your early unduly playful self, your secret self, you offer up to the world's judgment, derision, attack, etc. *If* you have given it to the world on paper, you might find that the folks bring things back and rub your nose in it. As Lion once told me in answer to whether I should take the offer from a publisher to 'tell all' or not, fuck them! It's nothing but prurient curiosity on their parts. Of course you are a cross between a slut and a nun, so am I. But let's not document it for the titulation of a few and the boomerang airborne that may some day hit you right in the back of the head.

I haven't heard from your Brother Buzz for a month. As you may know, I was the fellow who introduced him to Jack Wyman, where he started as a stock boy and now will probably own the company. As Lion told Greg, "Don't be the least bit remiss about climbing up and over the back of your father." The same goes for you.

My love and thoughts,

Dad

★ ★ ★

Dearest daughter,

I'm sure I've told you the story: It's about 10:30 in the

morning and a guy is digging in the backyard amongst his roses, and suddenly, next to him is a rather large, grey figure—the Angel of Death—and the Angel of Death says "Listen, ol' guy, about 4 a.m. tomorrow morn I have to come back down here and take you out of the scene. If there is anything you want to do today, you better get with it." To which the fellow replies, "I'll just keep on with what I'm doing, if you don't mind, because I'm doing exactly what I really want to do."

Oh! To be able to say that at any given time of the day. What a blessed life that would be. The happiest humans I know, interviewed, whatever, have been those people who, regardless of anything else, are doing exactly what *they* feel joyfully fulfilled doing. I don't care whether they are musicians, scientists, teachers, gardeners, dishwashers, drinkers, smokers, non-smokers, writers, etc. *To find what it is that YOU feel is important and satisfying.*

I love you,

Dad

★ ★ ★

October 16, 1982

My dearest daughter,

Thank you for the Mail-gram and your concern. I would have replied sooner but have been very busy trying not to have too many anaerobic attacks. The Palm Springs area has not proven to be that much better than the city. I guess I have to extend my search to less polluted areas. Too many golf courses, too many surprise L.A. smog days, too much goddamn gardening. Everyone's moved to the desert and now are trying desperately to convert it into the tropics . . .!

Under separate cover I shall send you the photos that were taken for the Chronicle article a few months back—in case anyone that Greg or Diane ever meet might say, "Well, who was your father and what did he do?" You are the Family Historian, which is, on the face of it, rather unique. The way my mother has it figured, I shall become raindrops first and then she will go to the great child-beating playground in the sky.

I shall never be able to thank you enough for the Pooh
book—it has been a true inspiration. I hope that you carry
the beauty of forgiveness in your heart forever.

Vaya con Dios,

As another Christmas approached, Greg received the
following letter from his father:

Dear Gregor,

All seasons should be merry if one is to believe Epictetus.
This gift of the phenomena of existence is rather unique
when applied to us humans.

I've made quite a study of them, and can say, without
qualification, that cockroaches do not get "into" Christmas.
So, as long as we are here we should try and feel as good
about it as is possible.

I started to scratch the surface of the times in my life
when *you* have made it so much more easy for me:
overlooking my discourtesy as a "star" and weekend father,
my tardiness and sometimes my not showing up at all,
coming to my aid on innumerable occasions when alcohol
had taken its toll—trying desperately to save me and my
marriage from the clutches of the wicked witch of
Broadway, etc.!

What's even more important, you have been the best son
and friend I have ever heard of in all my born days.

What can you do for a person like this? Well, other than
the standard response of a deep love and respect, may I,
during this Yule season, forgive and absolve the current
fiscal agreement. As of this date, you don't owe me a cent.

Much love,

That Christmas, for the first time in *twenty years*, Don
and his three children spent the day together. Throughout
the afternoon, they talked, laughed, teased, cried, and
laughed again—and then the subject of Don's death came
up.

When Robin said, "I can't believe you're going to die,"

Don's response was, "How do you think I feel? I can't believe it either!"

"How can we prepare for this?" Robin asked. "All my life I have had you, in this love-hate relationship. You've always been such a stimulating force in my life. . ."

"Well, it's going to be rough. . . I don't want that! Ah, Jesus, I've got a better idea"

"Yeah, one of us go!" Greg chimed in for Don. "There's three of us and only one of you!"

"Yeah, let's take a dog and pick on him!" Don said.

The laughter echoed long and hard, petering out as he focussed once again on what was before them.

"Me? I get this feeling that now it's time for me to figure things out. I've got to go on all by *myself*—that's a bitch and a half." Don was talking almost as much to himself as he was to his children. "What do I say to myself—that I've had enough? I'm getting tired of being so frightened every night. It's always there, just *there*. You think all the thoughts you're ever going to think. It's ridiculous! We're dealing with a person who's run out of options, and you've got to know that's the way it is. I want so much to go to sleep forever, but then I want to see more things—such a dichotomy. One more . . . one more."

Don lit a cigarette, and as he did, he said, "If you realize how much a person like me, who has never been feeling, cannot handle feeling, you'll know why I had a cigarette. I can't handle feelings. I know that feeling means pain."

Looking at Greg, he surely saw a young man who, in the same way as himself, seemed closed. He had once said that if there were one gift he could give his son, it would be passion.

"In the early fifties," he said, pouring himself another glass of wine, "when you three were blumping around wondering where your father was, Dr. Lion said to me, 'After all the headlines, and all the bullshit, all the great Don Sherwood is going to have when it's all said and done —what really matters in the world—are those three.' 'Those little lumps, those farts, the bitch that screams at me and the other one who sits on the corner waiting for me?' I asked. 'Yeah, those people.' 'Well, I'll try,' I said, 'but it ain't going to be easy.' And it wasn't easy. The son of a bitch was right. You're all I have in the world now. You all know now, don't you?"

And know they did.

As they sat around eating their pie—with a crust so light, Greg called it "layered angel farts"—they talked of living together in a house. The dream of being a family was very much alive.

"Dr. Lion would puke in his grave if we lived together!" Don said. "That would be so selfish of me. You've got lives to live." He went off on a maudlin speech about how he just wanted to be "in earshot" of his kids, surrounded by their loved ones and "those presently in your favor," like a patriarch "sitting there farting a lot."

They broke into fits of laughter. So much for the Grandpa Walton role. Don would always be center stage.

"You're not buying that, huh?" Don laughed along with the rest of them until his laughter turned to tears. "I've got to do a lot more thinking than I've done. I've got to do this alone. It's my turn."

For a while no one spoke. Don broke the silence. "I've got to give you up," he said, "and I don't want to do that yet! We haven't had each other that much or that much of each other."

No Place to Run

In the Spring of 1983, Jack Erdmann was introduced to Don through Alcoholics Anonymous. Even AA had not succeeded in helping Don control his drinking.

JACK ERDMANN:

In early 1983, a friend of mine in Alcoholics Anonymous was talking to Don at *Enrico's*, telling him about me—that I was a very low-bottom drunk. Don had been in AA but hadn't stuck with it. He was still getting a euphoria from his drink. Don wanted to meet me, so I called him, and he said, "I've got to meet you. You're a junkyard dog like I am." We talked the same language, and I wasn't a fan of his. I told him I listened to jazz, not him.

I stood in the lobby of his place—he'd moved off the houseboat by now to Russian Hill—wondering what I was going to find when I walked in. When I came into his place, I saw this thin man with oxygen tubes coming out of his nose, threatening to kill himself with a gun that he said he had. Then I saw a mason jar filled with about forty or fifty cigarette butts floating in it. He had his favorite booze out, pinot noir, and a bottle of potato vodka in the icebox.

JACK...

My first impression when he looked at me was that his eyes were bright, brilliant, and I knew he was alive and that I could talk to him. We started to talk, and I convinced him to go in for detox. He went into Presbyterian Hospital and came back to his apartment. Then I'd come by and spend a couple of hours with him every day. We became real and best of friends, human being to human being.

By now, when Don drank, his euphoria lasted all of ten seconds. When I asked him if it was worth it, he said yes. His drinking also made him chain smoke, which meant going back to the hospital because it made him so sick.

I kept working with him, promising that if he'd stick with me and stay off the booze, he would have a moment of clarity where he would realize his whole life had been worth it. Everything would be good. We talked about pursuing a spiritual path, a loving power, something that doesn't have to be God or Christ. We called it "infinite love," the power that keeps us balanced and keeps us going. He wanted this.

Don still went to *Enrico's* whenever he felt up to it. "One day he asked me what I was going to do with my body when I die," Enrico remembers. "I told him that first of all, I have put aside money for everyone to go out and have a good time, get drunk, have fun. For my body, I've got a tree picked out in Muir Woods where I've put a pipe twenty feet into the ground, all capped, where my ashes will be poured to go into the tree's roots and be absorbed. Trees love ash. Then I'm going to be alive, up there looking at you, I told him.

'Yeah, and I'm going to be a bird and I'm going to come by you and shit on you!' Don said, laughing himself silly."

Though he joked about Enrico's plans, Don was very serious about his own plans that needed to be made. He

began to get rid of things and return other people's memo-
rabilia. He even rented furniture, so that no one would
have to worry about it.

GREG :

What ultimately cracked the barrier in his life was having a physically degenerative disease. Relatively suddenly, he became physically and emotionally dependent
on people, making him very angry. He realized now he
needed somebody.

He could outsmart himself, like playing chess with
himself, but when those pieces started to break down, it
was too late to make the changes in his life. In his relationships with family and friends, he lost control and
couldn't run away anymore.

He learned that he could survive his dependency, and
he started to appreciate those who were helping him.
The world had to close in on him before he would take
that chance. Then he pursued these relationships with
more intensity and clarity than most people do.

Shirley met Don for dinner about once a month at *Jack
Schutz's Village Pub* in Woodside or at the *Skywood Lodge*.
"Even towards the end he demanded complete attention!"
Shirley says. "If I so much as glanced sideways for a moment, something caught my eye, he'd say, 'Okay, the evening's over.' But we could never not see each other, no
matter what else went on."

"I had pneumonia at this time and was off work, and
Don came to see me," Diane's mother, Sally, says. "I
hadn't seen him in a long time. We went to a restaurant
nearby and sat out on a deck overlooking the river and
talked about our illnesses and medication and especially
about how I'd quit smoking. He was very interested in
that, thinking the doctor had slipped me something!

"I was glad to have that lunch because it was probably
the only time the two of us sat down, as mature adults,

and talked. Don had changed so very much. I saw vestiges of the boy I'd known, but he was very serious now."

JACK ERDMANN:

I managed to keep him sober for about three months, which was really an accomplishment, but then one day at *Enrico's* I came back from the men's room and he had the pinot noir on the bar. I didn't lecture him.

When he drank he became overbearing, demanding that full attention and eye contact, as always. Don didn't really feel sorry for himself, he was furious with life.

Sober, he was fascinated with the television series "Ascent of Man," and we'd watch it together. He had a love affair with the brain. What he wanted to do was write a children's book on the brain, with drawings that would teach them what goes on in the language center. We were going to do it together and it was exciting, but then he'd get drunk.

Another thing he wanted to do was go and live in his van down in the high desert. The van was all fixed up with tinted windows, air conditioning, and an air filtering system. He had kept virtually no possessions. He wanted to create a center in the desert where lots of people could come and stay, exchanging ideas, a meeting of the minds, a creative oasis. The problem with getting to the desert was that he couldn't make it through the valley, there was too much mold.

Don wanted to give something back. Spending time with him was spending time with a mind like I've never encountered since. He didn't talk about business, women, toys, cars. . . He talked about art, philosophy, music, literature, the mind, the world around him.

One day he got a call that his mother had died. He carried on with "Oh, my God, she's dead," all emotional. I said, "Bullshit." He sure wasn't crying over his mother! I wasn't buying his act. He hated the power that mothers have over their children, saying they were like praying mantes. When Don had first called her to tell her about

JACK...

his emphysema, her response was, "Listen, can I call you back? My bridge group is here." He hated her so much, he told everyone that he refused to give her the satisfaction of dying before she did!

Ultimately, Don didn't find anything spiritual to hang on to. I've always thought that if he had just been a little dumber, he might have gotten it.

Jack Erdmann introduced Don to a friend of his, Anne Lamott—a San Francisco author—hoping she could help him help Don.

"Don and I were the best of friends from the first day," Anne says. "We talked and laughed. The next day I called him to ask if I could hang out with him for a while. He was ecstatic. I'm an alcoholic, and I was drinking. What Don needed more than anything was friends. He was absolutely the loneliest man. Between Jack and I, he had two friends who deeply loved him and who would be there with him every single day."

Jack went to Don's every day, and Anne stayed over at Don's apartment every other night. She slept in his room while he stayed on the sofa. He gradually came to believe that they truly cared about him.

"For those two months Don wasn't drinking," Anne says, "he was so clear, hopeful, and funny. He was a different man. He started to feel better.

"We talked about religion a lot. He wanted to know that his soul would survive, that there was a reason for all this. I suggested he try pretending he believed in God for a while. He thought this was a great idea. He'd tell me he'd spoken to his 'higher power.' It really calmed him down, and he began to make plans to do radio and television spots about alcohol and smoking. He wanted to redeem his life by saving others."

They rented movies, talked, went for drives, and read. "Don never knew it, but Jack hat to borrow all kinds of money, because he wanted to take Don places and do things for him."

Through Jack's generosity of spirit, the three of them enjoyed a magic two months together.

Then one day, Don summoned Anne to *Enrico's*. She instantly saw from the expression on his face that something was going on. She was right; he was planning to start drinking again.

"As all alcoholics do, he tried to rationalize. 'It will relax me,' 'I need the calories,' 'I'll drink slowly.' As soon as he'd drink, he would be out of control again, and then so angry. 'I've just flushed myself down the toilet!' he'd sob."

There wasn't anything anyone could say to Don about Don that he didn't already know.

The Last Ride

"I always felt if you didn't commit yourself heart and soul, it was all right, because you always had tomorrow," Don said to his friends. He made no secret of the fact that he was dying, telling people, "Death is nothing. It's the dying that kills you!"

"By this time Dad was really testing me, calling me all of the time, insisting, 'I need you,'" Diane says. "I'd fly or drive from Eureka, to put him in or take him out of the hospital. I *had* to be there, I needed him to know how much I loved him. He finally said to me, 'You really did it.'

"I was always there. I idolized him, and he knew the influence he had on me. One day he said, 'God, I hope you can forgive me for the legacy I have left you—your hopeless attraction to men who cannot love.'"

Don did not have the strength to be at the big roast given for Ronnie Schell in his friend's home town of Richmond that fall. He asked Greg to go in his place and give Ronnie a message: "I wanted to send my regrets, then thought about it and realized I don't have any."

In their private time together, Don told Greg, "I have met God . . . and it is us."

True to their pattern, Don and Robin ultimately came full circle as the end drew near. This was the final letter Don wrote to Robin:

September 11, 1983

Robin,

Once again you miss the point.

I have not rejected you. I shall be on the ready to help any time you are needful. However, until you have reached a state of self-understanding whereupon you can tell when there is a "waxy build-up" of resentment, hate, whatever, that then causes a blind striking out—I cannot be in your strike zone. I am too wise, too old, too tired, too covetous of beautiful days.

Dad

Robin continued to pour out letters to her father, trying to heal this sudden split, but he didn't answer them. Then one day he called.

Robin says, "Two weeks before my father's call, my best friend, Steven, had a brain seizure and was dying. I had told Dad this in a letter, so when he finally called I thanked him, assuming it was because of Steven. He said, 'I didn't call you because some faggot had a brain seizure! I called you because you're my daughter, and although you're a pain in the ass, I love you.' He proposed we get together, but the day he suggested was my one day alone with Steven at the hospital. And to be honest, I wasn't sure I could handle Dad in my emotional state. So I did what I never did — I said no to my father. We left it that he'd call me later, and we'd get together.

"When I didn't hear from him, I knew he felt rejected. I wrote him another letter. I told him that beyond all this drama, he and I were one. As I mailed it, I flashed that he might not get it in time. He didn't.

"Why it ended this way, after all we'd been through, God knows. Maybe it had to be this way so we could finally let go. . . ."

At the same time as Robin was mailing her letter, Don was on the phone calling friends. "Come around the city with me, for a last look," he said to them.

For one reason or another, no one could make it.

It seemed like any other night, and there was always tomorrow. . .

HERB CAEN

November 6, 1983

Last Friday started out gray and drizzly and it didn't get any better. Don Sherwood was found dead in his Russian Hill apartment.

"I'm dying, Herb, going fast," he kept saying at Enrico's, then he'd go into his dirty laugh. The muck and mire of commercial radio produces a rare species like Don Sherwood once in a lifetime, and the lifetime is over. It was all too short, but god it was fun while it lasted.

He crossed me right down to the end, dying on a Friday. I have no Saturday column, the Sunday column is locked up on Wednesday, and here it is Monday. I can hear him laughing now, and rolling his eyes: "Scooped again, eh?"

A week ago, Don hired a Rolls Royce limo to drive all around San Francisco, to drink up the views, soak up the old sights, for what turned out to be the last time.

The late John Wasserman once asked Don to define the meaning of life, and he replied, "Shakespeare said it—a tale told by an idiot, full of sound and fury, signifying nothing." Pause. "But it's the only game in town." And now it's over.

Out of the mud grew a lotus.

—L.H.

Index